Godnesia:

Keeping God in Mind Each Day

Denise Larson Cooper

ROCKFORD, ILLINOIS

https://www.facebook.com/DeniseLarsonCooper

Cover photograph Copyright © by Jacob A. Pearson

Book Layout © 2014 BookDesignTemplates.com

Godnesia: Remembering God Each Day/ **Denise Larson Cooper**. — 1st ed.

ISBN-13: 978-1981401284

ISBN-10: 1981401288

Thank you, Duane and Martha, for working with me on Godnesia *and my two previous books. These projects would still be lying dead in a mound of paper on my office floor were it not for your expertise in editing, generous giving of your time and tireless work to see them completed.*

Your patience, humor and friendship were a great encouragement to me through this process. I am grateful that God brought us together to spread His Word through the Spirit. I appreciate your deep commitment to our Lord, Jesus Christ, and your desire to bring Him glory and honor through your work.

I am looking forward to future projects together.

About This Book

The Bible translations used in the citations is the 1984 New International Version (NIV) unless otherwise stated: English Standard Version (ESV); God's Word Translation; Christian Standard Bible (CSB, formerly Holman Christian Standard Bible [HCSB]); International Standard Version (ISV); King James Version (KJV); New American Standard Bible (NASB); NET Bible; NIV 2011; New Living Translation (NLT); and the World English Bible (WEB).

CONTENTS

January

JANUARY 1

Michigan State football fans celebrated because the Spartans overcame a 20-point deficit in the fourth quarter to beat Baylor and win the 2015 Cotton Bowl. By the end of the third quarter many Michigan fans had already surrendered to defeat. But when Baylor missed a field goal, the Spartans became energized, and new life blossomed for them. Now those who had lost hope were suddenly full of hope. Players also felt a resurgence of power and confidence. And when the game was over, all who had experienced that new life were the victors.

As Jesus Christ hung on the cross, the disciples felt the weight of hopelessness as the Lord took His last breath. They watched as His chest failed to expand, His cries fell silent and His body hung motionless. His promise of salvation seemed dashed. For three days the cloud of despair oppressed believers. But then a resurgence of hope began to bloom: the tomb was empty. He was indeed risen.

Christ's triumph over death is the believer's triumph over death. "We have been born into a new life that has a confidence which is alive because Jesus Christ has come back to life" (1 Peter 1:3 GWT). By faith we believe in the resurrection of Jesus

Christ, and He fills us with new life and the power of the Holy Spirit.

Those who have received new life are the victors.

JANUARY 2

We sometimes forget that the Spirit is God. He is the third Person of the Trinity: Like the Father and the Son, the Holy Spirit is omnipotent and omniscient. He abides in the world to continue Jesus' earthly ministry, which is to reconcile men to God. God's almighty Spirit testifies about the atoning work of Jesus Christ on the cross. The Spirit is in the world to expose the sin of the world, so all men will know they are sinners before God and will cry out for salvation that comes through Christ (John 16:8).

Through the power of the Holy Spirit a sinner comes to know the truth that Jesus has reconciled men to God by shedding His blood on the cross. By the power of the Holy Spirit human hearts are transformed and minds are illuminated with knowledge of God's saving acts in Christ Jesus. The Spirit instills faith in the believer and teachers the believer all things of God in Christ and "remind them of everything I (Jesus) have said" (John 14:26) in the world through the Scriptures.

The everlasting, divine Spirit was with God and Christ in the beginning. He participated in creation—"the Spirit of God was hovering over the waters" (Genesis 1:2)—and is active in the lives of all believers, cleansing them of unrighteousness and empowering them to live obedient lives to God to the glory and honor of Christ. The Spirit is Almighty God at work in the believer, so the believer can be at work in the world proclaiming the gospel to all people wanting to know God, His saving grace in Jesus Christ and the reality of His eternal kingdom.

JANUARY 3

A close friend of mine is 97 years old and lives in a rehab hospital recovering from a stroke that paralyzed her left arm and severely weakened her left leg. Several times she has mentioned to me that this was not the direction she thought her life would go. She is not complaining. In fact, she seems to accept her circumstances. Of course, she would rather be at home, but she works hard in therapy, compliments the staff and always remains pleasant. Not once have I seen her lash out or fight the situation.

My friend's example reminds me of how I am to live my life in faith. There are days that I claim faith and then fight God about everything. I find myself complaining to Him instead of accepting the circumstances: Whatever He brings to my life must be necessary for me to grow strong as His disciple.

I need to pray to accept God's will through the power of the Holy Spirit. And then I can put down these childish uprisings and surrender my will to His. Living a submissive life to God in Christ will calm the troubles in my days. Proverbs 19:23 says, "The fear of the Lord leads to life: Then one rests content, untouched by trouble." To surrender is to respect God's work in my life and accept my circumstances as being for my own good. Respecting God leads to life; fighting God leads to strife.

Yielding to the Spirit allows me to rest in the assurance that all God does is in my best interest. "And we know that in all things God works for the good of those who love Him, who have been called according to His purpose" (Romans 8:28).

JANUARY 4

All athletes run into problems in training. They are usually aware of the problem, they can identify the problem and they can even articulate the solution. Yet, with all that knowledge about the skill and their understanding about their own strengths and weaknesses, they still won't act to resolve the difficulty. These athletes will talk about the problem but do nothing concrete to solve it. Instead they have the misconception that talking about it is the same as solving it.

Spiritually we find ourselves like these athletes. We recognize the problem of sin in our lives, talk about it, but don't take steps with the Lord to settle it. Initially we avoid the subject. However, God will make it plain that we must deal with sin. Once He makes us aware of our sin, we need to work with Christ to rid our lives of sin. We know there is no solution for sin apart from Christ Jesus, yet we are reluctant to approach Him.

But Jesus says, "Come to me" (Matthew 11:28) at the cross. where you will understand His atoning sacrifice and receive forgiveness for your sin. Next He says, "Leave your life of sin"

(John 8:11), and be washed in His blood, and He will be the "Lord Our Righteousness" (Jeremiah 23:6). Finally, He says, "I will send to you from the Father, the Spirit of truth" (John 15:26) so that you can "obey my commands . . . and remain in my love" (John 15:10).

Going to Jesus is action against sin.

JANUARY 5

A lone male cardinal was sitting quietly on the far end of a small, thin tree branch this afternoon. His vibrant red color drew my attention as I glanced out my office window at the backyard. He was a beautiful sight against the bare backdrop of winter.

Immediately my mind moved to the precious red blood of Jesus Christ spilling down the naked, gnarled wood of a Roman cross. The Savior hung bleeding and dying on that rugged tree as the nails in His hands and feet shredded His human flesh. This is the sight of God's beautiful love suspended against the bare, dark background of the sinful world.

That vivid crimson river runs through the world cleansing sinners of their foulest crimes, washing those who repent and believe in forgiveness and regenerating their souls with redemption. Christ's pure blood brings an acquittal to the guilty, a pardon to the transgressor and rescues the perishing from the forces of evil. Christ's "blood is the life" (Deuteronomy 12: 23) of God poured out in the world to free it from Sin's grip and Death's bondage. As hymn writer Lewis E. Jones wrote, "There is power, power, wonder working power in the blood of the Lamb. There is power, power, wonder working power in the precious blood of the Lamb."

Jesus Christ offered Himself "unblemished to God" (Hebrews 9:14) to "cleanse our consciences from acts that lead to death, so that we may serve the living God!" (Hebrews 9:14b)

JANUARY 6

When I returned home from work, I found that my daughter's car was blocking the driveway on my side of the garage. I had to park on the other side. Silently, I groused about not having "my spot." Then God used it to point out my lack of humility.

I was reluctant to take a parking space in the garage that I had deemed "lower" than my usual place. That may sound silly or even ridiculous, but I realized for one moment that I had decided I was more important than other family members. Instead, I should be willing to put others ahead of myself, even in little things like garage parking places. In 1 Peter 5:5, Peter says to us, "All of you, clothe yourselves with humility toward one another."

Doing little things to put others first teaches us humility. When we clean up someone else's mess, or do the chore no one else wants to do, if we hold open a door or throw away litter, we are exercising humility. Doing things for others reminds us of what God did for us through His Son, Jesus Christ. We practice humility out of love for Christ and others.

Jesus demonstrated abject humility by leaving the heavenly realm to come and clean up our mess of sin and rebellion from the cross. He made Himself equal with us by surrendering His equality with God. The divine son of God made a world full of sinners more important than He was, and He died on the cross so we might be exalted through Him.

Only through humility can our attitude "be the same as that of Christ Jesus" (Philippians 2:5).

JANUARY 7

Entering my dark office early this morning I stepped on a cascade of light that had splashed onto my floor through the window. Immediately I knew that these bright beams were radiating from a full moon. I followed the streak across the carpet, looked out the window, and stared high into the western sky spotting the moon. In the morning sky the beams shone brightly against the black heavens. The bold light emanating from its source formed a perfect cross athwart the heavens.

For a few quiet moments I stood soaking in the wonder and majesty of God's creation. Psalm 19:1 came to mind: "The heavens declare the glory of God; the skies proclaim the work of His hands." Washed in the rapturous moment, I thought that, not just the skies, but I, too, am the work of His hands.

I am a sinner saved by grace by the nail scarred hands of Christ my Savior. His hands, ripped and bleeding were working to secure my salvation. Those nails tore through His flesh binding Him to the cross, even though "His love would have held

Him there" (Michael Card). God's mangled hands worked for my redemption, cleansing me of unrighteousness so I could be born again. Everything I am in Christ is the work of His hands.

If a silent sky can proclaim the "work of His hands," then let "everything that has breath praise the Lord" (Psalm 150:6).

JANUARY 8

Gymnasts receive coaching and tools to master skills. Some athletes add many skills; others add fewer. Those gymnasts who increase their skill output are usually stronger than those who don't.

The apostle Peter wrote a long list of godly qualities that we should "make every effort to add to your faith" (2 Peter 1:5) to "keep you from being ineffective and unproductive in your knowledge of our Lord Jesus Christ" (2 Peter 1:8).

How often do we consider adding to our faith to be effective and productive in our knowledge of Christ? Typically, we swim in the shallow end of that pool. For whatever reason, we play in the baby pool of theology. The Holy Spirit is willing to instruct us to further our knowledge of God in Christ, but we settle for limited thinking and minimal pursuit. Then when the worries of the day strike, our faith in omniscient Christ wavers, and we question or doubt Him. Or, when evil attacks, our faith withers for lack of understanding in omnipotent Christ, and we stumble.

Peter doesn't want us just to sit back and hope our faith gets stronger. He expects us to put energy toward godliness so the

Spirit's energy will reveal the life of Christ dwelling in us and mold us to that life. "Our wishes, our desires, control; Mold every purpose of the soul; O'er all may we victorious prove That stands between us and thy love" ("O Thou, who Hast at Thy Command," Jane Cotterill).

JANUARY 9

Tonight I am really feeling the crunch to get this reflection done. I have just returned from gymnastics meet, and I must be on the road early in the morning to return to the venue and coach three more sessions tomorrow. My haste creates more starts and stops. When I hurry, I don't listen to God. I just want Him to run with any old idea, just so we can get done.

When I hurry, I am being lazy. I am not showing God proper diligence in the work He has assigned to me. Instead, I am focused on my own needs, putting them ahead of His. My impatience toward God is an insult to Christ, who patiently endured the cross for my sin. He placed the will of the Father and the needs of humanity above His own will. Bearing humanity's sin and God's punishment for sin on the cross, Christ hung over the chasm of holy redemption and holy retribution for the sake of salvation. He didn't provoke God to hurry and finish the work: He waited for God to finish so the work of reconciliation would be complete once and for all.

When I enter Christ's presence, I recognize that God is always able to bring to completion His work of salvation in my life. "Bear in mind that our Lord's patience means salvation" (2 Peter 3:15).

Rushing, hurrying and being impatient to fulfill my will means that I have gotten lazy about letting God in Christ complete His work in my life.

JANUARY 10

It has been a long day. That is to be expected when the gymnastic-meet season begins. Usually coaches spend about 12 hours working on the day of a meet. The work isn't physically demanding, but it is mentally taxing and can occasionally be emotionally draining. By the end of a day during meet season, one of two things happen, a coach is either so tired he or she can barely stay awake or so past the point of exhaustion that he or she can't get to sleep. With both cases, what the coach is craving is rest—undisturbed, uninterrupted, peaceful rest away from work.

God created us with a need for rest. Foolishly we pride ourselves on ignoring this essential requirement. We boast about how tired we are. For some reason, we are under the delusion that exhaustion, not rest, is good for the soul.

God designed a day of rest. "There remains, then, a Sabbath-rest for the people of God; for anyone who enters God's rest also rests from His own work, just as God did from his" (Hebrews 4:9-10). Drink deeply from God's rest. Inhale the fragrance of His eternal life. Feel His presence caress your weary soul, and slip into the wonder of His grace. Let Him calm your anxious heart and quiet your unsettled thoughts. Think of God. Worship the Father, Son and Spirit. Obey God's command to keep the Sabbath.

Rest in God.

JANUARY 11

My daughter decided to venture out on her own phone plan, so she generously offered me her old one. I am now trying a smart phone. Fortunately, the current power cord and charger for my other electronic devices also works for this phone.

I thought how much that is like the Holy Spirit; He is the power cord of God charging believers with strength and faith. The power of the omnipotent God dwells within us through the Spirit. Yet, so many Christians fail to tap this resource. We attempt to live faithfully by relying on our own strength and might. Using only human energy, we cannot accomplish the things of God. Only God can achieve the things of God because the things of God are redemption, salvation and reconciliation. God has accomplished these things once and for all by and through the God-Man Jesus. When we tap the resource of the Holy Spirit then Christ will accomplish the things of God in and through us.

Paul wrote that Christ "is able to do immeasurably more than all we ask or imagine, according to His power that is at work within us" (Ephesians 3:20). To live through the power of the Spirit is to live as Christ lived. While He was in the world Jesus' human body was the same as ours. His body was fragile, weak, and bound by the same rules of nature which bind our bodies. He was not Superman. He could not "leap tall buildings with a single bound" nor was He "faster than a speeding bullet." No, He was just an ordinary human like us. Yet, while He was in the world, He was, "full of the Holy Spirit" (Luke 4:1). Through the Spirit of God He healed the sick, raised the dead and endured the cross for our salvation. When we let the Spirit of God dwell in us, Christ will accomplish His purpose in our lives. Christ charges us with the power of His Spirit so we can accomplish His ministry on earth.

Be charged with the power of the Spirit.

JANUARY 12

In the winter I wear several layers of clothes to protect my body from the cold. Besides a shirt, I also wear a sweatshirt and vest underneath my jacket when I venture outside. I wear a pair of gloves to guard my hands against the frigid weather and keep my head covered with a hat. My boots have a thin layer of insulation, which keep my feet warm even if the temperatures dip below freezing.

People who live in the northern US have clothing and outerwear that protect them against the stinging winter weather.

This preparation reminds me that we also need to be protecting our hearts and souls against the cold, harsh elements of the world. As Christians we need to guard our hearts and minds against false teachings, destructive heresies that pull us away from the truth of the gospel, and teachers who "exploit you with stories they have made up" (2 Peter 2:3). We need to take precautions against false prophets and wolves in sheep's clothing who want to lure us away from sound doctrine and the truth of Scripture.

Those who try to deceive believers are clever and convincing. So, believers must insulate themselves against these spiritual predators. We need to develop layers of protection against false teachings by studying the Gospel of Christ. We need to study the Scriptures diligently and let the Holy Spirit teach us the truth about Jesus the Godman. We need to read great theologians, discuss sermons, know the creeds of the faith and delve into Church history. These are all ways we can strengthen our faith and protect ourselves against the world's deception.

"Through the power of the Holy Spirit who lives within us, carefully guard the precious truth that has been entrusted to you" (2 Timothy 1:14 NLT).

JANUARY 13

I coached an athlete who struggled with vault because she did not run as fast as she was able. Finally, she made up her mind to put all her energy into the run. Her face filled with joy as she landed her first vault in a competition. And the glory of that moment was to her a great prize.

Paul told the members of the Corinthian church, "Do you not know that in a race all the runners run, but only one gets the prize? Run in such a way as to get the prize" (1 Corinthians

9:24). The King James Version translates the last line: "So run, that ye may obtain."

As Christians we are to run in such a way to obtain the glory of God's heavenly kingdom. We cannot sit in our sin and expect to be rewarded. We are to run from sin as fast as possible and arrive at the bleeding side of our Savior on the cross and be cleansed of unrighteousness through His blood.

We must run from Satan who chases us with his lies and deceitful ways, trying to make us stumble and fall off the path of righteousness.

We must run to the waiting arms of "The Lord our Righteousness" (Jeremiah 23:6) who will protect us from the evil one.

And finally, we must run "with endurance the race set out for us" (Hebrews 12:1ESV), so by Christ's death and resurrection and through the power of the Holy Spirit we can obtain eternal life in God's kingdom.

JANUARY 14

Often athletes struggle to improve their gymnastic skills because they cling to old habits and bad technique. Coaches design drills, work with mental choreography, and encourage good technique; however, if an athlete is comfortable with her execution of the skill, she resists coaching suggestions and rejects proper technique. Athletes know good technique and new habits will make them stronger competitors; still, sometimes they refuse to change.

Sadly, I run my spiritual life like some of my athletes run their training sessions. My fallen human nature insists I cling to sin. But, clinging to sin and disobedience will not strengthen my faith in God in Christ, yet I persist. I recognize and embrace Christ as Savior, but cling to my sinful ways. I do not listen to Christ when He calls me to repentance and confession, and often I resist the Holy Spirit's work of sanctification in my life. Scripture says, "They would not listen, however, but persisted in their former practices" (2 Kings 17:40).

Clinging to my old ways of sin, disobedience and rebellion is much easier than clinging to Christ and living a life of obedience to Him. Even with the power of the Holy Spirit providing all I need to walk in the new ways of obedience, I sometimes refuse.

But Christ calls me to a new life: He is forming His pure, holy life in my heart and soul through the Holy Spirit. So, I must submit to the Spirit, so He can break my hard heart and rid my life of old sinful habits. In this way, my new life in Christ will flourish, and I will grow stronger in faith, hope and love.

JANUARY 15

The other day, my daughter left the garage door opened when she left the house. Since I was upstairs in my office at the time, I didn't realize that the door was open. Later, I reminded her that, with the door open, I was vulnerable. She failed to see the potential danger. Her excuse for failing to close the door was that she had no remote. Of course, she could get out of the car, walk to the key pad and close it, but that didn't enter her mind.

When it comes to our spiritual lives we sometimes make ourselves vulnerable. We leave the door open to misguided thinking about God when we accept any teaching just because someone who teaches it claims to be Christian. All teaching should be tested by the Spirit and through Scripture. If the cross isn't central to the teaching, that should raise a red flag. If a speaker does not acknowledge that Jesus Christ has "come in the flesh" (1 John 4:2), his teaching is not sound doctrine. If a person claims to be a Christian teacher and yet refutes the resurrection, be wary—run away—Paul says if there's no resurrection there's no faith—he or she is a wolf.

Deception has always been a problem in the Christian church. Jesus warned, "Watch out that no one deceives you. Many will come in my name, claiming, 'I am he,' and will deceive many" (Mark 13:5-6).

Not everything we hear about God and Jesus Christ is true. However, Christ left His Spirit of truth in the world: "He will guide you into all truth" (John 16:13). The Spirit protects us from deception through the truth of Scripture.

JANUARY 16

At the gymnastic competition last night several of my gymnasts struggled in the event warmups. They were falling on their floor passes, took the wrong steps on vault or missed leap connections on beam. However, they handled the problems calmly and made the necessary technique adjustments. They listened to their coaches, and by the time it was their turn to compete they had resolved the problems, and they successfully executed the routines. While these athletes went on to give strong performances what impressed me was the maturity they displayed throughout their struggles.

As Christians we sometimes fail to remember that our goal in this life should be to mature in our faith in Christ. We encounter problems in our lives every day that fill us with worry and fear. But we fail to pause and seek guidance from our Lord. Instead we tend to use our problems as an excuse to be disobedient to God in Christ. We need to calmly enquire of the Lord. He will use the struggles of our day to grow us into mature believers.

The goal of our Christian life should be to mature in faith by living obedient lives to Christ through the power of the Holy Spirit.

When we live mature, obedient lives in Christ through the Spirit, the body of Christ, the church is "built up until we all reach unity in the faith and in knowledge of the Son of God" (Ephesians 4:13). Maturing in faith brings unity to the community of faith, which brings glory to God and honor to Christ. And as we become mature in faith we gain "the whole measure of the fullness of Christ" (Ephesians 4:13b).

Therefore, "work so that you may be mature and complete, not lacking anything" (James 1:4).

JANUARY 17

Recently a situation surfaced at the gym that caused some disagreement between two staff members. It is highly unusual that something could force a wedge between these particular coworkers, since they are mutual friends, respect each other's work and share a commitment to strong professional goals. However, a storm began brewing, one that brought them to a division. Before the cohesion of the staff became shredded, a meeting was held, in which all the parties decided that the quality of the relationship between the staff members was more valuable than the circumstances that had created the conflict.

Likewise, there is always one who threatens a believer's relationship with Jesus Christ. The Evil One will always try to seduce us away from our Lord. He will offer us the kingdoms of the world if we will bow down and worship him. But chasing the desires of the world, these temptations from Satan, will only bring arguments, jealousy, and quarrels into the body of believers—causing divisions. These human divisions will also cause a great rift between God and His people.

In Romans 16:17-18a, Paul writes, "I urge you, brothers, to watch out for those who cause divisions, and put obstacles in your way that are contrary to the teachings you have learned. Keep away from them."

God has called us to be united with Him through Jesus Christ. We are to keep away from anything and anyone who attempts to hinder that unity. Jesus knew how fragile this unity would be, how vulnerable it would be to attacks from the Evil

One. Therefore, He prays on behalf of all His disciples, "May they be brought to complete unity to let the world know that You sent me and have loved them even as you have loved me" (John 17:23).

Satan wants to rupture the bound of unity between believers and their Lord. He will constantly put temptations before the church to try and separate the body from its Head. But Christ is at work praying for all His disciples in the presence of the Father and strengthening the bond of unity between Himself and His church.

JANUARY 18

The hospitality room at the gymnastic meet this weekend was full of delicious food. The room had a central location in the venue, which made it convenient for coaches and judges to grab food before returning to work. Its location also made it easy to sit with fellow coaches and talk. In other words, food and fellowship were readily available all weekend.

God's Word is spiritual food, and we must be able to feed on His word regularly. Jesus must hold the central place in our lives. His Word brings nourishment and refreshment to our souls. It is the revelation of God in Christ, and as we sit and read and listen to the Spirit's teaching, we are brought into deeper fellowship with God.

We have all heard the expression "You are what you eat" (credited to Jean Anthelme Brillat-Savarin). There is some spiritual application in this little phrase. If we take our food from

Jesus, then through the power of the Holy Spirit our hearts, minds and souls are conformed to Christ. Spiritually we are being "made in God's likeness" (James 3:9).

God provides an abundant table for His people. He offers the manna in the desert through His Word—so we can feast on the promises of God. The Lord makes us thirsty for the cup of salvation, so we will desire the new wine of His glory. As He gave the food of John the Baptist, God offers us the honey and locust of repentance. And He supplies grapes from the vineyard of the Kingdom of God to give us the wine of new life.

Share food and fellowship each day with our Lord.

JANUARY 19

Peter is my favorite disciple. Perhaps because we share similar characteristics. He spoke his mind, often without first thinking through his words. He jumped to action, usually at inopportune times. And after three years of living each day with Jesus, on the night before Christ's crucifixion, he hung back. He is concerned for Jesus, but doesn't want to get caught in the web of politics surrounding Him. So, Scripture says, he "followed him at a distance" (Mark 14:54).

There are so many times during the day that I am tempted to follow Jesus from a distance. He is easy to hang around with when He is healing, teaching, or feeding the people. But as He moves toward the cross, reason insists that I stay back, while faith insists I move ahead with Him.

Peter stayed away from Jesus and ended up denying Him three times that night: his faith collapsed.

The path of Christ is difficult for us to travel if we rely only on human reason and logic. In fact, if we only view Jesus through the lens of human logic our faith will collapse. We will stumble and fall when Jesus asks us to walk with Him to Calvary. Watching an innocent man go to a horrible death on a cross sends our logic into overload as we try to make sense of God in a situation that appears to make no sense. Only when we view the cross through the lens of faith do we see our Savior being nailed to a tree for our transgressions and we know He took on the punishment our sins deserved. Then faith will move us closer to the bleeding side of our Lord.

Faith requires close contact with Christ if it is to thrive and survive. And for our faith to stay strong we must stay close to Jesus as He walks the road of suffering and hangs dying on the cross, and then to watch as His lifeless body is sealed in a tomb.

Faith brings us to God in Christ on the cross, so we can repent of our sins, be redeemed by His blood and be reconciled to God through His perfect sacrifice.

JANUARY 20

My daughter had a particularly trying day. She spent an hour or so venting to me. Exhausted from our conversation and the events of the day, she went to her room and put on Celine Dion songs. For my daughter, this artist's voice is soothing and calming. She has listened to Celine for so long that she recognizes her voice whenever it comes over the airwaves.

I thought about the verse in John 10 I read this morning, "The man who enters by the gate is the shepherd of His sheep. The watchman opens the gate for him, and the sheep listen to His voice. He calls His own sheep by name, and leads them out" (2-3).

In this crazy, hectic, anxious world, believers in Jesus Christ hear the voice of the "good shepherd" (John 10:11) and their fears are relieved. When stress beats on the door, His calming, soothing voice assures us that "all things work together for good" (Romans 8:28 ESV) through Him.

As the world rants and rages the faithful can rely on the voice of God to lead them into quiet pastures and to pools of still waters. When disobedience tempts us, the voice of our Shepherd calls us to lead lives of righteousness. When sin tries to seduce us toward the road that leads to death, the voice of our Lord speaks "words of life" (John 6:68). And finally when our time on earth is done the Savior's voice will lead us home.

JANUARY 21

Today I watched a gymnast try to set the record for pertinacious behavior. She spent a disproportional amount of time on an event because she had refused to make the one correction that was necessary to complete the assignment that I had given her. I puzzled as to why she could apply this much tenacity to doing the skill incorrectly but not apply the same persistence to doing the skill the right way.

I would have handed her a trophy for obstinacy myself until I realized I had spent nearly 30 years in a bullheaded state before God. I would still be in that stubborn condition except for the power of the Holy Spirit, who turned my head toward the cross of Christ.

Jesus said, "But I, when I am lifted up from the earth, will draw all men to myself" (John 12:32). Christ's cross is a head turner. Through the cross, God confronts us with our sin and our stubborn attitude toward salvation, redemption and reconciliation. Our sinful nature insists that we need none of these things offered to us by God through Jesus Christ. Still, in God's great mercy, the Holy Spirit draws us to Christ so we can see our need and turn and be saved.

Without the work of the Holy Spirit and the sacrifice of Jesus Christ on our behalf, we would stay fixed in sin. Yet, once Christ enters our life, He transforms our stubborn attitude so we can stay fixed on the purposes of God.

JANUARY 22

After several hectic weeks, I returned to the workout gym today. Carrying my Kindle and a bottle of water I made my way to the stationary bikes. The gym was busier than I had remembered, so I had to settle for a recumbent rather than an upright bike. Then it occurred to me: it's January, and people's New

Year's resolution goals of weight loss, better health habits and fitness—adopted so enthusiastically—had not yet worn off.

When life gets hectic we also might seem to put a few worldly pounds onto our soul. What that means is we get busy and tired and don't take the same care to guard our heart, mind and soul against the influence of the world. We let unwholesome talk sneak out of our mouths and fail to recognize it as unhealthy spiritual behavior. Instead of "doing something useful with his [our] own hands" so we "have something to share with those in need" (Ephesians 4:28), we allow our hands to be idle. Perhaps we fail to be totally truthful, or we let anger get the better of us. Maybe we've even harbored rage, malice and bitterness in our hearts.

Paul instructs us to get rid of all worldly baggage by "putting off the old self . . . to put on the new self, created to be like God in true righteousness and holiness" (Ephesians 22, 24).

Let the Holy Spirit work in your life to trim the fat of the world from your soul.

JANUARY 23

I am ready to just throw up my hands and scream. I can't get the layers of the world out of my mind and heart to hear God. Everything about my day keeps coming back to me. I can hear the popular songs that were blaring on the radio all afternoon at the gym. I can hear pieces of conversations that I had with coworkers and friends. My mind is still full of the theme song from the Rockford Files that was playing on the TV downstairs.

My ears hurt, my soul is agitated and I am getting grouchy. I want to shut the world up but the more I try to silence it, the more of it I hear. This just makes me madder.

It has taken me most of the evening to figure out that the more I was protesting the world, the more I behaved like it. Through my attitude and actions, I have befriended the world rather than close it out. Tonight as much as I want to say that the world and I are not friends, I must admit that we are.

This relationship with the world puts me at odds with God. James says, "Don't you know that friendship with the world is hatred toward God?" (James 4:4) Ouch! Well, I know it now.

But there is something else I know now too "But He gives us more grace" (James 4:6).

Tonight all I can do is fall at the foot of the cross, empty my heart of my friendship with the world and receive God's grace through the power of the Holy Spirit.

JANUARY 24

The Psalmist wrote, "[H]e frustrates the ways of the wicked" (Psalm 146:9). God frustrates the wicked by what He does. He defeats the plans of the wicked through the work of salvation in Jesus Christ. Christ's death on the cross is the eternal obstacle that thwarts the evil intention of the wicked.

The wicked seek to deceive sinners into choosing eternal death. However, on that road, God has placed the cross. He draws the sinner to the dying Savior to hear "Father forgive them, for they do not know what they are doing" (Luke 23:34).

The sinner who hears these words and believes comes to repentance. The repentant soul leaves the path of the ungodly and follows the cleansing blood of the Lord to the "city of God" (Psalm 46:4).

At the cross and through the blood, souls once destined to perish are rescued from damnation. The wicked gnash their teeth at God for foiling their plans and defeating their evil purpose of dragging the sinner to death.

The wicked cringe at the sight of the dying man on the cross. They scorn His torment and anguish. The wicked cannot persuade Him to "come down from the cross" (Matthew 27:40). The Lord will not be moved, but He remains steadfast to God. Yet when sinners traveling on the road of condemnation see His faithfulness and love for God and man, they come to repentance and are saved.

JANUARY 25

We sometimes forget that people before us have paved the way for what we can accomplish today. For example, John Wesley's preaching had a tremendous spiritual impact on England's poor. His faith, work and commitment to God inspired William Wilberforce to change England's attitude toward slavery. England then influenced America. Today, we cannot even imagine our society's failing to extend help to the lowly and the needy.

Also consider John the Baptist, God's premier forerunner to Christ. His ministry prepared the hearts and minds of the people of Israel to receive Jesus Christ, the Messiah. His message was simple: repent and receive forgiveness for sin. We cannot imagine our spiritual lives without the possibility of forgiveness.

God prepares all His disciples to be forerunners. When we become Christians, we join the relay team of God. Our conversion results from the forerunners who extended the baton of salvation to us through the power of the Holy Spirit. Once we receive that baton, Christ's Spirit directs us to extend it to others.

When our hidden life in Christ is made visible through the Holy Spirit, He moves others according to God's great plan of salvation. Each leg of this race called life is meticulously executed by God in Christ so all the world will hear the Gospel and be transformed through the "Lamb of God, who takes away the sin of the world" (John 1:29).

JANUARY 26

I will be traveling to a warmer climate in the next few days. So, I have to think about what clothes to pack. Winter clothes will be important for my departure and return. However, once I have reached my destination summer clothes will be appropriate.

We spend hours shopping for appropriate clothing. Besides seasonal attire our wardrobes also must include attire for work, casual events, funerals, weddings, leisure activities, exercise, formal affairs, and so on. And whether we like it or not, clothes make an impression.

God is also clothed in fitting robes. The Psalmist wrote that God clothes Himself in splendor and majesty (104:1). According to the book of Job He is adorned with glory and honor (40:10). His glory fills the everlasting temple. His splendor reaches beyond the skies. His majesty and honor fill creation. These clothes make an impression. This is the wardrobe of the Almighty. It is His exclusive collection. It reminds us we are corruptible flesh and bone and finite, but He is magnificent, timeless and radiant. This splendid array caused the prophet to exclaim "No one is like you, O Lord; you are great, and your name is mighty in power" (Jeremiah 10:6).

God's accoutrement is dazzling and stunning and luminous. They are clothes worthy of His perfect nature, and He wears them to remind humanity of the respect due His name.

"The Lord reigns, He is robed in majesty" (Psalm 93:1). "Let us kneel before the Lord our Maker" (Psalm 95:6).

JANUARY 27

Let me try to unravel Christ's analogy in John 10:3, "The watchman opens the gate for him, and the sheep listen to his voice. He calls his own sheep by name and leads them out." This verse has intrigued me for several days, primarily because in Hebrew one definition of name is nature.

The shepherd is calling his sheep by their nature. Now let's put the cast of characters together. The Shepherd is Christ, the sheep are people seeking salvation and the watchman is the Holy Spirit.

I am not going to carry this too far, but here's my thought: The Watchman-Spirit opens the heart of a sheep-sinner for Jesus Christ. The ears that had been deaf to Christ's voice are now able to hear the voice of the Savior. As a sheep-sinner hears "the Good Shepherd" (John 10:11), he is, by the power of the Spirit, compelled to follow. The Shepherd takes the sheep on a journey of faith, which begins at the cross. At the foot of the cross, the sheep become aware of the price Christ has paid for their sin. Through faith in the atoning work of Jesus on the cross, the sheep are set free from sin. And the Savior imparts His righteous nature into the sheep through the power of the Holy Spirit. Through this work of the Spirit, the Righteous Shepherd calls His righteous sheep, and He leads them out of sin and death into life.

JANUARY 28

Recently I lined up our young gymnasts to give them instructions. They listened as I explained the drills and the order in which they were to be done. Most of the girls heard and followed the directions. However, one athlete moved randomly about doing her own thing. She failed to listen well. As a result, she was in the way of the others, causing a few of her teammates to stumble, and she almost hurt herself. It took only a few moments to recognize that a bad listener destroys order.

Easy lesson here: God created a world of perfect order for Adam and before him set the instructions for maintaining it.

Unfortunately, Adam was a bad listener. He failed to follow God's instructions, so God's created order was destroyed.

Desiring to restore order, God sent Jesus Christ into the chaos of this fallen creation. He was a good listener. He was so attuned to God that He spoke only what He heard His Father say "I do nothing on my own but speak just what the Father has taught me" (John 8:28). By listening to the Father, the Son was perfectly obedient to the Father. And through the Son's obedience, He reconciled the world to the Father.

We have two choices. We, like Adam, can continue, to run through this world without listening to the Word of God. Or we can by faith in the Lord Jesus Christ and by the power of the Holy Spirit listen to God and live as His obedient children.

JANUARY 29

The way things are going, writing my Evening Reflection and my For the Weekend devotionals are going to bump into each other in the night. I am numb from traveling from Columbus, Ohio, to Phoenix Arizona, to Houston, Texas, for gymnastic competitions.

My weariness reminds me of a spiritual dilemma I face. Some days, I don't feel like a sinner. I can keep myself so busy during the day that I don't think about it. I can keep my mind occupied with other things. This forgetting my sin is denial, but it doesn't change the fact that I am a sinner.

Sometimes, I get into a state I call *sin numb*. This numbness means my heart is hard and calloused toward God. When I am sin numb I am also Savior numb. "If we claim we have not sinned, we make Him (Christ) out to be a liar and his word has no place in our lives" (1 John 1:10). If I deny my sin, I deny my need for the Savior who came into this world to take away my sin.

While my essential nature is sin, Jesus Christ's essential nature is salvific. It is as natural for Christ to save as it is for me to sin. Just because I don't feel like a sinner doesn't change the fact that my nature is sinful. I know it because Scripture confirms it, the Holy Spirit exposes it and Jesus Christ died to save me from it.

"I know that nothing good lives in me, that is, in my sinful nature" (Romans 7:18).

JANUARY 30

I have always loved the ocean. Walking on the beach fills my mind with wonder and my soul with joy. All that water sparks my imagination as I consider the wonders and mystery within that vast body of water. Ocean beaches captivate me. There is always something new to discover because the waters wash ashore remnants from the deep, or draw ripple patterns in the sand, or bring forth the sounds of the underwater caverns to the surface.

This wonder and fascination with the ocean makes me appreciate the Creator. In Isaiah 51:15, God says, "For I am the Lord your God, who churns up the sea so that its waves roar."

The ocean reflects God's nature: deep and mysterious. And, yet, He willingly sent His Son into the world to reveal those mysteries and draw us down into His depths. From the shore, He gives us a view of His greatness and invites us to swim deeper and deeper into life with Him. He does not remain a mystery, but through His Son brings us into more knowledge and understanding about who He is and what He has done on behalf of humankind.

God's creation displays His glory and the glory of His Son. Walk the beach with God.

JANUARY 31

After the meet this weekend, I realized that a gymnastic competition is just a trial and test to evaluate the training habits of the gymnasts. As I looked at this test, one thing became clear: gymnasts who had been impatient and worried during practice exhibited greater frustration, anxiety and disappointment at the competition than those gymnasts who had submitted to coaches' directions, assignments and corrections.

Every day we face many trials. The world accosts us with evil, sorrow comes our way, friends are burdened or we are suffering with heartache. If we respond to our trials with impatience and worry, that will lead to greater frustration, anxiety and suffering. Our hearts become heavy with burdens and restlessness. We have no peace; our minds fill with thoughts of hopelessness and our soul despairs. We crumble under the pressure of the trial.

However, if we respond to the trials with patience and prayer, God empowers us with His Holy Spirit to endure the trails we face. With the aid of the Spirit our minds calm and fill with the hope of Christ. As Christ dominates our thoughts our hearts find His peace, and our souls rest in the assurance that Jesus walks through our trials with us. Through our trial and testing, Jesus guides us, sustains us and strengthens our faith through the power of the Holy Spirit.

Christ will "strengthen and encourage you in your faith, so that no one would be unsettled by these trials" (1 Thessalonians 3:2-3).

February

FEBRUARY 1

As I write this, I've just watched Super Bowl XLIX. It will occupy our conversations for the next several weeks. We saw spectacular plays and a stunning conclusion. It was a Super Bowl like no other. And whether your team won or lost the last thing any of us could say was WOW!

The final 30 seconds changed the game. It looked as though Seattle would finish the game as the victors. But that never happened. And the victory went, once again, to the Patriots.

More than 2,000 years ago, history records six hours that changed the world. During those six hours, a Jewish man, Jesus Christ, hung on a Roman cross to die as a felon. It looked as though His death would put an end to His message, purpose and will. Crowds lined the streets to watch this man die. Once the last breath escaped from Christ, the spectators were certain that would be the end of this insurrectionist.

But His death changed everything. When Jesus died on the cross, sin and death appeared victorious. However, His death was the vehicle to His conquest and when the six hours passed, and three days went by, the game changed. Sin and death were conquered by the Savior and everlasting life was the prize of the victor.

For those of us who believe in the saving grace of Jesus Christ all we can say is WOW. Through His resurrection we to are raised to life. "Since then you have been raised with Christ, set your hearts on things above, where Christ is seated at the right hand of God" (Colossians 3:1).

FEBRUARY 2

My girls chatted with me for several hours tonight, filling me with stories about their weekend. I enjoyed every facial expression, gesture and detail of their recaps. We sat for nearly three hours in the upstairs hall. None of us wanted to leave the presence of the others.

Yes, the temperature in Rockford is 1 degree tonight with a minus 8 wind chill; there are 16 inches of snow on the ground, and I am wrapped in three layers plus a blanket as I write. But this is home. And home is where your family can sit in a hallway enjoying one another's presence.

Scripture says, "In the shelter of Your presence you hide them . . . in Your dwelling you keep them safe" (Psalm 31:20). For a Christian, home is God's presence. We don't have to wait for eternity, He is near now. And where the presence of the Lord is there is shelter, protection and safety.

The problem is many of us do not seek the presence of God through the Holy Spirit. We endure the cold of the world, instead of taking refuge in God. We race through this world, trying to find a place where we belong instead of settling at home in God's presence to receive His comfort and security. We fail to come into God's presence through Christ to embrace the love and joy and peace God offers through His Son.

God is home. Come in out of the cold of the world.

FEBRUARY 3

It's strange for me to be tired. However, the schedule over the last few days has finally taken its toll, and both my mind and body are fatigued. I don't appreciate the vulnerability that accompanies this state of weariness. I prefer the feelings of power and strength that energy produces. My energy level usually runs on high, so this low is uncharacteristic. But I know that a little rest will recharge my system, and I will be full throttle again tomorrow.

As strange as this feeling is to me, I am reminded of how unusual it had to be to Jesus. In John 4:6, Jesus' ministry schedule had caught up with Him. He had traveled between Judah and Galilee at least twice and on this day, the trip wore Him out. John says, "Jesus, tired as He was from the journey, sat down by the well." How strange is it to think that the eternal Son of God sat down because He was tired?

How uncharacteristic for the everlasting God, the immortal, omnipotent God to feel fatigue. He who was infinite in power and might was tired from walking. Perhaps His feet were sore, His legs were weak and His body ached from walking. "Very God of very God" (Nicene Creed) was exhausted.

My own fatigue reminds me of just how much God sacrificed for me. Jesus chose to live the human life, within the limitations of a body. He labored, He tired and He died. God sat down so we could rise up.

FEBRUARY 4

Gymnasts frequently struggle with Yurchenko vaults. This skill is very difficult to execute properly because the athlete must run as fast as she can toward the vault table, round off onto the vault board, do a back handspring onto the table, use her hands and shoulders to block (a very quick push) off the table, do a full twist in the air and land. In order for this skill to be powerful, the gymnast must focus on the approach to the table. If they run too slowly and do not get the round off turned over quickly they will have problems blocking off the vault. The approach determines the strength or weakness of the vault.

Likewise, if our prayer lives seem dull and weak, and we think God is not listening, perhaps we should consider our approach to Him. The Lord said to Moses, "Among those who approach me I will show myself holy" (Leviticus 10:3).

When we pray we are entering the presence of Holy God. Still, we tend to ignore the holiness and purity of His essence. We race into His throne room spouting requests, usually without even pausing to appreciate His wonder and majesty. We hasten from His presence without offering Him the respect and homage He deserves. Then we're baffled when we don't hear Him answer.

We need to demonstrate adoration of and admiration for God. Part of prayer is learning to sit in awe of God and wait for the Spirit to usher us into His presence. God is eager to grant us audience, but we must approach Him offering the honor due His name.

Approaching God is an aspect of prayer. Read in Scripture how Abraham, Moses, David, Isaiah and others entered the presence of God. Then allow the Spirit to teach us to enter God's presence with awe and wonder and humility. In this way our approach will be worthy of His majesty and holiness.

FEBRUARY 5

People have many reasons for not attending church on Sunday or participating in spiritual activities during the week. In fact, excuses are abundant. For instance, I have heard people say, "I'd like to go to church, but I was up late." And, "I really should join a Bible study, but I'm just so busy." Or, "My children would like to attend youth group, but I just can't add one more thing to my schedule." These might all seem to be legitimate reasons for not observing the Sabbath, but they are, ultimately, excuses. People are not easily roused to action, but they are quick to defend why they don't act.

These are just typical examples. However, our proficiency in making excuse spills over into other areas of our spiritual lives. Instead of facing and confessing our sin, we make excuses for the sin in our lives. Making an excuse for our sin does not remedy sin. We know the solution is faith in Jesus Christ, but we do not heed the call to come to Christ for salvation, through the power and conviction of the Holy Spirit. Instead, we let sin fester in our hearts, minds and souls. An excuse does not change the condition of sin.

Christ is the change agent. Christ did not come into the world to listen to our excuses for sin. Nor did He come to excuse our sin. Christ came into the world to endure our sin on the cross and take the punishment we deserved for our transgressions against God.

Jesus bled and died for our sin. His atoning sacrifice set us free from sin and its consequence, death. Therefore, we no longer have an excuse for our sin; the cross is God's divine remedy for sin.

Jesus said, "If I had not come and spoken to them, they would not be guilty of sin. Now, however, they have no excuse for their sin" (John 15:22).

FEBRUARY 6

My gym clothes are comfortable and appropriate for work. It is clothing that is useful and functional for the job that I have as a gymnastics coach. I would guess that most of us have work, casual and dress clothes. The malls, lined with retail clothing stores, confirm that we have clothes in our closets for all occasions. We should wear clothing appropriate to specific functions. Depending upon the social engagement, certain types of clothing are expected. A person should not wear beach-party attire to a funeral. Nor should anyone wear a muscle shirt and spandex to a wedding.

In Scripture, Jesus tells a parable about a man attending a king's wedding. The king arrives, and as he greets his guests, he notices one guest has not worn wedding clothes. Without hesitation, the king removes him from the celebration.

God has a dress code. Our carnal human nature is not appropriate dress before the Almighty. Our sinful nature is an affront to God, so it is not welcome in His presence. God Himself sent His Son to die on the cross so that through Him our sinful wardrobe could be changed into a wardrobe of holiness. Through faith in Jesus Christ, we receive apparel fitting to wear in the presence of God.

Isaiah 61:10 says, "I delight greatly in the Lord; my soul rejoices in my God. For He has clothed me with garments of salvation and arrayed me in a robe of righteousness."

FEBRUARY 7

At the moment, we are surrounded by snow. Turning onto busy streets, I have to inch the car forward to see around a snow mound. Snow is piled up to the mailbox. Parking lots are missing spaces because the plows had to push the snow into hills along the border of the lot. The main streets have been cleared, but side streets are still white. Snow is everywhere.

The Psalmist wrote this simile, "As the mountains surround Jerusalem, so the Lord surrounds His people both now and forever" (125:2). Let me take poetic license here: "As the snow surrounds Rockford, so the Lord surrounds His people."

When I look at the snow surrounding me, I remember that God encircles His people in this city and every city. We are surrounded by Almighty God. His glory, His holiness, His majesty encircles us through the power of the Holy Spirit.

We often come to a wrong conclusion: that since Jesus is no longer physically present among us, God has left us all alone. However, this verse contradicts our erroneous conclusion. God is with us always in the Person of the Holy Spirit. He continues to minister in the world as Christ ministered in the world. He exposes our sin. He reveals the Savior's work of salvation on the cross. He grants us the gift of faith, administers redemption and brings reconciliation to those who believe.

God remains always around us in the Person of the Holy Spirit.

FEBRUARY 8

One of my gymnasts is a huge Elvis Presley fan. Not only does she own his movies, songs, t-shirts, and other memorabilia but she also possesses a vast knowledge of his career and personal life. Of course, she has never actually seen him perform. Since Elvis is no longer living, she will never attend one of his concerts or see him live or have any chance of meeting him in person. She can know him only second-hand.

But one day Elvis will be forgotten by most people. Because Elvis, like all of us, had a life span. He was very popular during his day. However, no one in the 1700s knew who he was, and anyone born in 2305 probably won't know him either. That's what it means to be a finite being. We have a beginning and an end.

However, there is one being who had no beginning or end and who will never be forgotten: Psalm 90:2 says of the Lord, "Before the mountains were born or you brought forth the earth and the world, from everlasting to everlasting you are God." This eternity is what it means to be God: He has no beginning and no end. He has no life span. He was present before He created Adam and Eve, and He will be present when the last finite being dies. God simply is forever.

Being infinite also means that every generation past, present and future can know God through the Person of the Holy Spirit. All human beings from the beginning of time to the end of time have an opportunity to enter into a relationship with God and know Him personally through the work of the Spirit. God is eternal, absolute, unending.

FEBRUARY 9

In John chapter 10 the Jews are ready once again to stone Jesus. So Jesus says, "I have shown you many great miracles from the Father. For which of these do you stone me?" (32).

The Jews respond, "We are not stoning you for any of these, but for blasphemy, because you, a mere man, claim to be God" (33).

The Jews did not object to Christ's miracles, but they could not tolerate His claim of divinity. Didn't the miracles point out that Jesus was not a mere man?

Many of us want miracles from Jesus, but we don't want them to be entangled with or point to the truth that He is God. We like miracles so long as Jesus remains a mere man. We prefer to consider Jesus a mere man, so we can receive the benefit of a miracle and then go about our lives as though that experience does not change it and that the truth of His divinity does not demand something of us.

However, if we accept the miracles as proof that Jesus is God, then our lives will be changed. When we come to understand that, through the Holy Spirit, Jesus is divine, then we will also come to understand through the Holy Spirit that we are sinners. We don't want to know we are sinners. We want to believe we are good people whose meritorious acts and deeds invoked Jesus to give us a miracle and put us in favor with God.

But Jesus is God. We are sinners. And it is Christ's meritorious life of righteousness that puts us in favor with God.

FEBRUARY 10

Coaches must justify to gymnasts that the corrections that they insist upon are reasonable for that particular athlete's level of difficulty and experience in the sport. Sometimes gymnasts don't want to recognize that coaches' corrections are reasonable. Sure gymnasts will usually agree that the coaches' corrections are reasonable particularly when it applies to a teammate. However, sometimes a gymnast does not trust a coach enough to implement a correction. Then there's a problem. In fact, a gymnast who applies a correction personally reveals a high level of trust in her coach.

Often we consider things asked of others more reasonable than things asked of us. Even the disciples had this problem. Jesus told Peter to "Follow me!" (John 21:19). As Jesus says this, Peter points to John and says to Jesus, "Lord, what about him?" (John 21:21). Peter was struggling with the reasonableness of Jesus' command to follow and was wondering if John was going to get a better offer.

Jesus then said to Peter, "If I want him to remain alive until I return, what is that to you? you must follow me" (John 21:22). Peter was sure Jesus would give John something reasonable, but he wasn't sure that Jesus' request of him was reasonable.

We all behave this way with the Lord. We struggle with what the Lord requires of us. We find His requests unreasonable. But Jesus asks of us what is reasonable according to the maturity of our faith and the strength of our relationship with Him. His requests are also reasonable because they deepen our understanding of God and grow us in knowledge of Him.

Jesus makes reasonable requests of each of us. Our response to His requests reveals our trust in Him.

FEBRUARY 11

Going into fourth grade, I heard all sorts of horror stories about the teacher. The playground buzzed with upper-level students telling us lowly third graders about the terror of fourth grade and the tyrannical teacher.

I was not looking forward to fourth grade. On the first day, I entered the classroom with great fear and trepidation. My dreams had produced a picture of a Herculean-sized woman standing at the classroom door wielding a paddle in each hand smacking students about like ping pong balls.

As it turned out, the rumors were wrong, and my dreams were even further from the truth. She turned out to be the best teacher I have ever had. Some things you must find out for yourself.

We spend many hours listening to the world tell us about God. It yammers on about how frightful the Lord is. It points to the cross and tells us how unloving the Creator can be. It smears the name of Jesus and ridicules anyone foolish enough to believe in Him. There are many, many rumors about God, and sadly, we listen to them instead of the Holy Spirit.

The truth about God is found in Scripture, not the world. When it comes to finding out who God really is we must find out for ourselves through the help of the Holy Spirit.

"I am the Lord your God, Who teaches you what is best for you, who directs you in the way you should go" (Isaiah 48:17). Does this sound like a frightful tyrant?

FEBRUARY 12

Several years ago, I chose a vegetarian lifestyle that has helped me keep my body healthy. I supplemented my new lifestyle with additional rules to help me monitor and guard my health. Of course there are times when I break the rules, but my commitment to health is greater than my desire to break the rules.

Becoming a Christian means that we undergo a lifestyle change. We can no longer live according to our "old self with its practices" (Colossians 3:9b), but "have to put on the new self, which is being renewed in knowledge in the image of its Creator" (Colossians 3:10).

To help maintain the health of our "new self," Paul gives us some practical rules to incorporate into our daily lives. In 2 Timothy 2:16 he writes, "Avoid godless chatter, because those who indulge in it will become more and more ungodly." He also wrote, "but set an example for the believers in speech, in life, in love, in faith and in purity" (1 Timothy 4:12). And he cautions Timothy to "watch your life and doctrine closely" (1Timothy 4:16). All these rules can be kept only through the power of the Holy Spirit, and we stay close to the Holy Spirit through diligent reading of the Scriptures.

These rules simply offer a means of monitoring the health of our "new self," and when we keep the rules, we are testifying to our pledge to live in a manner pleasing to Jesus Christ through the Holy Spirit. Certainly, we will err; however, we should want our commitment to the Lord to be greater than our desire to break the rules.

FEBRUARY 13

There is a comfort in knowing what to expect each year. Every year I can predict my day at the Chicago Style Gymnastic Meet, in Chicago, Illinois. This event is one of my favorite meets of the season. I look forward to it every year. I have an opportunity to see old friends and encounter new ones.

But this year the meet presented something unexpected. I got to experience something new, thanks to a very good friend who invited me to her favorite vegetarian restaurant in Chicago. I ordered a buffalo-chicken wrap, made with meatless chicken. (Yes, I know that seems to be an oxymoron.) However, this vegan meatless chicken tasted very similar to chicken. After all these years of not tasting meat, my taste buds were shocked by the taste, and I began to question whether this might actually be meat. It was shocking to taste meat. It was also a delicious surprise.

See, I thought that today was going to be the same. I thought I knew what to expect. But today was very different and new and a blast.

Sometimes we think we know what to expect from God each day, but He very often surprises us. But we must be open to His surprises. He likes to bring the unexpected into our lives. We have to be open to receiving it.

God makes all things new in our lives.

FEBRUARY 14

I spend a great many hours reminding gymnasts that they must expect to make their routines at a meet. This past weekend, I could tell easily by a gymnast's body language and facial expressions whether she had expected to perform well at the competition. I could tell who hadn't, too.

Gymnasts with an attitude of expectation exhibit certain traits at the meet that the others do not display. There is a confidence and calmness about them. I can sense that they trust their coaches and believe that the hours they have spent practicing in the gym have made them ready for the competition.

As Christians we should be living with an expectation: that our Lord and Savior Jesus Christ will return. Jesus said, "You also must be ready, because the Son of Man will come at an hour when you do not expect him" (Luke 12:40).

Like athletes who expect the expected, Christians should be prepared for the arrival of our Lord. We should also be training for His return. In this way, we will live as an example to the world that Christ will indeed come again. We must be diligent in prayer, asking for Christ to come. We should be invested in the study of Scripture and committed to attending worship.

When we are persistent in our training, our lives will be full of confidence in Christ's promises, particularly His promise to come again. And we will have the calm assurance of knowing that His return will create a new world and we will be transformed in His likeness. "Dear friends, now we are children of God, and what we will be has not yet been made known. But we know that when He appears, we shall be like Him, for we shall see Him as He is" (1 John 3:2).

FEBRUARY 15

Over the weekend, I had an opportunity to watch the sun rise over Chicago. Its rays shimmered across the icy waters of Lake Michigan and bounced off the windows of the high rises and towers reflecting columns of light across the frozen waters. While splashing light across the awakening city, the sun also painted soft hues of pink across the heavens.

I like watching the sun's glory mingle with man's magnificent buildings and structures. It reminds me that God and man belong together. Each daybreak is an opportunity to recall that God is exalted over all the earth. Man, as a creature, is to walk with God, the giver of Light, in a posture of humble adoration. As the sun continues to rise higher in the morning sky, God's abundant light pours into the world, casting out the darkness.

God's Son mingled on earth a man with men. He said, "While I am in the world, I am the light of the world" (John 9:5). While Jesus was in the world He sent the light of God into the shadows of sin and death, casting out the darkness. He shines brightest on the cross, where the piercing light of Holy God could not be vanquished by the charging forces of darkness. "Light has come into the world" (John 3:19) "and the darkness has not overcome it" (John 1:5).

Brighter than any sun, Christ's light still shines in the world through the power of the Holy Spirit, who brings the truth to mankind that God and man belong together.

FEBRUARY 16

If you're like me, your personal life takes precedence over the work day. But some days we don't know how to carve out time for that priority when the demands and responsibilities of work suck the hours from our days.

Beyond that, Christians must also prioritize our spiritual lives. Yet you might find that rarely does our spiritual life get precedence over our physical life. As a result, we are tired, uninspired to rise early for prayer and powerless to answer Christ's call to ministry. We are even faithless at times.

When we place our spiritual lives in highest regard, we are giving God His rightful place in our lives. And He will order our days so we can accomplish the things that most matter to Him. And each week, Sunday, He will give us an entire day to devote to Him and the significant others in our lives.

However, we are too weak to prioritize our own spiritual lives without depending upon the Holy Spirit. Each day, we should sit with Him and let Him show us where we waste our time. He can show us the ways in which each of us can make Him the priority in our daily schedules.

He has shown me how to simplify my meals so I can pray more. He has taught me how to monitor my phone and computer time so I can spend personal time with Him and my family and friends. He has swayed me from TV viewing to Scripture reading and memorizing. All this is what God has shown to me, but it is different for everyone. "Seek ye first the kingdom of God" (Matthew 6:33 KJV).

FEBRUARY 17

Tonight, one of my daughters spied a bag of candy on the counter. Since it belonged to her sister, she tried to sneak a piece, certain that her sister would never notice. Her sister did notice, so she was busted. My daughter's best attempt to cover up her candy crime had failed.

I was reminded of how we try to cover up and hide our sin from God. Even King David thought he could cover up an affair and murder, Moses thought he had hidden a murder, and Ananias lied to the Holy Spirit. These men could hide their crimes from men. However, their crimes were never hidden from God's sight.

We sometimes act as though God is old, deaf and blind and so far away in heaven that He can't possibly notice our actions or hear our words. We carry on in a sinful fashion thinking we are hiding everything from Him. We forget that, "Nothing in all creation is hidden from God's sight. Everything is uncovered and laid bare before the eyes of Him to whom we must give account" (Hebrews 4:13).

God exposes our sin to us through the conviction of the Holy Spirit, so He can save us from the consequences of our sin through the saving work of His Son, Jesus Christ. Remember

God sees our sin, and Christ carries it to the cross so we can receive eternal life. "Salvation is found in no one else, for there is no other name under heaven given to men by which we must be saved" (Acts 4:12).

FEBRUARY 18

John 4:32 and 34 have intrigued me for a long time, and I am using one period of Lent to study and ask the Holy Spirit to show me what Jesus means in these verses. "I have food to eat that you know nothing about," and, "My food is to do the will of Him who sent me and to finish His work."

Food is any nourishing substance that sustains life. Substance is the essential part or element of anything and it belongs intrinsically to a thing by its very nature. Jesus is saying that His substance sustains life. That is, His nature sustains life and His nature is divine. He is God. Jesus says, "I am the resurrection and the life. He who believes in me will live, even though he dies; and whoever lives and believes in me will never die" (John 11:25-26).

However, Jesus also has a human nature and experienced all that we do as humans. God incarnate felt the necessities of life as the Son of Man. Think about this, Jesus needed to eat to survive, yet He is the Lord, the giver of Life. Jesus came to die for sinners, but He had no sin. Jesus died on the cross and was buried but He rose again from the dead. The immortal becomes mortal; God becomes man; and the Crucified becomes the

Risen. Within One Person, Jesus Christ, all the fullness of human nature and the fullness of divine nature exist.

God the Father gave the Son a human existence to accomplish what must be done on the cross so the world would be saved through Him.

Let Jesus, the Son of Man and the Son of God, be your Lenten focus.

FEBRUARY 19

As children, many of us were, at one time or another, afraid of the dark. Our parents would remedy the situation with a night light. Though the wattage of these bulbs was low, it cast enough light into the room to chase away the monsters.

As adults we still sometimes find ourselves afraid of the dark in this world. Hostilities in the world, political uncertainty, marital problems, and family hardships can all cast shadows of darkness across our days. Trouble, anxiety, confusion and skepticism have us reaching to turn on the night light. We need something to chase away the uneasiness in our hearts.

Psalm 27:1 reminds us that God gives us His light: "The Lord is my light and my salvation—whom shall I fear? The Lord is the stronghold of my life—of whom shall I be afraid?" The everlasting light of God shines in this world. When we look at God all the shadows, grays and darkness of this world are dispelled. Our worries about the day, our angst about life and even our dread of tomorrow are swallowed by the inextinguishable Light of God in Christ.

Christ's light casts away the darkness of this world and opens our eyes to the reality of God's glorious kingdom. Therefore, "Walk while you have the light, before darkness overtakes you . . . Put your trust in the light while you have it, so that you may become sons of light" (John 12:35, 36).

The Light of Christ shines in this world, so we do not have to be afraid of the dark.

FEBRUARY 20

Occasionally we coaches have our older gymnasts demonstrate a skill or drill for our younger athletes so they can get a visual understanding of the trick. We do so on everything from basic body shapes to high-level skills. Giving the younger gymnasts a picture of what has just been explained is very beneficial for them. Once they see the skill, they are in a better position to imitate the actions they've seen. A young gymnast can't attempt a skill without first seeing it done and imitating what she sees. Young gymnasts, in essence, become imitators of their older teammates.

Paul writes in his letter to the Ephesians, "Be imitators of God, therefore, as dearly loved children and live a life of love, just as Christ loved us and gave himself up for us" (5:1-2). How is it possible for human beings to imitate God? God made sure He sent us an example in Jesus Christ.

Jesus Christ modeled a life of perfect obedience to God. He walked among us as an example to demonstrate the life God wants us to lead through the power of the Holy Spirit.

Without the picture of Christ's perfect life, we can't live a life pleasing to God, because our sinful life is rebellious to obedience. We need to see that it is possible to live in a manner pleasing to God. Among sinful humanity there was no one to demonstrate an obedient life. And, we couldn't even attempt to obey God without first seeing it done. So Christ, the perfect man, walked among us, and then He sent the Holy Spirit to dwell within believers so we might live the obedient life to God.

FEBRUARY 21

I attend a book study one morning a week at a local restaurant. This week, I arrived a little early and talked with the leader as he buttered a bagel. A few minutes later, several members of the group arrived, and one lady took a seat behind the leader. She settled into the chair. The leader kindly placed a strong hand on the slender shoulder of the woman and slid the bagel in front of her. It was from that simple touch, that gentle gesture that I was made aware that this woman was the man's wife.

Touch is a powerful communicator. It expresses our deepest emotions when words cannot. A touch makes our thoughts tangible to another. How we touch and how we use touch reveals our character.

Consider the ministry of Jesus. He used touch. He raised a dead girl by taking her hand. He touched a man with leprosy and healed him. He touched Simon's mother-in-law and cured her fever. And Luke records, "[The] people brought to Jesus all who had various kinds of sickness, and laying His hands on each one, He healed them" (4:40).

Jesus's touch communicated the most powerful message in history: God was on earth. Each time Jesus touched a person and brought healing or restored life, His character was revealed. His divine nature, which was hidden in human skin, was manifest through His touch. His human frame testified to the truth of His humanity. His touch, and the signs He performed, testified to the truth that He was God.

FEBRUARY 22

On Sundays I visit my friend in a nursing home. We chat. She asks about her friends from church and if anyone is sick. She also wonders what must change so she can go home. She is comfortable and well taken care, but she wants to go back home. Of course, I can't change her circumstances, but I remind her that there are agencies that could help her.

Driving home I realized that my situation is similar to my friend's. I also want to return to my lost life in the kingdom of God. However, when Adam rebelled, God locked the door, and, like all sinners, I was banned from re-entry. "After He drove the man out, He placed on the east side of the Garden of Eden cherubim and a flaming sword flashing back and forth to guard the way to the tree of life" (Genesis 3:24).

As a sinner, I can't change my circumstances. However, someone came to give me a way home: God sent His agent of change into the world in the person of Jesus Christ. God sent

His Son into the world to pay the penalty for all sin. By faith in Jesus's work on the cross, I can one day return to the Garden. Lent is the time we remember that "God made Him who had no sin to be sin for us" (2 Corinthians 5:21), so that through faith in Christ my circumstance would change and the ban on the life-to-come would be lifted.

FEBRUARY 23

A coworker told me that over the weekend he and his family had helped search for a missing child at a waterpark. After looking for 30 minutes, they stopped and prayed. Within three minutes the little girl was found.

Tonight, when I returned home there was a message on my phone from a good friend who told me that her husband had received a job offer in Chicago. There have been several of us praying over the last seven years for my friend's husband to find lucrative work. And today we saw God's answer.

I can't tell you why one prayer took three minutes to answer and another took seven years. What I do know is that the Father of our Lord Jesus Christ answered them both. Why do I know this? I know this because Scripture tells us that both the Spirit and Christ Jesus "intercede for God's people in accordance with the will of God" and "Christ Jesus who died . . . is at the right hand of God and is also interceding for us" (Romans 8:27, 34).

God prays with us, and God prays for us. God's involvement in our prayer life is the exact reason we can come to prayer confident of an answer. John 3:35 states, "The Father loves the Son and has placed everything in His hands."

Every prayer we lift to God is placed in the hands of His Beloved Son, who takes it before the Father. Through Christ and the Spirit, our prayers are heard by the Father, and He will answer our prayers to the honor and glory of God.

FEBRUARY 24

This morning a young man on the stationary bike next to me at the gym joined in the chorus of Billy Joel's "My Life," which was playing on the gym radio. He isn't going to win *The Voice*, but he put plenty of heart and enthusiasm into the last verse.

The song basically describes a man who decides to live life on his own terms. Today it occurred to me that this song depicts Adam's attitude toward God during his rebellion in the Garden. Once sin entered the heart and mind of Adam, he wanted life on his own terms.

Our sinful nature wants life on our own terms, without interference from God. Yet, life apart from God is dark and without hope. We human beings quickly despair over our hard and tumultuous circumstances.

God knew the consequences of Adam's decision: that Adam's sin would be credited to all human beings. However, instead of leaving mankind to suffer for Adam's choice, God sent His Son into the world to show us how to live life on God's terms. And Jesus Christ's sacrificial death on the cross satisfied all the demands necessary for sinners to be restored to life in God.

When by faith we accept Christ's grace into our lives, our lives are no longer our own; they belong to God in Christ, and with the help of the Holy Spirit we live life not on our terms any longer, but God's. The Christian has no "My Life." Our self, our will and our life "belong to the Messiah" (Mark 9:41 NLT).

FEBRUARY 25

During the gymnastics meet season, the coaching staff is focused on the needs of each athlete. This focus can encompass a wide range of concerns, from the coaches' insisting on adequate nutrition, to practicing the necessary number of skill repetitions, to giving extra time on events for which gymnasts show a weakness, or to taking time off from training. Coaches address an athlete's weaknesses and deficiencies and create a course of training that addresses these needs.

We humans are always assessing the needs in our life. We are usually focused on them to the point of obsession. But most of our needs are not needs at all. They are physical desires that we pursue in an attempt to overcome our spiritual deficiencies caused by sin. We are broken people using objects or experiences to try to ease our guilt and cover our shame before God. Sin has destroyed our lives and left us lacking the righteous essentials we need to reconcile with God.

We spend thousands of dollars every year trying to soothe our weary, sorrowing soul with the tangibles of life, only to tangle it more deeply in hopelessness and despair, because the real need of every person is grace, forgiveness and redemption from God.

Through Jesus Christ, God has provided these essentials. In Christ, "we have redemption, the forgiveness of sins" (Colossians 1:14). Through Christ's death on the cross and His resurrection He has satisfied for us our deepest need, and this "is by grace . . . through faith" (Ephesians 2:8).

Our fixes won't remedy our deepest affliction. Christ's cross is our cure.

FEBRUARY 26

This morning as I was reading through John 14 the Lord grabbed my attention with these words "in my name" (14). After a quick word study, I inserted a different definition for the words in and name. The phrase then read "within my nature."

This substitution changed my perspective. How many times in prayer do I make requests of God based on His nature? According to Scripture, God's nature is "compassionate, and gracious . . . slow to anger, abounding in love and faithfulness . . . and forgiving" (Exodus 34:6-7; Jonah 4:2; Nehemiah 9:17 and Psalm 145:8). These attributes of God are worth praying for. When I ask God to pour His attributes into my corrupt nature, I am asking Him to transform my life into Christ's likeness. To be formed in the image of God is to allow the Holy

Spirit to shape Christ's perfect qualities into my imperfect life and being. When I pray for others I should be asking God to make them in Christ's likeness through the power of the Holy Spirit, what I pray Jesus will form in my life through the power of the Holy Spirit. These are the attributes of holy God that I should pray will fill the lives of those around me.

Imagine how dramatically lives will change if we are praying for people to be formed in the nature and likeness of God the Father, as demonstrated by God the Son through the power of God the Spirit? People who are unfaithful will be faithful. Those who have a quick temper will be slow to anger. Friends who are bitter and discontented will find forgiveness. Families will know how to love as Christ loves.

"You may ask me for anything in my name, and I will do it" (John 14:14). By praying in Christ's name we are calling on the Holy Spirit to transform and regenerate the world one life at a time.

FEBRUARY 27

Focus is essential to gymnastics training. When athletes fail to keep their focus their minds become undisciplined and the result is, as people say these days, "a hot mess." A loss of focus leads to stumbles and falls, and the gymnast who loses focus will become preoccupied with making excuses and obsessing about fears. Suddenly consistency exits, and confidence wanes.

As Christians, we also have difficulty when we lose our focus on Christ's cross. The author of Hebrews knew the importance of focus. He writes, "Let us fix our eyes on Jesus, the author and perfecter of our faith, who for the joy set before Him endured the cross, scorning its shame, and sat down at the right hand of the throne of God" (12:2).

When we take our eyes off the cross, our minds become filled with the fears of this world. Suddenly our faith is shaken, and we begin to doubt God's love in our lives. We wonder if He hears us when we pray or even cares about our lives. We are, in effect, a hot spiritual mess.

However, when we keep our eyes focused on Christ's sacrifice, the love of God grows ever larger in our hearts and minds. When we focus on the cross, Christ's enduring love for us becomes plain, and the grace and mercy of God becomes evident. Focused on the cross we see Jesus' righteousness, which He imparts to us through the Holy Spirit. Through His righteousness, we can boldly go where sinners dared not go before: God's throne room.

FEBRUARY 28

I learned that my cousin, after 30 years of service to a local hospital, will now have to relocate to keep her current position. Another friend has lost his job. My husband has been told there are work projects for him, but nothing crosses his desk. Jobs, careers, relationships, college degrees, happiness, love, and so on and so on; this world guarantees none of it. However, the world does lure us into long hours, stress, heartache and aggravation by promising things and then reneging on the promise.

In God, however, anything that He has promised has been fulfilled and kept through Jesus Christ. Since God has kept His promise of sending a Savior who "takes away the sin of the world" (John 1:29) and the Savior has kept His promise and finished God's work through His sacrifice on the cross and resurrection, then God's guarantee of eternal life for all who believe is full proof.

To assure the faithful, Paul says God has "anointed us, set His seal of ownership on us, and put His Spirit in our hearts as a deposit, guaranteeing what is to come" (2 Corinthians 1:22). The Holy Spirit dwells in the hearts of believers assuring us and testifying to the truth that God's accomplishments in Jesus Christ will bring us into everlasting life with Him.

We can continue to let the world's broken promises and false hopes frustrate and exasperate us, or we can listen to the testimony of the Holy Spirit and know He is the deposit guaranteeing us eternal life.

March

MARCH 1

A few years ago, I heard the expression "even a flat pancake has two sides," meaning that every story has two sides. That thought came to mind this morning during the Gospel reading from Mark 8.

In that passage, Jesus explains the suffering He was going to endure, and Peter scolds Jesus for speaking such. Jesus then admonishes Peter with these harsh words, "Get behind me, Satan" (33)! Then He tells him, "You do not have in mind the things of God, but the things of men" (Mark 8:33). In other words, Peter was looking at only one side of the pancake.

Maybe Peter's rebuke of Jesus seems appropriate, since he did not want His friend talking about such horrible suffering and death. Peter might have witnessed criminals dying such brutal, grotesque and excruciating deaths at the hands of Rome. He couldn't picture His Lord enduring such horror.

But even a rugged cross has two sides.

From the human view, Christ's cross is that of a criminal. It is shameful, humiliating and agonizing. On the front of the cross is Jesus' bleeding, dying, marred, disfigured body, writhing in pain. This picture was actually God at work redeeming the world through His Son.

However, behind the cross is the glorified Son in His resurrection body. Behind the cross is the reconciled world, the spotless church and the perfect Kingdom of God.

In front of the cross is Christ's sacrifice for us; behind the cross is His glory and our eternal life.

MARCH 2

Delays are part of life. Road construction signage makes it plain: Expect delays. The airlines are subtler, since they pretend to be on time and then keep us waiting on the tarmac, at the gate, or on the runway. Delays are everywhere. Perhaps an important phone call has been delayed. Maybe a promotion at work has been promised but held up. Are test results slow in returning? Delays kick our impatience into overdrive and are a source of irritation.

But the Bible offers us a different perspective: perfectly timed delays. John 11:6 says, "Yet when [Jesus] heard that Lazarus was sick, He stayed where He was two more days." Jesus deliberately delayed His departure, and, as a result, Lazarus died. However, this delay is not the end of the story. After His arrival, He went to Lazarus' tomb, and in front of Lazarus' family and friends, He raised His friend from the dead.

Jesus had a specific reason for His delay. "[It] is for God's glory so that God's Son may be glorified through it" (John

11:4). In the great mystery of God, delays are necessary so God's Son will be glorified.

When we pray and Jesus delays His answer, the delay is for the greater purpose of God's glory. Delays are not irritants, but they are reverent moments in time used by God to bring glory to the Son. We must understand and accept that God uses delays to reveal the glory of His Son.

MARCH 3

My daughter wandered into my office and sat down. So for the next thirty minutes she and I had a pleasant conversation. We were not discussing anything particularly profound or earth shattering. It's just the two of us catching up on the day and enjoying each other's company. This private time brings us closer.

Jesus also made private time with His disciples. John 6:3 says, "Then Jesus went up on a mountainside and sat down with His disciples." As news of Jesus' appearance spread, more and more people demanded His time. The Pharisees questioned Him. Political leaders threatened Him. The sick sought His healing touch. Somebody always wanted something from Him. At the end of these grueling days, He needed some private time with His disciples.

Scripture doesn't record all of the conversations between Jesus and His disciples, but I can imagine how many questions the Lord answered for His closest friends. He settled disputes between them, taught them the meanings of His parables and listened to them sort out the mystery of "God with us" (Matthew 1:23). What happened during these private moments would sustain the disciples when Jesus was arrested and killed.

As disciples of Christ, Jesus still calls us to a countryside, outside the hectic pace of the world, where He can spend time with us. When He calls us to a private moment, by all means go and sit with Him. Jesus uses private moments to draw us closer to Him and God.

MARCH 4

I find that when athletes are struggling, the first thing they do is blame someone besides themselves for their problems. The second thing they do is reject coaches' assignments that would help them end the struggle. Only when athletes can take instruction can they overcome their struggles and solve their problems.

We are a lot like these athletes when it comes to our struggles with God.

Our biggest struggle is the alienation from God caused by sin. Like the athletes who blame others, we blame God. Our sinful human nature insists that He is the One who has abandoned us. However, Scripture states that we abandoned God by following the road of rebellion, which led to separation from God.

How does God help us to remedy that struggle? He places the cross of Christ on that road, so we can see that through faith in Jesus we can receive peace and be reconciled to God

(Colossians 1:20). Since our perspective has also been warped by sin, we reject Christ's cross, demanding, instead, that God provide a solution more palatable to our human nature. However, God is not trying to placate our human nature; He is transforming our sinful nature through His Son. Once the righteousness of Christ is shed in our hearts through the Spirit we are no longer alienated from God.

God's solution to our problem was to send His Son into the world to die on the cross and end the estrangement. Paul makes it plain that God "reconciled us to himself through Christ" (2 Corinthians 5:18). We no longer have to live alienated from God, because God has done all that is necessary to restore the world, and us, to Himself through Jesus Christ. Paul reiterates, "God was reconciling the world to himself in Christ" (2 Corinthians 5:19).

Struggle over. Problem solved.

MARCH 5

At the end of the *Big Bang Theory* episode tonight, the screen held a picture of Leonard Nimoy, who had recently died, and the caption read, "The impact you had on our show and on our lives is everlasting." I can appreciate the cast's sentiment. *Star Trek*'s Mr. Spock was a fan favorite, and fans will miss him. But, as always, life will move on eventually, and Leonard Nimoy and Mr. Spock will be forgotten.

There is only One Person who can have an everlasting impact on our lives, and He is the Lord Jesus Christ. When He conquered death and rose from the dead, He brought eternal life to the world through the power of the Holy Spirit.

To those who believe in Christ's work on the cross and the reality of His resurrection, Jesus says, "Verily, verily, I say unto you, He that believes on me has everlasting life" (John 6:47 KJ 2000).

Jesus Christ can offer everlasting life to all who believe because He is the eternal Son of the infinite Father. "For as the Father has life in himself, so He has granted the Son to have life in himself" (John 5:26).

God is life. He is immortal. Before the creation of the world, God lives. God is living and active in the world today and when the world is restored and the consummation of the kingdom of God is complete when Jesus comes again, God lives. And He has given us the gift of His Son so that through Him we might live forever. "He who has the Son has life" (1 John 5:12).

MARCH 6

Today the GPS on my smart phone led me astray. It took me down wrong streets and repeatedly had me doing U turns. Needless to say, the experience was frustrating. I finally arrived at my destination, but not by using the GPS. I had printed directions from MapQuest.

During this period of frustration, I figured out that there are many things in my life that try to make me take a U turn from God. The world is full of spiritual gimmicks and gadgets that it promotes as tools and devices that will give us inner peace. These tricks will leave us frustrated and far from peace.

However, there is no gimmick. If you want peace and a deeper faith and knowledge of God then you have to go to the cross of Christ. At the cross, Jesus died for our sin. Sin cancelled our peace with God, diminished our understanding of God and robbed us of faith in God.

However, on the cross Christ conquered sin and restored to those who believe all that was lost. Paul said, "Now may the Lord of peace himself give you peace at all times and in every way" (2Thessalonians 3:16).

If you are tired of doing U turns in your faith journey, get to the cross of Christ and the "peace of God which transcends all understanding" (Philippians 4:7) will be given to you along with anything else you lack.

MARCH 7

In this digital age keeping our identity safe is an ongoing struggle. My husband and I have each had our identity stolen. Friends of mine have also been victims of identity theft. Even the best safeguards cannot prevent it.

The book of Genesis gives an account of the first identity theft: in the Garden of Eden when Satan tricked Adam into disobeying God. Adam was created in the likeness of God. His character was holy, pure and noble. But Satan stole Adam's identity when he enticed him to sin. The image of God that Adam bore was shattered, broken and ruined by sin. His perfection was destroyed, and the purity, holiness and nobility of man collapsed under the weight of wickedness, rebellion and sin.

Of course, God had designed a plan to restore human identity. He sent His Son, who "is the radiance of God's glory and the exact representation of His being" (Hebrews 1:3), into the world to bring a new identity to those who believe in His name. Those who believe in Jesus Christ's work of salvation on the cross are given a new identity. When we receive redemption, righteousness and sanctification from Jesus through the power of the Holy Spirit, our identity becomes one with Christ's.

A new identity means our nature is made whole in Christ, and we are made fit to dwell in the presence of holy God. Through Christ and by the power of the Holy Spirit, our identity is protected and cannot be stolen. Jesus said, "[N]o one can snatch them out of my Father's hand" (John 10:29).

MARCH 8

Sundays are my favorite day of the week. I get to rest from work, go to worship God in His sanctuary, visit sick and shut in friends and family. This day has a slow ease to it. This day has an unhurried, kick back feel to it. The hectic pace of the work week is quelled by the tranquility of the Sabbath.

A day of rest does not mean that we have to sit around and do nothing, though that is sometimes also helpful. It means that we enjoy a refreshing ease to our hours. By making one day a week different from the others, we gain new perspective, insight and energy to tackle the norm of the work week.

God commanded us to set this day apart to worship Him. And what better way to worship Him than to give Him one day when our priorities match those of our Savior Jesus Christ. On the Sabbath, Christ went out among the people. He didn't hurry or rush to appointments. He tarried where He needed to so He could proclaim the Good News of God to His friends, followers and curious bystanders.

When we rest from work, we show God that He matters in our lives. When we rest from work and spend time with friends and family we show them that they matter in our lives.

Jesus said, "The Sabbath was made for man, not man for the Sabbath" (Mark 2:27). When we rest on the Sabbath we are renewed by God.

MARCH 9

Tears welled in my eyes tonight as I read the gym sign: *Eric Singer, you will be missed.*

Death is a harsh reality. I listened as friends told stories about Eric. I heard them exclaim their disbelief that a person so young could be gone. His passing has left a trail of hurt and heartache and tears.

When it comes to death, this world offers no solace. With a menacing attitude the world seems to shout, "Ha, told you so." As if it takes great pleasure in our pain.

However, there is solace and compassion and hope in God. Jesus Christ, God's Son, is our hope. He has triumphed over death, and just as His tomb was empty, so our graves will be empty when we are raised with Christ and brought into the glorious Kingdom of God on the Last Day. Jesus says, "No one can come to me unless the Father who sent me draws him, and I will raise him up at the last day" (John 6:44).

The glorious Savior is risen, and death is no longer our captor. We have been set free from its bondage. By Christ's own death, our death is vanquished. Believers live because Christ lives.

Death could not hold Christ in the grave, and we who are in Christ will not be held in the grave either. We have been given eternal life through Jesus Christ. There will be a glorious resurrection for us, and that is our hope. "We believe that Jesus died and rose again and so we believe that God will bring with Jesus those who have fallen asleep in him" (1Thessalonians 4:14).

MARCH 10

This afternoon a couple of the gymnasts were not putting effort into their workouts. The coaching staff tried to motivate them, but with little success. They did not make corrections. Effort continued to wane. They ignored their assignments. On their last event, I was sent to find out why their workouts had been so shoddy.

Their reasons were so flimsy that I knew they weren't being honest with their answers. Without honesty, I can't help them change anything.

God has the same difficulty with us. He shows us our sin, but we are not honest about our sin. We try to convince God that our sin is just a tiny mistake. We treat it like a passing fad or an illness that we can cure with chicken soup in a couple of days. We tell God our sin doesn't require anything as dramatic as Jesus' death.

Still God shows us His Son, His cross, His sacrifice and His forgiveness. And we give God any number of reasons to convince Him that we have no need of such things.

When we are honest about our sin then we have to be honest about our need for the Savior, Jesus Christ. Sin isn't something we can change by ourselves. Only through Jesus' atoning death on the cross and the power of the Holy Spirit can our sin be reckoned with.

When we are honest about our sin, we can accept help from God, and He will "purify us from all unrighteousness" (1 John 1:9).

MARCH 11

Tonight marks a milestone for me. Thanks to the Holy Spirit, the power of prayer and God's impeccable timing to bring a wonderful college friend back into my life along with her husband, I have a book on Amazon. (I know, everybody does.)

But this isn't just a story about my being a writer; this is a story about God's revealing Himself to me day in and day out. There is no way I can even sit here tonight and write out this reflection, except for the power of the Holy Spirit, who faithfully meets me in my office and shares His wisdom and insight with me. The Spirit has taught me more about Jesus, His incarnation, His cross and His resurrection than I ever dreamed possible. He has taught me through the Scriptures, exposed my sin and given my self a smack down when needed. He has taught me obedience, though I am a poor student.

I am a sinful human being who gets alone with God, so God will get alone with me. And the cool thing? He does this for everyone.

I have written down what He has taught me during these times, so I won't forget it. (A real possibility at my age.) And that is why I have a book.

Our God is amazing. And after today, I know with absolute certainty that the Psalmist is right, "Delight yourself in the Lord, and He will give you the desires of your heart" (Psalm 37:4).

MARCH 12

Last week I bit my lip, hard. Eating has become a painful experience, and even swallowing water stings. While trying to protect that area from further discomfort, I have managed to bite other parts of my lip. It's annoying and the healing process slow.

The heart like the mouth is a slow healer. We have all experienced wounds of the heart. Sometimes these wounds are self-inflicted like when we fail to forgive others, or we harbor anger or hatred. Other times, our heart has had pain inflicted upon it through loss or rejection or harm. When the heart is filled with pain and ache, we try to protect it from further affliction. We keep people at a distance, lash out at the innocent or hide ourselves away. These attempts at remedy don't heal, but cause further injury. That is what Solomon discovered and wrote, "heartache crushes the spirit" (Proverbs 15:13).

When we don't let Christ deal with the pain in our heart, we soon find that our spirit and physical body also suffer. The wounds of the heart are not limited to the heart, but find their way into our bodies through stress and anxiety and produce a restlessness in our spirit.

Jesus knew the consequences of a troubled heart, and He imparted the true remedy to His disciples on the night before their hearts would be troubled by His death. He said, "Trust in God; trust also in me" (John 14:1).

The wounds of the heart are healed through faith in God.

MARCH 13

In the Gospel of Mark, Jesus heals a boy "possessed by a spirit" (9:17). The father approaches Jesus for help by saying, "If you can do anything . . . help us" (9:22). Jesus is stunned by the father's conditional word, "if." When the father hears the surprised tone in Jesus' voice, he cries out, "Help me overcome my unbelief" (9:24). The father says this as though, suddenly, his own words have just caught his ear and he realizes the depth of his sin of unbelief.

Jesus filled with compassion helps the father overcome his unbelief by casting out the spirit in the boy, but not without allowing the spirit to give the boy a terrible seizure, possibly one of the worst the boy has ever had. As the boy convulses the father can only watch and trust Jesus. It is during this chaos, this terrible sight of his son lashing around in a grand mal seizure, that the father is saved from his unbelief. After the seizure the nature of God is revealed to the father as the boy finally becomes calm, and he is healed.

Like this father, we all have places in our lives in which we suffer from the sin of unbelief. When we ask to be cured of unbelief, we should expect chaos to ensue as Satan whips into a frenzy to dissuade us. But we need to stand firm in the truth that God will banish the chaos, and we will see the glory of the Son.

MARCH 14

The kids and I left the gym after the morning workout and walked into a clear warm day. We squinted into the bright sunshine and celebrated that gorgeous weather had arrived. We hurried to our cars, eager to embrace a spring-like weekend. After the cold and dark of the long winter months, we happily received these warm, sunny, early days of spring.

In the spring the world blossoms with new birth. Flowers dot the drab ground with color. Young animals can be seen following their mothers, while baby birds are rocked in the branches of breeze-blown trees. All around us the miracle of birth fills us with wonder and hope.

Equally miraculous is spiritual rebirth. Jesus told Nicodemus, "You must be born again" (John 3:7). Spiritual birth is the spring time of the soul. When we receive the truth from the Holy Spirit that Jesus Christ has died for our sins, the long days of sin and darkness are over.

Through the power of the Holy Spirit, Christ's life is born into our hearts. Our hearts blossom with righteousness, forgiveness, and grace through faith in Jesus' atoning sacrifice on the cross. Through the work of the Holy Spirit, we are filled with the wonder of God and the hope of eternal life through His Son.

When we are born again, sin and death no longer have a claim on us, for by the Spirit and through Christ we are now children of God.

MARCH 15

Social media is making people socially awkward. Society's dependence on Twitter, Facebook, snap chat, and so on has many people incapable of reading their social surroundings and situations. As a result, relationships that would have formed naturally go undeveloped.

The more we fail to build personal relationships with our fellow human beings, meaning those people whom we can see, the further we fall away from building a personal relationship with God, whom we cannot see.

The habits we have for building relationships are the same habits we exercise toward God in Christ. If you expect God to answer you on Twitter or snap chat, you will be disappointed. He will, however, answer your prayers. you can't creep on God's Facebook page, but you can meet Him every Sunday morning in worship. He won't call you on your cell phone, but He will invite you to His communion table and introduce you to His Son, who died to save you.

God knew the difficulty we would have building a relationship with Him, so He took on the responsibility to build the relationship with us. Truth is, our sinful nature is so hostile to God that we don't want a relationship with Him. We can come to God only when the Holy Spirit opens our eyes to Christ's work on the cross and transforms our lives through His enduring love.

"This is love: not that we loved God, but that He loved us" (1 John 4:10).

MARCH 16

Today things started to unravel when three groups of gymnasts arrived at bars, with two coaches, one of whom was leaving shortly to fulfill other obligations in the gym. Out of a sense of urgency I was compelled to act, so everyone could complete the skill as quickly as possible: As swiftly as I could, I did everything necessary to make sure assignments were finished and needs met.

The first disciples worked under a sense of urgency. They were certain that after Christ's ascension it would be only a short while before His return. Equipped by the Holy Spirit, they worked tirelessly to proclaim the Good News of Christ's death and resurrection throughout Jerusalem and beyond. The Spirit compelled them to act, so the news of salvation could reach the masses. They were diligent in prayer, faithful to the Word and empowered by the Spirit to preach the Gospel. It was critical that they finish the work the Spirit had given them to do before Christ's return.

As the time between Jesus' ascension and His return lengthened, the sense of urgency to proclaim the Gospel waned. We must remember that Jesus will return, and until then the Word of salvation and redemption has to go into all the world. Jesus calls His disciples to the urgent work of proclaiming the Gospel. His delay in returning should not lead His followers into complacency concerning the message of Good News but inspire them to go forth into all the world preaching and teaching the truth about Jesus Christ. By the power of the Holy Spirit, Christ equips His disciples to participate in His "ministry of reconciliation" (2 Corinthians 5:18) through the proclamation of the Word. Then the world will be ready and filled with believers when Christ returns.

MARCH 17

Today before practice our coaching staff explained to the athletes that the only way to overcome fear of a skill or event was to put the words of proper technique into their minds. Through the consistent execution of technique, fear soon vanishes.

As Christians we spend many of our days living in fear. We fret over the headlines, we worry about the future, we have concerns about life, death, disease, job, children, violence, drugs, war, and so on. There will always be something to be afraid of in this world.

There is a remedy for fear: The words of Scripture, the Word of God and the wondrous life, death and resurrection of Jesus Christ. We fear because we take our eyes off God. We read Scripture once in a while. Then, when fear strikes, we don't have enough understanding to consider it helpful, so we look for solutions in the world. However, the world cannot offer freedom from fear, because the world is a fear monger. The world peddles fear. And if we listen to the world, we will be overcome with fear.

1 John 4:16 says, "God is love." And verse 18 states, "There is no fear in love, but perfect love drives out fear." So, there is no fear in God.

Let the love of God in Christ fill you, by reading His word and listening to Him speak, and, by the power of the Holy Spirit, the fears of this world will be driven from your life.

MARCH 18

"Going a little farther, He fell with His face to the ground and prayed, 'My Father, if it is possible, may this cup be taken from me. Yet not as I will, but as you will'" (Matthew 26:39). With this prayer, Jesus, the Son of God, willingly delivered His life to the Father. The Son puts Himself in the hands of the Father, and the Father hands Him over to His enemies. God's enemies put His Son to death on a cross. Jesus delivers Himself to His Father; the Father delivers Jesus to His enemies; God's enemies deliver Jesus to the Romans; the Romans crucify Him, thereby delivering Him to death. All this was God's plan so that those who believe that Jesus is the Son of God can be delivered from sin and death. This is what the body of believers, the church, remembers at the communion table. In 1 Corinthians 11:24, Paul records the words of Jesus on the night of the Last Supper, "This is my body, which shall be delivered for you" (Douay-Rheims).

As the treasured Son of the Father, Jesus Christ surrendered His will to the Father's by coming down to earth. Here, He was put under the authority of death to conquer it. God the Father allowed His beloved Son to be possessed by death. Jesus, the "resurrection and the life" (John 11:25), obeyed the natural law of death and became subject to death.

In dying on the cross, Christ had to be possessed by death so He could go into hell and destroy the authority and control that death had in the world. According to Philippians 2:8, Christ, "humbled himself and became obedient to death." He surrendered His superior power so He could be overcome by death. However, God would not let His "Holy One see decay" (Psalm 16:10), and He raised Him from death to life. Because He is the "firstborn from among the dead" (Colossians 1:18), we too can be raised in Him from death to life.

MARCH 19

It drives me crazy when I ask an athlete a question about her gymnastics and get no response. She looks at me, but her lips remain still. She sees me standing right in front of her, but she remains silent, as though she is unaware of my presence. She ignores my questions. Even when she makes mistakes repeatedly, she seems to shun my involvement. Eventually she ends up in tears, but utters no response to my inquiry.

I have noted that many Christians behave like this toward God. They go through their days without talking with Him. Even though they believe in God, they spend little or no time developing an awareness of His presence in their lives. Then, when troubles and storms threaten, they are frustrated, stressed and anxious because they do not recognize Him. "He was in the world, and though the world was made through him, the world did not recognize him" (John 1:10).

There are ways to build an awareness of God. Pray for the Spirit to illuminate your mind with the truth of Christ's presence in the world. Read the Scriptures; what God has done in the past for His people He still does for His people today. Look at the cross of Jesus and notice that God kept His promise to send a Savior. Find a way to celebrate communion with frequency. God in Christ will meet you at His table. Embrace worship. The Holy Spirit will reveal God in Christ to all who long to abide in His presence.

The Lord replied, "My Presence will go with you" (Exodus 33:15).

MARCH 20

John Lennon's song "Imagine" came to my mind. I don't really know why a song I haven't listened to for years suddenly comes to mind. But it did. The first line of that song is "Imagine there's no heaven/It's easy if you try."

I hate to disagree with Lennon, but, as a Christian, I can't "imagine there's no heaven." In fact, the opposite is true. I like to spend some time imagining heaven. Jesus told us that His Father is in heaven. The Son is seated at the Father's right hand, and the Holy Spirit is present. God's majesty and glory fill the eternal kingdom. And we will see the Lord in all His fullness.

The book of Revelation says that heaven is a "Holy City" (21:2). God and His people will live together and "He will wipe every tear from their eyes. There will be no more death or mourning or crying or pain" (21:4).

Imagine heaven and then live like a citizen of heaven on earth. Where there is sorrow in this world, be ministers of comfort. Where there is death, offer the hope of the resurrection. Where there is pain administer prayers of healing. If a person has wronged you, forgive him as God has forgiven you in

Christ Jesus. Let the Holy Spirit create a pure heart in you, so you will "see God" (Matthew 5:8).

Imagine heaven, and live it on earth.

MARCH 21

This morning, when Lori woke up too sick to coach at the gymnastic competition, who's she gonna call? Well, she's not gonna call Ghostbusters. I received the call at 4:45 a.m. After a brief discussion, I left for the meet. How did she know I would go? Well, for thirteen years, day in and day out, Lori and I talk. We are always there for each other. We have developed that trust daily.

Driving to the meet, the massive orange sun rose over the horizon spilling light onto route 176. The sunrise reminded me that faithful God always answers us. Our certainty in God comes from sharing our days with Him.

When Jesus walked on earth, He was always in communion with God. In fact, before raising Lazarus from the dead He prayed, "Father, I thank you that you have heard me. I knew that you always hear me" (John 11:41). Through daily communication with the Father, Jesus could boldly declare those words of truth.

Martha, Lazarus's sister, also knew Jesus trusted in God. She said, "I know that even now God will give you whatever you ask" (John 11:24).

And Jesus tells us that God always hears us and responds, "If you remain in me and my words remain in you, ask whatever you wish, and it will be given you" (John 15:7).

If you are not convinced God hears and responds to you, increase the time you spend with Him and listen to His Word.

MARCH 22

My elderly friend now receives around-the-clock care. Her caregiver is a Mongolian woman who obtained a visa for herself and children to come to the States. She could neither speak nor read English. She taught herself the language by watching TV and reading subtitles. Her knowledge of America came from a friend who had emigrated earlier. But she says that many people helped her along the way. She courageously entered a strange country on the word of a friend and made a new life for herself.

When the Holy Spirit draws us from our sinful life into a life of faith, our experience is similar. We know very little about the life of faith we have just entered into with God. We believe in Jesus Christ as our Savior, but we wrestle with understanding just what that means in our daily lives. We try to read the Bible, but so much of it is still a mystery. Simply, we don't understand the language.

Yet, God does not leave us alone in our life of faith. The Holy Spirit remains steadfast to the task of "teaching, rebuking, correcting and training in righteousness" (2 Timothy 3:16), so we will grow deeper in the knowledge of our Lord.

We must enter the life of faith with courage and conviction, trusting the Spirit to guide and direct us through the process until He has grown our new life to maturity.

MARCH 23

The gym was full of a mixed bag of emotions today. It's the start of the post season. Over the weekend some of the gymnasts finished their state meets and were successful, so they were running on high energy. Others have their state meet this coming weekend, so they are feeling the stress of competition.

Emotions cannot be trusted. They are too unstable, too unpredictable. They can build gradually or explode suddenly. Emotions can create extreme highs or lows in an athlete or any person for that matter. They can sabotage a training session or enhance a workout. The problem is a gymnast can't tell how emotions will affect them until they fall during a routine, or are suddenly unable to complete a training task.

Christians sometimes confuse emotions with faith. If our emotions are joy and happiness, we equate that with God's presence. However, when we feel unhappy or experience sorrow, we tend to think God has abandoned us.

Emotions are driven by our attitude toward our circumstances. Faith is driven by the Gospel, the certainty of God in Christ and His work of salvation. Faith is rooted in the truth that God became a man, Jesus. Faith digs spiritual roots deeply into the ground of redemption at the cross of Christ. Faith confirms the reality of God's presence in our lives. "So faith comes from hearing, and hearing by the word of Christ" (Romans 10:17 NASB).

Faith is anchored in reliable, dependable God. And the more we allow the Holy Spirit to anchor us in the Scriptures, grow us in knowledge of Christ, and teach us to pray, the stronger and more certain our faith in God becomes.

MARCH 24

It was a busy day for my family today, and the house was alive with stories as each person took a turn sharing the most humorous, infuriating or surprising moments. The evening was alive with talk of work or friends or plans. Our conversation was filled with details from the day. We learned about each other, and we laughed with each other. And the storytelling brought us all a little closer together.

The Bible is filled with stories that teach us how God interacts and engages with the world. In the Old Testament He speaks through Moses and the prophets to assure the people that He understands their struggles with sin and death. He assures His people with the promise of a Savior.

In the New Testament, the four Gospels are the stories of God's keeping His promise of a Savior in Jesus Christ. Through Christ we see how God interacts with the sinful world to bring salvation, forgiveness and redemption. As we look to the cross we see Jesus, the Love of God, dying for our sins. We are told the story of His anguish on our behalf. And we celebrate His triumph over sin and death in His resurrection.

The rest of the New Testament gives us stories of the Church, formed by God through the power of the Holy Spirit, and its charge to preach the truth of Jesus Christ in all the world.

These are the stories of God, given to us so we can gain deeper understanding and faith in our Lord.

MARCH 25

This morning the Today show ran a segment on Ivonne Mosquera-Schmidt, a blind woman who has run 14 marathons. She trains and competes in these grueling races with her husband, who serves as her guide runner. Using a short tether the couple stay hooked together as they race over trails and streets building trust and courage with each step. We are inspired and influenced by her story of determination and overcoming.

Jesus Christ is the ultimate overcomer. The night before His crucifixion He told His disciples, "In this world you will have trouble. But take heart! I have overcome the world" (John 16:33). The Son of Man went to the cross, died for our sin and then triumphed over death.

Even in the face of Christ's triumph, spiritual blindness caused by sin stops many people from seeing the truth of Christ's victory over the grave. They do not see God's love in Christ, receive forgiveness or accept grace. Those people "grope in the darkness with no light" (Job 12:25).

However, by faith the blind can see. But even with sight the faithful can struggle with darkness. We fear living exclusively for God. We succumb to the temptations of the world. We want to please God but trip over our own desires.

God sent Christ into the world so we could be tethered to Him through the Holy Spirit. With guidance from the Holy Spirit we can overcome the world in Christ and remain obedient to Him as we journey through life.

MARCH 26

I met an absolutely delightful and charming woman today. Her eyes sparkled as she told me about her teaching career and her accomplishments as a flutist. She learned that I had authored a book and graciously asked me about the process. We engaged in conversation for several minutes. I will see her next week, but she will not know me. She has Alzheimer's disease, so all memory of our talk will vanish from her mind.

I see a parallel when it comes to God: We also suffer from forgetfulness. Sin has distorted or erased our memory of God. Adam's rebellion shattered his perfect knowledge of God. His mind had once been filled with thoughts of God, but after he sinned it filled with thoughts of self. Adam's sin gave him a sort of amnesia about God, a condition I call Godnesia. Sin has cleared our minds of the truth of God, His kingdom and the world to come.

However, One Man, Jesus Christ, did not suffer from Godnesia. He came into the world to help us remember God and all that we had lost. John the Baptist testified, "The One who comes from heaven is above all. He testifies to what He has seen and heard, but no one accepts His testimony" (John 3:31b, 32).

The cure for Godnesia is to accept the testimony of Jesus Christ. Through faith in Christ our minds are opened to the truth of God's existence, and through the power of the Holy Spirit, we regain the capacity to remember God.

MARCH 27

I would like to be asleep right now. The fatigue of a long day is hanging on my body, my eyes are heavy and my mind can think only of the sweet respite of slumber. Requiring sleep is part of our human frailty. Our bodies and minds need rest. Experts insist that people need eight hours of undisturbed sleep to be productive and healthy. I'd get bed sores if I lay in bed that long, but still I understand that an adequate amount of rest is needed for me to be functional.

God, on the other hand, is infinite and immortal and requires no sleep. In fact, Psalm 121:3 states, "He [the Lord] Who watches over you will not slumber." There is a calm assurance that comes from knowing that God our Creator and Redeemer is always awake and keeping vigil over all of us. His eternal essence cannot retire for the night. He is always awake and always at His work of salvation.

So, even when we rest, He is still saving. He is still about His work of reconciling the world to Himself through Jesus Christ. He never rests from offering His grace, love and forgiveness to mankind.

God watches. He will NOT take His eyes off those whom He loves. Nor will He take His eyes off those still trapped in the sin of unbelief. Instead, He is always watchful, waiting to bring the hope of salvation to all who need redemption.

MARCH 28

After the gymnastic meet this afternoon, one of my gymnasts and I sat and talked as we waited for others to finish. We shared a pleasant conversation about her life and friends. We exchanged opinions, talked about her family and had a good time just getting to know each other.

It's difficult to have conversations with people today because so many are plugged into something electronic. So today was unique. It was a spontaneous moment free of technology. It was the way life should be: two people engaged in the fine art of communication. It was fun.

Spontaneity should also be part of our relationship with God. While having time set aside for prayer is valuable, it doesn't have to be the only time we communicate with God. When He shows you a stunning sunset, take a moment to sit and thank Him. When a beautiful bird alights on your deck or a tree branch, stop and ponder the Creator. If the Holy Spirit reveals a new truth to you from Scripture take the time to write it down and explore its meaning further. When God gives you a spur-of-the-moment blessing, give Him a blessing back by lifting words of praise to Him.

God is waiting for us to unplug from the hectic pace and harsh noises of life to share some unexpected moments with Him.

Jeremiah 33:3 says, "Call to me and I will answer you and tell you great and unsearchable things you do not know."

MARCH 29

This weekend the scoreboard was the center of attention at the State gymnastic competition. When a gymnast finished an event performance she and her coach would fixate on the board waiting for the judges' results to flash across the screen. Some gymnasts were exuberant about the scores they received from the judges; others were disappointed and still others expected the score they were given.

Roughly 2,000 years ago the people in Jerusalem raced into the city streets to see Jesus as He came riding into town on a donkey. The crowd was shouting praises to Him as He rode past.

Jesus was the center of attention as He rode through the crowd. All eyes were riveted on this man. Some of the onlookers were filled with excitement and awe as they looked at Jesus, anticipating His rule to be as great as King David's. Others were disappointed when they saw this ordinary man riding slowly through the streets on a donkey, not a strong, powerful horse. They had been hoping for a king strong enough to conquer Rome.

Finally there were those for whom Jesus met their every expectation. These people looked at the face of Jesus and saw God. They put the Scriptures into the context of His words and deeds and realized He was the Savior. They knew the donkey was the right animal, and they rejoiced that their sins would soon be forgiven.

Make Christ the center of your attention, and pray the Holy Spirit will show you that He is God who meets our expectations. "Blessed is He who comes in the name of the Lord" (John 12:13b).

MARCH 30

The day before I wrote these words, Indiana Governor Mike Pence had signed Indiana's Religious Freedom Restoration Act. The act gives business owners who oppose homosexuality for religious reasons the right to turn away gay, lesbian and transgendered people.

Indiana businesses such as Angie's List, Apple, the NBA, WNBA and the NCAA have all denounced the law. I hope that the Christian Church has spoken out against it as well.

Faith in our Lord and Savior Jesus Christ means that we respectfully oppose a law when the well-being of others is at stake. As followers of Christ, we are not allowed to choose whom we love; indeed, we are simply to love all people as Christ has loved us and in turn we are to love our neighbors as ourselves. How did Christ love us? Paul wrote, "Christ redeemed us from the curse of the law by becoming a curse for us" (Galatians 3:13). On the cross He was judged by the law of God and condemned for our sin against God and His law. He endured our punishment so we would be forgiven. He received punishment and death, so we could receive grace and the gift of the Spirit.

By faith we have been saved by Christ's gracious act and freed from the law of sin and death to love one another through the power of the Holy Spirit. As believers we must now "live by the Spirit" (Galatians 5:16) and allow the fruit of the Spirit to extend to all "love, joy, peace, patience, kindness, goodness, faithfulness, gentleness and self-control. Against such things there is no law" (Galatians 5:22-24).

MARCH 31

Jerusalem was packed with people who had come to celebrate the Passover Feast. Jesus had also made His entrance into Jerusalem to prepare for the Passover meal with the disciples. His arrival in the city created great concern for the Pharisees. They watched as the crowds around Jesus grew larger and larger. Many in the crowd had been present when Jesus raised Lazarus from the dead, and they continued talking about Him and spreading the word about this miracle.

The Pharisees' hatred toward Jesus seemed to be proportional to the size of the crowd nearby. At one point, they decided the time to act against this man had come. They exclaimed, "Look how the whole world has gone after him!" (John 12:19).

At that time, the Pharisees thought that Jesus had convinced the masses to follow Him instead of the Law of Moses. They believed that they must maintain the religious status quo and that they had to prove the superiority of the law over Christ's superiority, so they manipulated Pilate to condemn Jesus, because they could not put Him to death according to Jewish law.

However, the Pharisees' view of the law was not superior to Christ. So, they had to break Jewish law and conspire with Roman authorities to stop Jesus. The very laws that God had given Israel to establish them as His chosen people were the same laws they broke to take down God's Son.

The leaders thought that by twisting the law they could rid the world of Christ. But God fulfilled the law in Christ and saved the world.

April

APRIL 1

Soon believers will commemorate the closing hours of Jesus' earthly life: His arrest, His trial, His beatings, His humiliation and passion on the cross.

On Good Friday, as the cross casts its shadow across the world, the sounds of Christ's cries of anguish echo from eternity into the world. For those of us who stand in that shadow, we will face the truth: The man dying on the tree will have to be dealt with. Some people will see Jesus Christ, God's Savior, bleeding and dying to save them from their sin. But many will think Jesus was a foolish dreamer whose crucifixion was inevitable. Paul wrote in 1 Corinthians 1:18, "For the message of the cross is foolishness to those who are perishing, but to those who are being saved it is the power of God."

The cross divides the foolish from the wise. The foolish live in the sin of unbelief and see the cross as a shameful act of a diabolical God. They are blind to their sin or need for a Savior. They have no knowledge, experience or understanding of God in Christ. The wise live a life of faith and receive from Christ through the power of the Holy Spirit knowledge, experience and understanding of God. Through Christ they are able to clearly see their corrupt nature and need for salvation.

The foolish man builds upon the sinking sand of sin. The wise man builds his house upon the rock of Christ the Lord.

APRIL 2

I left the Maundy Thursday service in silence tonight. It is a somber, sobering experience to walk away from the sanctuary of God without a sound. Silence forces me to spend time alone with my thoughts.

These thoughts center on the last meal that the disciples shared with Jesus. He spoke of service, and love and the disciples worked through the tension and sorrow in the room to try to understand Jesus' teaching.

Across town, the religious leaders and teachers of the law were meeting; theirs was not a meeting of silence, but one that was loud and boisterous, as these men created false charges and accusations, which would enable them to arrest Christ. After the Sanhedrin (comprising the Pharisees, Sadducees, and the chief priests) convened, the consensus became "it is better . . . that one man die for the people than that the whole nation perish" (John 11:50). They failed to recognize the truth of those words. Indeed, Jesus was going to die for all people. At that moment, however, they were simply trying to silence the man.

On that night as the world bellowed and conspired against Jesus, God stayed silent. It's not the noise of the world we remember from those many years ago. It's the silence of Christ, who spent the night in prayer, calling for strength from God to accomplish salvation for all people.

This night, God let the world silence His Word, so three days later, God's Word would rise from the dead and silence the world.

APRIL 3

For believers this is a night of grief. Jesus' cries of anguish have been silenced by death. But by faith we still hear His voice cry out, "My God, my God, why have you forsaken me?" (Psalm 22:1; Matthew 27:46; Mark 15:34)

I have wondered whether on this night 2,000 years ago the disciples might have asked God similar questions: "Why have you forsaken us? Why did you send your Son into the world to die in the world?" They had been so certain that Jesus was the Christ, who would reign as king of Israel. Instead, their Messiah had died on a Roman cross.

These men and women longed to hear Christ's voice one last time. They yearned for a parable or teaching from Jesus. Like all who grieve, they wanted more time, one last moment together. They regretted words left unspoken. They mourned His absence. And perhaps they even wondered how they could have been so wrong about Jesus. They questioned, as Christ did, if they were forsaken by God.

In their grief and pain of loss what else could they think? Christ left them. And if He was gone, then God must also be gone.

Tonight is the closest we will ever come to imagining the world without God. Christ had come into the world to reveal God, and now with His death, any revelations of God would cease with Him. Think long and hard about these disciples' feelings and thoughts as they contemplated an absent God.

The world is cloaked in a holy silence tonight. Jesus is dead.

APRIL 4

On Good Friday evening, I attended a cantata at church. Because of the somber mood of the Good Friday service the pastor asked the congregation to refrain from applause. When the cantata was over we joined in the Lord's Prayer and left the church in silence. It was a poignant moment.

Applause can also be distracting to worship. And we must be aware of when God is calling for silence and when He is calling for celebration. When applause is appropriate it is an offering that is pleasing to God. When it is inappropriate, it comes as a profane gesture.

Last night was an evening of grief and mourning, and applause for the choir's performance would have been inappropriate. And God through the power of the Holy Spirit was moving through the sanctuary, applying the truth of the cross into the hearts of those present through the words and music of each song. By the end of the service, a sacred silence filled the sanctuary and many felt the gentle touch of God. In His Church, God ministers in the silence opening our hearts to holy moments of intimacy with Him. If we are afraid of this holy silence, and fill it with the noise of applause, we risk missing quiet encounters with the Lord.

God is in the silence. It is His gift to us, and He uses it to draw us deeper into Him.

"It is good to wait quietly for the salvation of the Lord" (Lamentations 3:26).

APRIL 5

When gymnasts have great success in a competition, the coaching staff comes back to practice anticipating a lull in their training. The joy of triumph creates such an intense happiness in the gymnasts that when the euphoria dies away the athletes drop into a deep low. They want to feel that elation again, but they dread the work it will take to get there. In simple English: The higher the highs, the lower the lows.

On Easter Sunday Christians around the world came into sanctuaries to experience the exhilaration of Christ's victory over sin and death. By faith we passed through the suffering of our Lord and now by faith and through the power of the Holy Spirit we share His triumph. We hit the high.

There is a real temptation, however, to let the resurrection talk of today be silenced tomorrow. We want to keep holding on to the high of the morning but cringe at the spiritual work that will be required of us in the world. Instead, we will be tempted to tuck Jesus safely back into the tomb so life will return to normal.

But the Christian's life isn't normal. It is wrapped in the truth that God raised Jesus from the dead. The angel was clear, "He is not here; He is risen" (Luke 24:6). We cannot let the celebration of today fade into a low tomorrow. Jesus is alive! And His presence among us in the Holy Spirit means we have work to do.

APRIL 6

Today a young man whom I haven't seen in 25 years contacted me through Facebook. When I last saw him, he was a rambunctious 8-year-old. I lived with him and his family for one summer during my seminary days, when I was doing a ministry internship at the Methodist Church in their small Kentucky town. We were a perfect match of energy and mischief, much to his mother's dismay. My heart filled with joy when I saw his note.

This infusion of joy made me think of how the disciples must have felt when they realized that Christ was alive. The swing from sorrow to joy for those men couldn't be clocked with a stopwatch. One minute they were sitting in fear and grief and the next shock and elation. They thought they had lost their Lord to death. However, Almighty God raised Jesus to life. Joy flooded their hearts as they talked to the Lord, shared meals with Him and finally received the Spirit from Him after His ascension.

Not just the disciples but Jesus himself experienced the pure joy of triumphing over death. And through the gift of faith Jesus lets us share His joy of victory. For the Christian, joy is that indescribable happiness that comes from knowing that Christ has conquered sin, defeated death and lives and reigns forever. Jesus Christ gives us His joy so our "joy may be complete" (John 15:11). Our life is full of joy when it is full of Christ.

APRIL 7

We are in the most intense phase of the gymnastics season. The gymnasts are preparing for regional competitions. Now the emphasis of the workouts shifts from physical preparation to mental training. The rigors of mental preparedness tax their minds, and the girls become physically tired. When weariness sets in the gymnasts become less optimistic about achieving their goals. The coaches must keep the athletes' thinking aligned with their goals. By the end of a practice, both coaches and gymnasts imagine our brains oozing out of our ears.

The world inflicts a similar intensity upon the mind of the Christian. It constantly throws evil desires and temptations at the faithful. After Easter, the world mocks anyone who thinks the resurrection is real. At Christmas, the world invades the mind of a believer and fills it with questions about whether Jesus could really be the Son of God. On Good Friday, the world ridicules the mind that believes that Christ's cross was an atoning sacrifice for our sins. The constant battles with the world make Christians grow tired and weary.

On those days, we must seek refuge in Christ Jesus. We need to keep our thoughts centered on Him and let Him stifle the raucous, profane thoughts of the world lurking in the depths of our minds. As Christ silences the thoughts of unbelief and ungodliness in our minds, the Holy Spirit will bring refreshment to our lives.

God has promised, "I will refresh the weary and satisfy the faint" (Jeremiah 31:25).

APRIL 8

A young gymnast lied to her coach. She insisted her assignment had been completed when it wasn't. Her teammates listened to her try to deceive the coach. Because she had deliberately tried to mislead the coach, she was, as a consequence, given a double assignment.

When people lie, they are willfully trying to deceive another person. Even within the church this deception can be a problem. Some church goers claim to love God and then treat people shabbily. That is what the author of 1 John addresses, "If anyone says, 'I love God,' yet hates his brother, he is a liar" (4:20). To be a liar means a person is deliberately trying to dissuade another from knowing and following God and leading them away from faith in Jesus Christ.

In this early church the poor behavior of the liars created an obstacle to faith and hindered people from seeing the truth about God in Christ. These people lied about God through their calculated inconsistencies in word and action. People who willfully deceive others are undoubtedly trying to deceive God as well.

The world accepts lies, and even considers some of them harmless, say, for instance, the little white lie. But for God any word that does not speak the truth about Jesus Christ is a lie; and the one who delivers this untrue word is a liar and opposed to God. "Who is the liar? It is the man who denies that Jesus is the Christ" (1 John 2:22).

APRIL 9

Sirens blared tonight, warning residents about the possibilities of tornados. The gym staff evacuated all athletes from the main gym and moved them into safer areas of the building. Parents arriving to pick up children came inside the building to wait out the storm. Many people received further warnings on their phones. One man had an app that allowed him to hear the police radios. He knew the tornado was spotted over the airport. The television stations had streamed warnings across the screen, and weather maps highlighted areas that were most affected by the storm front. It was impossible to avoid the warnings tonight. The warnings were in place to help us stay safe.

God also sends us warnings about the devastating impact sin has on our lives. He warns us about the effect our disobedience has on our relationship with Him so that by the power of the Holy Spirit we can turn from our rebellion and find safety in Christ Jesus.

Warnings are not threats from God; they are words from Him that are intended to steer us away from the path of destruction onto the way of righteousness. We sometimes view His warnings as threats because we are reluctant to surrender our stubborn ways. God told the prophet Ezekiel, "But if you do warn the righteous man not to sin and he does not sin, he will surely live" (3:21).

God's warnings are words of life.

APRIL 10

Yesterday, our dog Buddy was acting strangely. He kept moving his head as if urgently looking for something. His body trembled, and he couldn't stand up. We got him to the vet immediately. He had an infection in his brain that caused extreme dizziness. His equilibrium improved; now he can walk short distances.

Buddy's lack of balance made me think of the number of times the sin of this world tries to knock us off our spiritual equilibrium. The world throws us off balance by insisting that sin has more power to ruin our lives than God has to save our lives. Suddenly we stagger in doubt, questioning whether Jesus Christ's death on the cross has the power to bring us salvation. Our sinful nature makes us question whether we need the cross at all. It deceives us into thinking that we are not sinful and have no need for a Savior.

Scripture tries to right our imbalance and speaks very clearly to our condition. "If we claim to be without sin, we deceive ourselves and the truth is not in us" (1 John 1:8).

The world tries to throw us off balance by insisting that we can by our own merits overcome our sins. In fact, the world won't even talk about our rebellion and disobedience towards God. It will instead tell us that Jesus was just a man.

Stay in balance; hear the Scriptures speak: "Christ Jesus came into the world to save sinners" (1 Timothy 1:15).

APRIL 11

My neighbor and I walk together regularly. Our first few steps are important because we use them to match our strides and speed so we are walking side by side. In this way we can carry on a conversation. If our steps don't match we can't walk together. One of us will always be ahead of the other. Walking together keeps us motivated and builds a stronger friendship. In other words, it's a good time.

In Galatians 5:25 Paul writes, "Since we live by the Spirit, let us keep in step with the Spirit." As Christians we need to work closely with the Spirit and match steps with Him. He is in the world to be our companion on our faith journey. We can't navigate the path of faith in this world without Him.

We sometimes think it is His job to match our strides, and we want to be the ones in charge of setting the pace and the course. We have neither the wisdom nor the foresight to chart our way. To keep in step with the Spirit is to walk with God. We are not to walk ahead of Him or behind Him, just with Him, conversing and growing deeper in faith. Matching the Spirit's stride keeps us inspired and strong when the path of faith is rough. As we walk with God we know we can trust the course and pace He has set for our journey.

APRIL 12

My pastor and the church worship committee had graciously given me the privilege and responsibility of leading the worship service this morning. On mornings like this, I arrive at the church very early, before the silence of the sanctuary is interrupted by the others.

After I go through the order of worship, practice my sermon and read through the Scripture passages for worship, I sit quietly and pray. Though I sit alone, I never feel lonely.

I have experienced some powerful worship services over the years. And I have seen some beautiful sanctuaries. At Christmas Eve services the glow of candles and the sense of God's presence are overwhelming. During a Tenebrae service, a profound hush falls across the sanctuary when the last candle is extinguished and the congregation is covered in darkness. When a congregation lifts glorious praise to God during an Easter celebration, God comes near. God's people have wept and rejoiced in sanctuaries. A sanctuary is no ordinary room. It is the holy place in which God joins His people in worship.

God says to Moses in Exodus 25:8, "Then have them make a sanctuary for me, and I will dwell among them." Just as God filled the Tabernacle with His presence, and His presence filled the temple of Jerusalem, so today God fills the sanctuaries of His people with His Being.

APRIL 13

Our gymnasts want to do well at regionals this weekend. However, instead of focusing on training today, some were already worrying about the outcome of the competition. As a result, these gymnasts suffered through a difficult workout because their minds and bodies hadn't been working together in the present. Once they allowed their minds to wander away from their daily training routine, they were filled with angst, worry and doubt.

Whenever we allow our minds to wander from the present into the future, we create worry and doubt. We know that we cannot predict the future, yet we consistently imagine ourselves in the future. We also know that tomorrow never comes, but we make plans for tomorrow. The challenge for my athletes and for us is to keep our thinking in the present.

Aligning our thoughts and actions with the present takes a tremendous amount of discipline. We have to focus on what is happening in our lives and accept whatever comes. We must allow the Holy Spirit to capture our minds and help us respond to our present circumstances through prayer, Scripture study and worship.

APRIL 14

Three of my little respectful, hardworking, obedient gymnasts were none of those things today. Their behavior in the workout was puzzling. They ignored their assignments, gave very little effort and demonstrated poor attitudes. They couldn't articulate the reason for the changes. And the coaches could only speculate about the problem. They received some hard consequences for their behavior.

I must admit that my behavior before God is sometimes similar to that of the girls. There are days I struggle to listen and obey the Lord. On those days my behavior is contrary to God.

When I find myself questioning the need to obey Christ, I know that I am spending more time listening to the lies of the world than the truth of God. At those times, I ignore the Holy Spirit and tune into the world. It is then I hear Paul say, "Bad company corrupts good character" (1 Corinthians 15:33).

The world offers up its ambitions and desires and corruption, and that is bad company for a believer. Yet, there are days we find that appealing. Unfortunately, God finds that appalling. Believers should part company with the world and keep company with God in Christ through the Spirit. When we hang around in the world, we eventually accept our sinfulness. Paul says, "Do not be misled . . . Come back to your senses as you ought and stop sinning" (1 Corinthians 15:33, 34).

To adjust our behavior God will take us to the cross and remind us just how unacceptable sin is to Him.

APRIL 15

My house has been full of laughter tonight. The girls and I have been telling jokes and sharing funny stories and humorous situations. There is a wonderful energy created by laughter. It melts away weariness and brings a renewed enthusiasm to life.

Laughter lifts a burdened heart and brings joy to the soul and harmony to a household. When we laugh pain is eased, stress is relieved and relationships strengthened.

The Psalmist wrote, "Our mouths were filled with laughter, our tongues with songs of joy" (126:2). When the Lord fills us with His joy and we can no longer contain the delight and happiness He has graciously lavished on us, we laugh. It is an expression of our appreciation to Him for all the wonderful things He has done on our behalf.

Laughter is an utterance of gladness. It is an offering we bring to the Lord, because He has secured our salvation through Jesus Christ. When we laugh we articulate our great relief that sin and death have been lifted from our lives through Jesus. We are no longer oppressed by sin and a slave to death. Through His blood shed on the cross, Christ has saved us from our rebellious ways and our disobedience toward God. When by faith we accept salvation from Jesus Christ and know that His work on the cross has brought us redemption; then God "will yet fill [y]our mouth with laughter and [y]our lips with shouts of joy" (Job 8:21).

APRIL 16

Right now there is a celebration going on at my house. My daughter has received some good news. My two girls are talking and planning and playing. They are including me through

Facebook and phone calls. I am feeling the excitement, even though I am eight hours away in a hotel room. The distance can't dampen my enthusiasm for their excitement.

Celebration is a central part of the Christian life. We tend to forget the joy and amazement that the disciples felt when they first saw the risen Lord. The women were elated to go back to the frightened disciples to share the news of Christ's resurrection.

"So the women hurried away from the tomb, afraid yet filled with joy, and ran to tell His disciples" (Matthew 28:8).

We sometimes forget that the resurrection is an event to be celebrated not just one day a year, Easter Sunday, but throughout the year. Christ is alive, and that fact gives us reason to celebrate and rejoice. The dark days of sin and death are over, and He is alive, in heaven and on earth. We should be celebrating "on earth as it is in heaven" (Matthew 6:10).

The Holy Spirit resides in the world to help us celebrate and rejoice in the truth that Christ is risen. As Christians we should celebrate the resurrection of Jesus Christ with the same enthusiasm and energy as the celestial beings who surround His throne singing, "Holy, holy, holy is the Lord God Almighty, who was, and is, and is to come" (Revelations 4:8).

Celebrate with great gusto and zeal the resurrection of our Lord.

APRIL 17

One of my gymnasts had a disappointing meet. She had done very well in the competition. Her routines were strong, and the mental and physical preparation she had worked so hard on was paying off. But, on her last event, she made a costly mistake that stopped her from advancing to the National competition.

As her coaches, we tried to offer solace, but the pain was too intense for her. However, time will help her cope with the disappointment.

For a brief moment I questioned my own work. Athletes and coaches spend hours and hours working together, preparing for these events. When athletes win, the recognition validates our work, but when they lose, our work sometimes appears meaningless.

However, Scripture tells us that our work is worthwhile. Ecclesiastes 2:24 says, "A man can do nothing better than to eat and drink and find satisfaction in his work." Work is satisfactory not because an athlete wins or loses, but because it is given to us by God. Regardless of the work we have chosen, it's meaningful when it springs from our faith and is rooted in Christ. God gives us work, and He chooses the work we have. In this way, all work has meaning.

APRIL 18

This weekend I am working out of town. I travel frequently at this point in the season as our team attends state, regional and even national competitions. Travel away from home is an aspect of my job. My family accepts this and has adjusted to it over the years. Even though we have adjusted to the schedule, my family and I still make sacrifices at home in order for me to travel.

Within the nature of work is the element of sacrifice. No matter what work, career or profession you are in, or are pursuing, you will have to surrender time and relationships to it.

God has designed work to include sacrifice. When we work we remember that Jesus Christ came to earth to work. In John 5:17 Jesus says, "My Father is always at His work to this very day, and I, too, am working."

Christ's work was His sacrifice on the cross so that the world would be saved through Him. He became a man to teach us that the sacrificial quality of work should be exercised to the glory of God the Father.

"Whatever you do, work at it with all your heart, as working for the Lord" (Colossians 3:23).

APRIL 19

Over the past 13 years I have developed a great many wonderful relationships through work. Though these relationships began as professional acquaintances, they have become strong friendships. Together we have shared stories about our families, faith and frustrations. We have consoled one other when sorrows hit our lives and celebrated when joys arrived. These people with whom I have the privilege of working come from all corners of the country and all walks of life. And I have learned something valuable from each one of them, because God has ordained our paths to cross.

Building relationship between God and mankind is the work of God in Christ. Christ came, walked among us, taught us and sacrificed for us, so we could have an intimate relationship with God. Through His work on the cross, Christ has given us the privilege of being children of God.

1 John 3:1 says, "How great is the love the Father has lavished on us, that we should be called children of God!" Through our faith in the work of Jesus Christ, we are given the opportunity to share intimacy with God. Through Christ and by the power of the Holy Spirit, we can be as close to God as God the Father is to His own Son. Christ's work for the Father on our behalf has created a very strong family bond between us and God.

APRIL 20

A friend and I were talking today about how much of a child's pain a parent shares. Regardless of the circumstances, when our children hurt, we hurt with them and we hurt for them. We do not want to see our children suffer, yet there are times when suffering cannot be avoided. As parents, we do not abandon our children during their time of hurt, rather we walk through it with them.

Christ also shared this kind of intimacy with His Father. He chose to come into the world to suffer and die on the cross so that the world would be saved through Him. Yet His Father did not abandon Him in His hour of need. Jesus knew that His disciples would scatter as the hour of His crucifixion grew closer, but He assured the disciples, "Yet I am not alone, for my Father is with me" (John 16:32).

When Christ suffered on the cross God the Father suffered as well.

When Jesus died in the flesh the Father felt the anguish of separation. His perfect Son carried the sins of humankind and paid the wage of death for our guilt. The Father could not allow the Son to escape suffering if the world was going to be set free from sin. So the Father abandoned the Son to endure the suffering and separation from Him. Theologian Jürgen Moltmann writes, "The Son suffers in His love being forsaken by the Father as He dies. The Father suffers in His love the grief of the death of the Son" (The Crucified God, 245). God suffers for the sake of mankind.

APRIL 21

We occasionally get gymnasts who come to us from other clubs, and the first thing I tell them is to forget everything from their former clubs and adopt our teaching, our methods and our techniques. An athlete must leave behind old methods of training if she is going to embrace a new way to train.

As Christians we sometimes struggle with this same problem. We want to leave our old way of sin and death behind, but we are afraid to move forward with Jesus Christ into the unknown way of discipleship. But we cannot mix our old life with our new life in Christ. It simply cannot happen. Our old life is corrupt and deceitful and ungodly. Our old self cannot dwell in the presence of God in its sinful condition. Only by abandoning our old way to Jesus Christ on the cross can we move forward in His holiness, righteousness and truth.

Paul wrote in Ephesians 4:22-24, "You were taught, with regard to your former way of life, to put off your old self, which is corrupted by its deceitful desires; to be made new in the attitude of your minds; and to put on the new self, created to be like God in true righteousness and holiness."

Our new self is our life in Jesus Christ. We are made righteous through His atoning work of the cross. He takes our old life and destroys it so we could have new life in Him.

APRIL 22

People who work out know the importance of doing something active every day. We also know that the pitfall of exercise can be taking off two days in a row. After that second day, a person lets down mentally, gets out of the routine and often wants to stop altogether. Instead of taking a day off, it's important to stay active on the off days.

In our spiritual lives, we should adopt a similar discipline and structure to our day. We should develop a routine of Scripture reading, prayer time, worship, and study. For many of us, we begin with the great expectation of rising early and reading a devotional before the world, particularly our families, wake up and infuse our quiet with noise and demands and needs. Perhaps, though, after a few days of success, we stay up too late trying to finish the days' responsibilities. We sleep in the next three mornings, and suddenly, our morning devotional time is gone. We won't return for many months.

The cure is to stay active spiritually: Do something for your spiritual life every day, no matter how small you think it may be. Spend one minute singing a praise song. Read a short Bible verse, and say a quick prayer. All these little steps will keep you from abandoning altogether your time alone with God. Eventually life will swing back around, and you will be ready to go back to more in-depth hours with God.

"Let us draw near to God with a sincere heart in full assurance of faith" (Hebrews 10:22).

APRIL 23

This morning, one member of the book study that I attend at church commented that our selection, *Surprised by Hope* by N.T. Wright, was giving her new insight into the pastor's sermons. Others agreed. I remarked that perhaps reading Scripture as frequently as other books would also help us gain greater understanding from sermons and more knowledge of God in Christ.

We read all types of material each day. We devour magazines, books, newspapers, blogs, devotionals, pamphlets and Facebook posts. Reading Scripture with that same enthusiasm would certainly benefit our lives.

However, many of us stay away from reading the Scriptures, for what I see are three reasons: 1) We are afraid that we won't understand what we read and 2) and that lack of understanding will cause us to question the reality of God. 3) Or, we are afraid that we will understand what we read, and that makes us fearful of what God will require of us. This avoidance causes many faithful Christians to be what I call scripturally illiterate.

When we fail to read the Scriptures, we can't receive what the Spirit can teach us through the Word. In essence, our faith lacks knowledge and understanding of God's purpose and work in Christ. Our belief becomes vulnerable to false teachings and errant doctrine. We find ourselves living in doubt instead of truth.

The Spirit relishes an opportunity to teach us through the Word. Jesus spoke of the teaching ministry of the Spirit by quoting Isaiah 54:13: "They will all be taught by God" (John 6:45).

Let the Spirit teach you the Scriptures.

APRIL 24

Our athletes' training includes cue words that we use to help them focus their minds on the tasks at hand. I tell the girls to stick to the script. They are not allowed to change these words or take their minds off them when they are competing on an event. These words—the script—help the gymnasts to anchor their thoughts and, thus, to alleviate the fear and anxiety that come with competition.

The Scriptures are the script from God, given to us so we can focus our minds on Christ and His work. When we read Scripture, we can anchor our thoughts to God through the power of the Holy Spirit. As we spend time reading God's Word, our fears and trepidation surrender to peace and hope.

The Scriptures contain the truth that God comes near to us in the person of Jesus Christ and remains with us in the Person of the Holy Spirit. In Scripture we are reminded, "If God is for us, who can be against us?" (Romans 8:31) Through the Word God reveals His might through all He has done in the life, death and resurrection of Christ. These words of assurance anchor our thoughts and focus our minds on the reality that God has reconciled the world to Himself in Christ.

We have nothing to fear because God is with us.

We often spend many hours of the day fretting and worrying and brooding over our circumstances. All this angst can be defeated by reading the Scriptures and allowing God to speak to you through His Word.

In other words, when life makes you fearful, stick to the script of Scripture.

APRIL 25

A week ago I was in Ohio in the Eastern Time zone. On Monday, I was back home in the Central Time zone. Yesterday, I traveled once again into the Eastern Time zone. When planning a trip to another time zone I make decisions for travel according to the loss or gain of an hour. I get ready for departure based on my current time zone while anticipating my arrival in the next.

As Christians, we live in different time zones as well: Now we live in the visible world; however, one day in the future, when the Son of God returns, this world will be recreated and reconciled to its original condition. Until that day, Christians live with the current condition of this world while anticipating the arrival of the heavenly kingdom. So, we have to make decisions by taking both worlds into account.

To make sound decisions for this life, we must be obedient to the Spirit of God. The work that He accomplishes through us in this world will continue in the realm of God through Him. All the work that we do in this world in cooperation with the Spirit is part of the reconciling work of God in Christ. Our work with the Spirit will bring change to this world and will ultimately be completed when the kingdom of God is revealed in all its fullness on the day of Christ's return.

James wrote, "Someone will say, 'You have faith and I have works.' Show me your faith apart from your works, and I will show you my faith by my works" (2:18 ESV). James reminds us that the work we do here with the Spirit reveals our belief in Christ's promise to return and demonstrates our faith in the reality of God's eternal kingdom.

APRIL 26

During practice today one of my gymnasts needed to make one correction that would help her complete a layout vault. I asked her to focus on that one correction. She chose to think about everything but that correction. After exhausting herself, she disciplined her mind to focus on that one particular correction and her vault was finally successful.

I thought about how many times as Christians we exhaust ourselves by failing to focus on Christ's cross. We exhaust ourselves following current events, questioning the brokenness in the world and, perhaps, in moments of real doubt, wondering whether Jesus accomplished anything while He walked on earth.

Here's the particular correction on which to focus: Christ's accomplishment was the cross.

When we focus on the cross the Holy Spirit shows us the Man-God dying for our sins. When we focus on the cross the Spirit shows us that our sinful hands jammed that crown of thorns onto the Innocent Victim's head. We know our sin caused His scourging. Our sinfulness hammered those nails into His holy hands. We know He was punished for our guilt.

When we focus on the cross the Holy Spirit shows us the God-Man dying for our salvation. On the cross the Spirit shows us Jesus, the willing, perfect sacrifice, offered to God for our redemption. The Spirit lets the holy words of Christ, "Father, forgive them" (Luke 23:34) pierce our hearts and heal our souls. And the Spirit makes us look at the Savior's blood shed for us so we can have peace with God.

APRIL 27

I visited an elderly friend today. After nearly ten decades on earth, her physical body has finally grown tired. The strength she once possessed to take on daily tasks has now slipped away. She is confined to bed, resting from the labors of this life. She is frail and sleeps most of the day. In the near future, she will quietly transition from this world into the unseen realm of God in Christ and be united with her Savior and loved ones. And her earthly body will be made new by the power of the Holy Spirit in the resurrection on the last day.

Paul writes in Philippians 3:20-21, "Jesus Christ . . . will transform our lowly bodies so that they will be like His glorious body."

God has given this promise and hope to my friend and to all Christians, secured for each of us through the resurrection of our Lord and Savior Jesus Christ. Death has been abolished by the almighty power of God, who raised Jesus from the dead and transformed His earthly body into a glorious heavenly body.

Just as Christ was raised to glory, we too will be raised in His glory and "clothed with power from on high" (Luke 24:49) to begin life anew, our everlasting life in the eternal kingdom of God.

The great mystery of God in Christ is that through Jesus' resurrection our mortal bodies will become immortal. We will celebrate that in Christ our perishable bodies become imperishable and "death has been swallowed up in victory" (1Corinthians 15:54).

APRIL 28

My friend died this morning. She surrendered her stubborn Scottish resolve to her Savior. As the last of her strength was exhausted, God filled her with His grace and she "passed from death to life" (John 3:14). Through Christ, my friend is now "filled with an inexpressible and glorious joy, for [she is] receiving the goal of [her] faith, the salvation of [her] soul" (1 Peter 1:8c). What a wondrous attainment!

Jesus Christ came to earth, died on the cross and rose from the grave so that my friend and all of us who believe would never taste death. The author of Hebrews writes, "But we see Jesus, who was made a little lower than the angels, now crowned with glory and honor because He suffered death, so that by the grace of God He might taste death for everyone" (2:9).

My friend did not have to taste the bitterness of death, but because of the work of Christ she is enjoying the "fragrance of life" (2 Corinthians 2:16) in the heavenly realm of eternal God.

Of course, it will seem strange not to call her each night or visit on Sunday and ream the Cubs or the Bulls with her. But she has now in Christ received the reward of her faithfulness to God, and so, instead of grieving her earthly life, I can celebrate the life she is now living in the fullness of our Lord.

APRIL 29

The gymnasts' routines become automatic this late in the season. They have done them repeatedly for months. The coaches' challenge becomes to keep the gymnasts' minds engaged in the process of honing the execution of the skills. At this point, the gymnasts can easily let their minds slip into neutral and let their bodies go simply through the motions of the routine.

To help the athletes stay focused, coaches create workouts designed to keep their brains stimulated and interested in the routines. Small changes like the introduction of a new drill or game fuel the athletes' desire to stay mentally connected to the routine.

Sometimes our spiritual lives become captives of routine. We start our day automatically with a Scripture verse, hurried prayer and short devotional reading before racing out the door to tackle the day. Without realizing it we have allowed our minds to slip into neutral and our hearts to become disengaged from God. What was once a fresh and vibrant aspect of our faith life then becomes stale and bland through repetition. We sometimes become more connected to the routine than to God.

The things of God that are "new every morning" (Lamentations 3:23) go unnoticed, because the routine dulls our minds to the unique activity of God in Christ in our lives. We need the Holy Spirit to stimulate our minds and open our hearts to the working of God. We need Him to jar us lose from our routines and reconnect us mind, body and soul to God.

APRIL 30

When I talk to children I instruct them in the way I want them to go. For instance, instead of saying, *Don't leave your plate on the table*, try *Please put your plate in the dishwasher*. Instead of *Don't throw your clothes on the floor*, say *Please put your clothes in the laundry basket.*

Plant in their minds the action you want them to take.

Jesus' words direct people toward the action He desires from them. When He called the disciples He said, "Follow me" (John 1:43). Healing the invalid, He said, "Get up! Pick up your mat and walk" (John 5:8). He instructed the blind man to "Go . . . wash in the Pool of Siloam" (John 9:7).

When we believe in Jesus Christ, we become children of God. Since we are God's children, Christ speaks directly to us through the Holy Spirit. He makes His directions clear, and His instructions to us will line up with His cross. Christ will always point us towards His cross. He will ask us to align our actions with His actions of sacrifice and commitment to God. Then He will direct His Spirit to teach us "all things and . . . remind [us] of everything" (John 14:26) that He has said to us.

Jesus applies straight talk to our lives through the Spirit. He tells us to forgive one another, love one another and treat one another with kindness. When Jesus speaks to us, He plants in our minds the actions He wants us to take to glorify God in the world.

May

MAY 1

I am awful with technology. I am illiterate when it comes to the language of technology, and I don't understand how any of the devices I own work. Technology baffles me and mocks me. I use it, but I'd rather lose it. My brain and today's technology are not friends.

Still God insists that my ministry require a computer, access to the Internet and Facebook. Lately He seems to be nudging me toward blogging. So I spent an hour this morning trying to figure out the difference between a blog and a website. Through this experience, I have come to understand Moses' position when God called him to speak to Pharaoh.

Moses had a stutter and wasn't comfortable speaking, so he asked God to let Aaron do the talking. So here I sit, stuttering and stammering with technology, praying God will send me an Aaron. I need someone with the capability to understand computers, blogs and the Internet and to explain this cyber world to me. Warning: you will have to explain things more than once.

My inabilities show me God's abilities. I must depend upon Him to meet the needs of this ministry. Every day, I am reminded of how truly helpless I am with technology, and then I marvel at what He accomplishes, in spite of my clumsy, faltering ways.

"Therefore I will boast all the more gladly about my weaknesses, so that Christ's power may rest on me" (2 Corinthians 12:9).

MAY 2

This afternoon I was reminded of two very painful periods in my life. The pain in both cases was delivered by the political hand of the church. The sad reality of these situations was not only did I get hurt but so did many members of the congregations.

I stayed away from the church for many years. I thought I was just avoiding more pain, but the Spirit pointed out to me that my absence was caused by my anger towards the church.

One day, while studying, I came across this verse, "Christ is the head of the church, His body, of which He is the Savior" (Ephesians 5:23). The church is the body of Christ. I could not say that I loved Christ but hated His body. That would make me a hypocrite. To abandon my life fully to Christ, I had to love His church. At the time, that realization was a hard pill to swallow. I wanted to hold a grudge. But the Spirit enabled me to release my anger toward the church, forgive and move on.

When I finally surrendered to the Spirit, my anger and hatred toward the church ended. Then God said, as He did to Peter, "Do you . . . love me?" (John 21:15). When I responded, "Yes, Lord" (John 21:15), He instructed me to make His church strong. I don't know exactly what that means or how it will look, so for now, I stay close to the Spirit and follow.

MAY 3

I was watching some of my young gymnasts train for vault today. As they sprinted down the vault run their heads moved up and down as their eyes looked down at the floor or up at the ceiling. One athlete ran while glancing from side to side. Apparently looking straight ahead at the vault table is a difficult thing to do. Watching these girls run, I realized the distractions in the gym were more interesting to them than the vault table directly in front of them.

Sometimes the world looks interesting. For instance a shiny, black Tesla can grab my attention. When my friends go on an exotic vacation I start choosing my own vacation spot. New clothes, technology and even houses can catch my eye. But if I am looking at all the baubles and beads of this world I am ignoring my Savior. Some days it is difficult to gaze directly at Christ on the cross—His tortured body writhing in pain for my sins, His precious blood dripping down His face for my peace, His side pierced for my iniquities. This sight is gruesome.

But I keep gazing straight into His divine face, and His holiness shines through. The glories of heaven are reflected in His loving eyes, and the things of this world fade away in the light of His resurrection.

Proverbs says, "Fix your gaze directly before you" (4:25). Directly before you is Christ the Savior and risen Lord.

MAY 4

Mastering the basics is imperative for developing good gymnastic skills. The basics are the foundation upon which more difficult gymnastic skills are built. Weak basics make weak skills; strong basics make strong skills.

As Christians we also should possess strong Scripture basics that help us grow deeper in faith and knowledge of God in Christ. When we focus on the basics, we allow the Holy Spirit to teach. He will bring clarity to the Word and increase our understanding of God's work in Christ.

Let's start with two basics of the faith:

The first is the doctrine of the Trinity—that we worship One God in Three Persons. God has One nature, and all Three Persons, the Father, Son and Spirit, are divine. God's nature is merciful, a trait that points to His desire to save all sinful humans, and the Three Persons are united in the work of salvation in the world. "The Lord our God, the Lord is one" (Deuteronomy 6:4).

The second is called concurrence—the doctrine that Scripture was written by human authors who were inspired by the Holy Spirit. The Spirit makes each book unique in the voice and tone of the particular author, yet the same, unified thread of salvation runs from Genesis to Revelation. Collectively, the Old and New Testaments affirm God's coming to earth in the flesh, His death on the cross to save us from sin, and His resurrection, which gives us new life through the Savior. Finally these sacred pages encourage us as we wait for Christ's return.

In other words, Scripture has nothing to do with us, but shows us everything that God has done for us in Jesus.

Let the Spirit take you back to basics.

MAY 5

My friend Marge Wold was a positive influence in the lives of many, many people. And today, at her funeral service, those who knew her came to pay respects and share stories. I heard new stories about Marge. As I listened to the memories, I realized how each of us had known Marge in a unique way. The stories filled in pieces of Marge's life I hadn't known, and each one revealed a new and wonderful side of my friend.

Jesus said, "I have called you friends, for everything that I learned from my Father I have made known to you" (John 15:15). Jesus Christ walked among us to tell us about the Father's eternal life in the kingdom. He shares different stories with each of us according to our unique relationship to the Father through the Holy Spirit. When we gather in corporate worship, we come together to tell these stories, and in so doing we discover new and wonderful attributes of God.

Christ reveals the Father to us. Jesus was very specific about His oneness with the Father when He spoke to Philip, "Anyone who has seen me has seen the Father" (John 14:9). And the Father reveals the Son to us through the Holy Spirit. When we seek the Father, He shows us the Son. When we seek the Son, He shows us the Father. In so doing the Spirit unfolds the larger picture of God for us.

Jesus called us friends so that "everything that I learned from my Father I have made known to you" (John 15:15).

MAY 6

It has been a long day of travel. I flew to Orlando, Florida, from Milwaukee, Wisconsin. The flight was quick. The conversation on the plane was pleasant and the landing smooth.

I have noticed that whenever I travel the time in the air goes by quickly. But the time after landing is always slow. We had to wait for luggage, the rental car, dinner, ice cream and the hotel room check-in.

When I travel like this I remember the trip that the Son of God made. Jesus said, "I have come down from heaven not to do my will but the will of Him who sent me" (John 6:38). Jesus made many stops before His travels on earth were over.

He entered this world as the newborn of a young virgin, and He lay in a humble manger. As a boy, He spent days in the temple of Jerusalem teaching about the Father. And as a man, He became a threat to the leaders, who once had been astounded by the knowledge of the boy.

This threat led to His suffering at the hand of Pilate and His death on the cross at the hand of the Roman soldiers. After His death on the cross, Joseph of Arimathea laid Him in a tomb. However, dark, cold death could not hold Him, and after He descended into hell He then rose again to life. Finally, He ascended into heaven.

These were the travels of God on earth, and He traveled every step for our salvation.

MAY 7

I have had a Mastercard since 1999. But when there was a problem with my card today and I called, they had no idea who I was. The first representative I spoke with could not comprehend the meaning of *customer* or *service*. So that conversation ended abruptly when he said he could no longer hear me. Funny, I could hear him.

It was a very frustrating few minutes as I tried to confirm my identity for this representative. It didn't matter that I had been a card holder for 16 years. It didn't matter that I pay my bill on time every month. It didn't matter that I could tell him the account number and other pertinent information. Because I couldn't answer his two questions, I had no identity.

Fortunately, when I called back, the next representative understood the meaning of both *customer* and *service* and she was able to confirm my identity and then quickly resolved my issue.

God has always known who I am. Our relationship is so intimate that, according to Psalm 139, He "perceives my thoughts"; He's "familiar with all my ways"; He knows "when I sit and when I rise"; and He even knows the words on my tongue before I say them. There is no identity crisis here, nor will there ever be.

God knows me. He knows you too. Now the only question that remains is do *you* know God?

MAY 8

The internet is so slow tonight that it is hardly worth using. It has taken the better part of 30 minutes to get this evening reflection posted because the technology is limping and stuttering along, causing me frustration.

Everything online is difficult. My pictures won't upload; my words won't post; and a black rectangle on my home page won't go away.

It occurs to me that this is how many of us live the Christian life. We are frustrated. We can't seem to read and make sense out of Scripture. Our prayers seem flat, and we doubt God hears. Worship seems lifeless.

Here's the problem: Many of us try to live the life of faith under our own power. We count on our human effort, which leads to frustration. When our human efforts fail, we think that the Christian life is hardly worth pursuing.

The risen Lord told His disciples to "stay in the city until you have been clothed with power from on high" (Luke 24:49). This power is the Holy Spirit, and it has been given to us to live a vibrant life of faith in God. We do not need to live powerless Christian lives. We need to call on Christ, who willingly sends us His Spirit. In this way we will live vital lives of faith.

MAY 9

This afternoon friends and I went kayaking down Shingles River in Florida. It was a dazzling day to be out. The river was clear and shallow, full of fish and turtles. Trees lined the bank; their images reflected on the water. It was an hour filled with beauty, quiet and pleasure.

Paddling slowly down the river made us appreciate the intricacies and grandeur of nature. The turtle had a design on its shell, the bird had a pattern to its feathers and the river itself had form. The beauty we see on the earth reminds us that a beautiful God reflected His glory in creation.

Psalm 50:2 says, "Perfect in beauty, God shines forth." When we see and experience beautiful things in the world we must remember that from beauty God shines forth. Beauty comes from God. When we see or experience beautiful things we see through them the beauty and splendor of God.

God fills the world with beauty so we will be reminded that we serve a beautiful God.

MAY 10

This weekend I had the opportunity to coach at the USA Gymnastics level 9 Eastern National Championships. Besides watching and cheering for young, talented gymnasts, I also had a chance to talk with coaching friends from around the country. One thing I noticed: The most successful clubs have a strong head coach.

Effective head coaches surround themselves with high-quality support coaches. These head coaches also communicate their plans, purposes and visions to the staff. They build a cohesive support staff by encouraging and exchanging ideas, delegating responsibility and empowering the other coaches with the authority to get the job done. Though the head coach is ultimately the final authority in all decisions, they never ignore the concerns and suggestions of their coaches.

This is a metaphor for how Christ runs His church in the world. He is the authority over the earthly church just as He is the authority in the heavenly kingdom. Then Jesus came to them and said, "All authority in heaven and on earth has been given to me" (Matthew 28:18).

The risen Lord communicates His plans, purposes and visions for the church in the world to His disciples. He gives them responsibilities and empowers them with the Holy Spirit to get His work done "on earth as it is in heaven" (Matthew 6:10). He is the final authority, yet, through the Holy Spirit He gives His disciples authority to complete the work He calls them to as the church.

In the world today, Jesus communicates with the earthly church through His Word as well the moving of the Holy Spirit. The church is Christ's support staff in the world.

MAY 11

Today, two athletes refused to conform to my expectations during practice. Even though the assignment was simple, they stubbornly dismissed corrections and help so they could complete the work in their own ways. I left them on the event. Finally, they finished, but not before they punished themselves. Their hands were hot and stinging. Their arms were tired, along with their shoulders. Tomorrow they will feel even more pain as their muscles stiffen overnight.

We respond in a similar way with sin. We know that we should surrender it to God in Christ, so He can take it to the cross. But, instead, we hang on to it. Even when the Spirit nudges us to surrender and receive the grace of God we refuse. We cling to our old ways, dismissing the Spirit and His guidance. We turn from God and fail to come to repentance. Our burden of sin makes our hearts heavy. We feel the pain of our decision not to relinquish sin. We end up punishing ourselves and locking ourselves in sin, estranged from God.

Jesus Christ came into the world to set us free from sin. We no longer need to be tangled in our transgressions. Paul said, "There is no difference, for all have sinned and fall short of the glory of God, and are justified freely by His grace through the redemption that came by Christ Jesus" (Romans 3: 22-24).

Christ sacrificed His life to free us from sin. We can be stubborn and hold on to it, or we can surrender our sin to Him.

MAY 12

I filled my car with gas the other day, which is hardly a milestone. Every time the tank empties, I go to a gas station and refuel. My car has a yellow light that alerts me when the gas level is low. This signal reminds me to get to a gas station and fill up so I don't get stranded.

When I fill up my car at the gas station, I remember that I must be working with God to keep my spiritual life fueled through the Holy Spirit. Some weeks, life is hectic, and I run all over town for work, my family, my writing and my friends. At these times, my body signals to me that I am running on empty: I tire easily, and I become apathetic. Finally the last ounce of energy drains from me, and I drop.

If I don't heed the signal, I will keep running on the fumes of my own human effort and truly collapse. I must take time to refuel my soul through the power of the Holy Spirit. I need to set apart time for reading Scripture, engaging in prayer and giving praise and worship to God. I must allow the Holy Spirit to show me insights into God through the Scriptures. I need to sit quietly with Christ as He "intercedes for us" (Romans 8:34), and I must welcome the Spirit to fill me with the awe and wonder of the Sovereign God.

If you are running on empty, stop. "Instead, be filled with the Spirit" (Ephesians 5:18).

MAY 13

One of my athletes earned a spot on the level 10 Regional team, so she will compete at the Junior Olympic National competition. Making this team was difficult. She has prepared herself for this meet every day in practice for the last year. She finally triumphed at the Regional competition. Her daily preparation was the key to her success.

To prepare His people to meet Him, God spoke to Israel through His prophets. To Amos He said, "prepare to meet your God" (Amos 4:12). These are practical words from God, who is reminding His people that a period of preparation is necessary to enter into a relationship with Him.

God must prepare us for such a relationship as well, because we are not like Him. We are imperfect, weak and sinful. God is perfect, powerful and holy. He is divine, omniscient and omnipotent. God sent His Son, Jesus Christ, into the world to prepare us and fit us for a relationship with Him. We have none of the qualities we need to meet God. Yet by faith in Christ and His work on the cross we are prepared to come to God. Through Christ's redemption, we are made holy and perfect.

MAY 14

My job tonight is to patrol the floors of the hotel to make sure all the gymnasts obey curfew. I will watch and listen and walk the halls to ensure that the athletes follow the rules. In that way, they will be rested and ready for their competition.

I don't anticipate any trouble. If the girls want to compete well, they will follow the rules. They have worked too hard to throw away their opportunity to succeed at Nationals just to stay up late.

As Christians we should also be diligent about watching and guarding our faith against the intrusion of temptations that may steer us away from God in Christ. On the night of His arrest, Jesus told His disciples, "Watch and pray so that you will not fall into temptation" (Matthew 26:41).

Staying strong in faith means partnering with the Holy Spirit in prayer and being alert to the pitfalls of temptation that come our way. It means letting the Spirit keep us close to God in Christ so we can follow Him instead of our sinful desires.

Let the Spirit guard your faith and take you to the cross of Christ, where you can watch and pray and see the salvation of our God.

MAY 15

This morning a thick fog cloaked Des Moines, Iowa. Along the river, only shadows of trees and bridges could be seen. A train lumbered down the tracks of the city. Only a few cars were visible; the rest seemed to vanish as they entered a tunnel of fog. Though covered by the misty cloud, the train's presence was still apparent by the trailing cars and the sound of its whistle.

Many people struggle to accept the invisibility of God. And, yet, God is not entirely invisible, because He sent His only Son to become a visible man so we could know the reality of God's existence. We also witness His handiwork through His creation. And the Holy Spirit continues to live in the world to enlighten us to the truth that God lives. Although invisible, the Holy Spirit helps us to discern God's presence through His direction and power.

Paul said it this way, "For since the creation of the world God's invisible qualities—his eternal power and divine nature—have been clearly seen, being understood from what has been made, so that men are without excuse" (Romans 1:20).

God reveals Himself to us through creation, the person of Jesus Christ and the power of the Holy Spirit. As Colossians 1:15 says, Christ "is the image of the invisible God, the firstborn over all creation." According to Scripture we don't have an excuse for claiming that we can't see God. He has made Himself visible in the world. If we struggle to see Him we need to ask the Spirit to show Him to us.

MAY 16

Stepping out of the car at the Sinissippi bike path, I noticed a pretty garden spot. So I made my way toward the small trees and shrubs to take a few quick photos. A red-winged blackbird dove at my head. As the bird took another pass at me I realized that its nest must be nearby. So, I moved quickly away.

A short time later, I watched a family of geese head down the bank into the river. One parent stayed behind. Approaching the goose was a man walking his golden retriever. When the dog spotted the goose, it began barking and lunging at the bird. The goose was undaunted. It hissed and flapped and snapped at the dog. The dog retreated. When babies are vulnerable, parents are strong.

God protects His children. As children of God in this world, we are still vulnerable to temptation and sin. We are exposed to wickedness and evil. We are threatened with death. However, Jesus Christ is God's strong arm, still protecting the children of God in the world through the Holy Spirit. On the night before His crucifixion Jesus prayed, "My prayer is not that You take them out of the world but that You protect them from the evil one" (John 17:15).

We cannot escape the trials and tribulations of this world. But the resurrection shows us the power of God in Christ to protect us while we live in this world.

MAY 17

One night last week I had an interesting conversation with a friend who asked me many questions about God, Christ and faith. When the conversation ended, she said, "I want to be like you, certain about what you believe."

My faith comes from years of the Holy Spirit's revealing Jesus Christ to me through the Scriptures. There is no secret formula. There is no gimmick. There is simply the Word of God speaking through Scripture.

Many of us don't possess certainty in our faith because we don't seek God in Christ in the Bible. The Bible exists in the world for one reason and one reason only: to reveal God in Christ. We are not the first generation to struggle with a lack of faith and we won't be the last. Even Jesus had to address this problem with His contemporaries. He said, "These are the Scriptures that testify about me" (John 5:39).

The Scriptures testify that God became the man Jesus. He walked among us, died for our sins and rose from the dead. The Bible also tells us that we will gain eternal life by believing in Jesus and coming to Him. John declares that his Gospel was "written that you may believe that Jesus is the Christ, the Son

of God, and that by believing you may have life in His name"
(20:31).

Certainty of faith comes from meeting God in Christ in the
Scriptures through the guidance of the Holy Spirit. you can be
sure about what you believe.

MAY 18

A friend has a young daughter who has cerebral palsy.
Caused by a brain injury, this disability affects body move-
ment, muscle control, muscle coordination, muscle tone, reflex,
posture and balance. In addition, the CP has also affected her
tongue and jaw, making it impossible for her to speak. Recently
her parents purchased an augmentative communication device,
known as her talker, which allows her to communicate with
others. Now when she pushes the buttons of the machine, it
talks for her, and she can express her ideas, her needs and her
wants.

God wanted to communicate what was in His heart and on
His mind, so He sent Jesus Christ into the world to be His
talker. As Hebrews 1:2 says, "God spoke . . . to us by His Son."
Jesus Christ is God's Word made flesh, and He came to earth
to reveal God's thoughts on sin, salvation, forgiveness, mercy
and love. Jesus did not express His own opinion but spoke the
truth about God because He is God. He made it clear that He
came to tell the world what God was thinking. Jesus said, "I do
nothing on my own but speak just what the Father has taught
me" (John 8:28).

God has made His intentions clear through His Word on the cross. When Jesus declared, "Father forgive them" (Luke 23:34), He made manifest the saving nature of God, and when He uttered, "It is finished" (John 19:30), He told the world that God's reconciling work was completed in HIs death and resurrection.

MAY 19

This morning I spoke to a couple of fellow walkers as we passed one another. The exchange was brief and centered on the weather. Our interaction is never deeper than a comment on weather, a greeting or have a nice day. Although we see each other almost daily, the depth of our relationship will not go beyond the current stage unless something changes.

I thought about how many people have this type of surface relationship with God in Christ. God is present in our lives every day, yet for so many people, interaction with Him is very shallow or nonexistent

However, we can share intimacy with God. In fact, the relationship God shared with Jesus Christ while He was on earth is the type of relationship God wants to have with each of us. God desires that we be as close to Him as He is to His own Son. He sent His Son to die on a cross so through His sacrifice we could come near to God.

James said, "Come near to God and He will come near to you" (4:8). God came near to us in Jesus Christ so through Christ we could come near to God. The Holy Spirit abides in the world to fill the hearts of the believers with affection for God so we will know God's affection for us.

Christ is our assurance that the living God desires an intimate relationship with us.

MAY 20

I had a brisk walk with my daughter after dinner tonight. We had a pleasant conversation, which covered a variety of subjects. I enjoy walking with her and listening to her talk about her day. It's just nice to get away from the house and share each other's company. Sometimes, she even asks my opinion on a subject. That's a bonus.

I have to approach my relationship with God similarly. There are many days that I get caught in the rut of work, household chores, and miscellaneous responsibilities. Before I know it, the day is over, and I haven't said two words to God. At those times, I need to take a walk with God.

There are many ways to walk with God. Isaiah tells us to walk in the way of holiness. Solomon instructs us to "walk in the way of understanding" (Proverbs 9:6) and to "walk in the way of righteousness, along the paths of justice" (Proverbs 8:20). Paul wrote that we are to "walk in love, just as Christ also loved you and gave Himself up for us, a fragrant offering and sacrifice to God" (Ephesians 5:2 NASB). John tells us, "And this is love: that we walk in obedience to His commands" (2 John 1:6). And finally remember the words of Moses, "Love the Lord your God, walk in all His ways and hold fast to him" (Deuteronomy 11:22).

Take a daily walk with God.

MAY 21

I spent many hours today listening to people talk. On the flip side, people listened to me talk as well. We humans are a talkative group. Sadly, we aren't very good listeners. Still, I found myself engaged in some very interesting conversations and a few that I probably could have avoided.

What I also find interesting is whom we find interesting: If a person of notoriety speaks, his or her comments will be quoted in the press, written about in the blogosphere, and shared thousands of times over Facebook. Whether famous people make a profound or a preposterous statement, it will be heard by millions around the country and possibly even the world.

The most influential person in all of history is Jesus Christ, yet we rarely listen to what He has to say to us. Jesus is the Word of God, and He came to engage all people in conversation. God came to earth so He could speak to us. He came to talk to us about salvation, redemption and forgiveness. And some of those conversations are recorded in the Gospels.

Scripture says, "Go and tell this people: be ever hearing but never understanding" (Isaiah 6:9). God in Christ is always speaking to us, but we don't give Him the attention He deserves so we can understand His plan of salvation and His work in our lives.

Challenge yourself to listen to God, who speaks to you.

MAY 22

Today, my daughter bought some new clothes. She pulled out her purchases to show me and realized two items were missing. She searched her bedroom and bathroom. Together we retraced her steps from the car to the house. Finally, I asked if she had put them in another bag. My words reminded her that the clothes were in the trunk of her car.

Losing things is part of this life. From pens to car keys and jewelry to money, we spend many hours of the week looking for something that has been lost to us. Some things we can retrieve. Some things we fail to find.

In the garden of Eden, Adam's disobedience caused him—and as result all of humanity—to lose the presence of God. Satan made sin look so desirable that Adam wandered away from the living God. So humanity strayed. Unfortunately, man found himself in a dark, broken, fearful world apart from God and subject to death. But God made certain that, while we had lost Him, He would not lose us. God made sure that He could find all those who were lost to sin and death. In Ezekiel the Sovereign Lord says, "I will search for the lost and bring back the strays" (34:16). Without hesitation, God sent His Son Jesus Christ into the world to find the lost.

In Christ Jesus, God made sure that we could find our way back to Him. "For the Son of Man came to seek and to save what was lost" (Luke 19:10).

MAY 23

Writers hope that people will read their work. We write with the expectation that someone will pick up the book and be inspired through the story and words that we put on paper. We want our words to get people thinking, motivate them to action or influence them to change.

God has also written a book. Yes, the title is familiar, the Bible. While many people own a copy, few people actually read it. The men who wrote the Scriptures were inspired by the Holy Spirit. Therefore, it is not a dusty old, outdated book. It is the living word of God. Hebrews 4:12 says, "For the word of God is living and active. Sharper than any double-edged sword, it penetrates even to dividing soul and spirit, joints and marrow; it judges the thoughts and attitudes of the heart."

When we are reading Scripture we are engaging with God. When we read the Bible we are giving God in Christ permission to apply His word to our hearts and transform our lives through the power of the Holy Spirit.

We need to read Scripture with the expectation that God will reveal Himself, declare His intentions to us and motivate us to a deeper understanding of Himself. Through the words of Scripture the Holy Spirit can bring thoughts of God to our mind, teach us about the activity of God in Christ and encourage us to act in accordance with our Lord.

"All Scripture is God-breathed" (2 Timothy 3:16).

MAY 24

While I was in Florida a few weeks ago, one of my colleagues went fishing in a pond near the hotel. He caught an alligator. Fortunately no one was hurt. Until my friend told me about his harrowing experience, I hadn't given much thought to alligators. I am from the Midwest. Alligators are not on my radar. However, after that, wherever I walked that weekend, I searched the streets and grasses for any signs of these dangerous reptiles. According to residents, alligators are always lurking about.

I am reminded how much sin behaves like an alligator. It is dangerous and always lurking in our lives. We have to be patrolling our hearts and minds with the Holy Spirit to guard against its deception and destructive forces.

Genesis 4:7 says, "If you do what is right, will you not be accepted? But if you do not do what is right, sin is crouching at your door; it desires to have you, but you must master it." Of course, we cannot master sin without the power of the Holy Spirit working in our lives. We are too weak and vulnerable to its treacherous ways. However, when we keep our faith grounded in the cross of Christ and cling to Him, He defeats our sin with His righteousness through the power of the Holy Spirit.

"But if anybody does sin, we have One who speaks to the Father in our defense—Jesus Christ, the Righteous One" (1 John 2:1).

MAY 25

I walked in the rain this morning. Yes, I am like Charlie Brown standing in a downpour on the pitcher's mound. I zipped up my rain coat and walked into a persistent drizzle. As I walked, the rain became heavier. It was relentless. Rain splashed against my legs, dripped off my shorts and filled my shoes. Soaking wet, I returned home.

A good soaking rain is necessary for growth. The plants relish its arrival. The grass, which I cut on Saturday, was already long. The flowers in my front yard opened. And the cardinals, birds that thrive on inclement weather, were happily feasting at our backyard feeders.

Sunday in the Church was Pentecost, the time when God gave His Holy Spirit to the believers and the church was borne into the world. In a nutshell, Pentecost was God's soaking His people with the Holy Spirit. Through God's giving of the Spirit, the apostles grew from frightened men to bold, dynamic ministers of the Word. They were filled with God's power and equipped to teach and preach the Gospel of Christ. The radical change in these men saw the fulfillment of God's words to His prophet Joel, "I will pour out my Spirit on all people" (2:28).

Even today God gives His Spirit to the Church. By the anointing of the Spirit the church is given new life, and the faithful are given a bold, dynamic Gospel message to proclaim to the world. Ask God to soak the church with His Spirit.

MAY 26

I went bike riding this morning. As I pedaled down a hill on Perryville, I noticed a jogger ahead of me. As I started to go around him, I called out, "On your left," to let him know I was present. Unfortunately, he had head phones on and didn't hear me. I slowed hoping he would not drift in front of me. When I realized it was safe, I sped past him.

I thought about the number of times we plug the world into our ears and fail to hear God when He approaches. God speaks to us in Scripture, but then the world calls, and we catch the news instead. He calls us to worship on Sunday, but soccer and gymnastics and baseball call so we grab our equipment and race out the door. God in Christ speaks to us from the cross, but we veer ever closer to the edge of destruction because the world vehemently denies the existence of sin and eternal death. Jesus has risen from the dead, but the world loudly refutes that possibility.

When we listen to the world, our lives become shaped by the world. When we listen to God, our lives become shaped by God. It is not by chance we hear God, it is by design. He spoke to us in Jesus Christ. We just need to take the world out of our ears to hear Him.

Jesus said, "He who has ears to hear, let him hear" (Luke 14:35).

MAY 27

There are days like today when life can seem overwhelming. Cancer is raging in the body of many of my friends. Young people I know are in crisis. Hatred in the world seems almost unbearable. Grief is an unwelcome visitor in the homes of many of my friends and family. On these days, when death, sin, wickedness, sorrow, hurt and despair are spitting in my face, I am reminded to turn the other cheek to see the glorious face of the risen Lord.

Some days when the world is in my face, I am tempted to stare back. Instead, I have to look at my Savior, who dealt on the cross with all the raging and raving of the world. When He died, sorrow and pain and anguish died with Him. When He rose from the dead, He left those evils behind and brought back into the world life and hope and joy through His resurrection.

Regardless of our circumstances, the reality of Christ's resurrection makes us "more than conquerors" (Romans 8:37). We do not have to live under the rubble of hopelessness; instead through the power of the Holy Spirit, we can live in the hope and glory of the risen Christ. The world will continue to stalk us and threaten us, but God in Christ will raise us with Him to be victorious over the world.

"Christ has indeed been raised from the dead!" (1 Corinthians 15:20)

MAY 28

Now that the mornings brighten early I can walk or ride my bike. Being outside in the morning makes me feel peaceful. During the early morning hours there is a hush, a serenity that draws me outside. When I am in creation, I tune my ear to hear the gentle voice of God speak to me.

I relish these solitary hours. To me there is nothing as tranquil and reassuring as creation. I witness God's created order in the rising of the sun. I witness the geese teach their young to flee from danger into the woods as I ride past. The wild turkeys gobble loudly, teaching their young to shout at intruders. A squirrel, with its baby on her back, scurries up a tree to teach her young that safety can be found in the nest. Teaching is a natural part of creation.

In the morning hours, God moves close to teach me. In the quiet I experience His presence. While I ride, Bible verses roll through my mind, and I know God is teaching me through these Scriptures. As I meditate on these verses, God teaches me a new insight or perspective about Himself, His Son or the Holy Spirit. I love the mornings, because then, more than at any other time of day, God teaches me.

"He awakens me morning by morning, wakens my ear to listen like one being taught" (Isaiah 50:4).

MAY 29

A good friend has joined Facebook. Over the years many of her friends, myself included, and her family tried to explain how useful Facebook could be. However, she held her ground, and even after persistent pleading, we could not convince her to join.

So, you can imagine my surprise when I found her friend request tonight. Somehow, after all the years of rejecting social media, she allowed her daughter to sign her up.

I tell this story to remind us of the number of friends and family members who say they will never accept the reality of God or the truth of Jesus Christ as Savior. To them I say: Stay in prayer. The Holy Spirit is always working to bring the reality of God into every life. It is the work of the Spirit to reveal God in Christ and to transform lives. We must persist in prayer, asking with sincerity of heart that the work of the Spirit be fulfilled in the lives of our loved ones, friends, coworkers, acquaintances and even enemies.

1 Samuel 14:6 reads, "Nothing can hinder the Lord from saving." God brought His Son into the world to save the world. Nothing on earth can stop God's plan of salvation in Jesus Christ. All that God intended to do for the purpose of salvation has come into the world in Christ.

Expect to be surprised one day because the Spirit is always at His work of transforming lives.

MAY 30

My daughter and I went out to lunch today. We noticed that the couple at the table next to ours did not speak one word to each other for more than forty minutes, but instead they texted on their cell phones. We watched sadly as these two people ignored each other. There was no interaction or personal conversation. They left the restaurant without sharing thoughts, revealing secrets, or expressing feelings.

Scripture states, "For anyone who does not love his brother, whom he has seen, cannot love God, whom he has not seen" (1 John 4:20). Here is the greater dilemma demonstrated by the couple at the table: They didn't even seem to see each other. So, if we, as a society, aren't even seeing each other, how will we ever see the invisible God and learn to love Him? It seems hopeless.

Of course, God has overcome the difficulty of our technological age. In other words, God is greater than the cell phone. "God is light; in Him there is no darkness at all" (1 John 1:5). Light makes things visible. God has made Himself visible in the person of Jesus Christ, and He continues to open our eyes to the truth of His Son through the power of the Holy Spirit.

By sending His Son into the world to die on the cross and then by raising Him from the dead, God made certain that He would not be ignored. "All the ends of the earth will see the salvation of our God" (Isaiah 52:10).

MAY 31

Yesterday a friend mentioned that she had said a little prayer. I have heard that phrase numerous times. However, this time, I spent the better part of the day thinking about those words until finally concluding that there is no such thing as a little prayer.

Prayer is always connected to the living God. It is His gift to us, so we can meet the risen Christ through the power of the Holy Spirit. When we pray, we are ushered into the presence of God in Christ. That is never a little thing. We may consider our time in prayer brief, but God does not clock our time in prayer. He sees our hearts set on Christ, and Christ's heart set on Him.

While we are on earth, our prayers will always be lacking, but Christ makes them complete. He prays with us, and through Him our incomplete thoughts, inadequate words and stumbling praises sound glorious to God. There is no gradation to prayer. Prayer is simply prayer. It is neither big nor small, right nor wrong if done through the Spirit in the presence of the risen Christ.

It is Christ who makes our prayers acceptable to God. He lives to intercede for us and through Him. "The words of my mouth and the meditation of my heart [are] pleasing in your sight, O Lord, my Rock and my Redeemer" (Psalm 19:14).

Don't consider the size of your prayer; consider Christ, who prays with you.

June

JUNE 1

Today I cleaned my office for the first time in a very long time. It was messy. Scraps of papers and old notes were layered on my desk. Books were thrown about the floor along with several pairs of shoes.

When I am busy writing, I pay very little attention to the clutter accumulating around me. Picking up isn't a priority so I don't do it daily. I convince myself that I like everything out where I can easily put my hands on it. However, now that I am sitting in a clean office, I'm wondering why I don't take more care to pick up each day.

I also let sin accumulate in my life. I go for several weeks neglecting repentance. I give other things priority over confession. But sin has to be dealt with daily. I need to humbly repent before the Lord. I need to come before my Savior confessing my sin so He can expose the areas of unrighteousness in my life through the power of the Holy Spirit.

When God exposes my sin He always reveals His Savior. There is not a delay or hesitation on the part of Christ. Let's put this in terms of time. When God exposes sin our Savior immediately responds to "purify us from all unrighteousness" (1

John 1:9). When we allow our sinful nature to harbor our sinfulness, we miss the opportunity to experience the grace, love and forgiveness of God in Christ.

Where sin is confessed, there is always God's Savior with His arms stretched out on the cross.

JUNE 2

My ego was yelling and flailing like a two-year-old today. It was storming and stomping, exclaiming about my worth, my talents, my, my, my. What a display of arrogance I put on before God.

I knew my thoughts had to sound ridiculous to Almighty God, yet I continued to let them spin out of control. These unbridled thoughts, focused on myself, romped through my mind for several minutes. I knew they were wrong, but I couldn't get control of my mind because I was consciously choosing to let my rebellious thoughts romp. Ugh! What a poor decision I was making.

At last I had had enough of my ego, arrogance and rebellious thoughts. So I redirected my mind to Scripture. As I read through verses my crazy thoughts began to slow and recede. Reading more verses finally put down the rebellion, especially when I read Mark 12:30, "Love the Lord your God with all your heart and with all your soul and with all your mind and with all your strength." My thoughts were nothing but arrogant wanderings that had absolutely nothing to do with my loving God.

God corralled my wild thoughts with His Word and then roped them to the cross. Loving God plunged the cross into the midst of my juvenile ramblings and deflated my ego by reminding me of Christ's suffering and dying.

There is never room for my ego next to Christ's humiliation on the cross.

JUNE 3

This morning the sky was clear, except for one wispy cloud stretching like taffy across the sun and reflecting the sun's rays across the sky. I considered the number of clouds that have passed in front of the sun. Some clouds change the intensity of the sun's heat; others hide the sun from view. A cloud in the sky floating across the path of the sun can change the look of the sky and even change the look of the sun itself.

We also have clouds in our lives. These clouds are the difficulties or problems or annoyances that we face each day. We sometimes permit our problems to obscure our view of the Son in our lives. But problems also have a way of showing us Christ as we have never seen Him before. And at other times of trouble, God illuminates our mind with a new knowledge about His Son.

Christ is always in our clouds. Struggles often press us into reexamining our relationship with the Son, our Savior. As we face each problem, God opens our eyes of faith and gives us an opportunity to see Christ through a different lens. Through these lenses we are able to see Christ's comfort, kindness, compassion and love during our times of trial. As our problems pass in front of God they are transformed into opportunities to reflect the Son.

"At that time men will see the Son of Man coming in clouds with great power and glory" (Mark 13:26).

JUNE 4

The phenomenal beauty of the Grand Canyon was formed by the running waters of the Colorado River. Melting glaciers increased the river's volume ten times. It overflowed and rushed across the earth's surface, eroding the ground. The weight of the water and the persistent raging current abraded the rock, dirt and land, carving out the magnificent canyon. It is a stunning, breathtaking, spectacular wonder that has been revealed through the river's destructive force.

The sanctifying work of the Holy Spirit runs like the course of the river. When the Spirit flows through the life of the believer, He destroys sin, churning and dislodging ungodliness and unrighteousness in the heart. The Spirit floods the soul, uprooting transgressions, exposing iniquity and uncovering wickedness. The Spirit then cuts a course to the cross, where this filthy water of sin is purified by the cleansing blood of the Lamb.

As the Spirit cuts more deeply into the sinful nature, Christ's stunning risen life, which resides within the believer, is revealed. The beauty of His holiness becomes evident, and the believer, aware of His presence abiding within, contemplates "the Lord's glory" (2 Corinthians 3:18). By the powerful work of the Spirit, believers "are being transformed into his likeness with ever-increasing glory, which comes from the Lord" (2 Corinthians 3:18).

JUNE 5

My friend's daughter is getting married. Today I listened to my friend describe the venue and the plans for the big day. I can hear the joy and the stress in my friend's voice as she talks about all the preparations that must be completed before the big day.

The church is also in the midst of planning a wedding. When believers gather on Sunday morning for worship, they should embrace the joy of knowing that the bridegroom, Jesus Christ, will one day come for His bride, the church. Scripture says, "Let us rejoice and be glad and give Him glory! For the wedding of the Lamb has come, and His bride has made herself ready" (Revelation 19:7).

The bride has made herself ready by accepting the sacrifice and love of her Savior. Christ has done everything through His death and resurrection to present His bride as "a radiant church, without stain or wrinkle or any other blemish, but holy and blameless" (Ephesians 5:27). Christ came down from the Father to be united to His bride. He died to save her and lives to love her. Therefore, the church should be a joyful place of preparation as believers celebrate and anticipate the day the bride and the bridegroom are united through the power of the Holy Spirit.

Christ is coming for His bride, and the faithful are invited to attend the wedding. "Blessed are those who are invited to the wedding supper of the Lamb" (Revelation 19:9)!

JUNE 6

This afternoon I attended two graduation parties. The food was plentiful, the pictures numerous and the memories abundant. It was fun, not only to reminisce, but also to hear the graduates describe their plans. These celebrations are a time to honor the accomplishments of the graduate and show support for their future endeavors.

God encourages His people to celebrate. He calls us to gather in worship to honor Him for His accomplishments in Jesus Christ. We come together as the family of God to remember all that His Son has done for us on the cross. We recall that through His shed blood we are saved from sin and death. Worship is about rejoicing that Christ our Savior has triumphed over death and has given us a future in the eternal kingdom of God.

In worship we have the privilege of joining Christ at the communion table through the power of the Holy Spirit. At the table we look back at the last night Jesus was on earth with His disciples. We remember that He shared the Passover meal with them. And when the meal was over "He took bread, gave thanks and broke it, and gave it to them, saying, 'This is my body given for you; do this in remembrance of me'" (Luke 22:19).

At the table we also look forward to the day when the world is reconciled to God, and we "will be with Him in paradise" (Luke 23:43).

Worship is the celebration of God in Christ.

JUNE 7

When I started walking this morning the clouds were low, thick and gray. I should have stayed close to home, because about halfway through my walk the sky grew dark, thunder rumbled and lightning flashed. I started jogging, but the rains came, and I had to seek shelter under a nearby building. Because it was early, I didn't want to disturb my husband and call him for a ride. Just then my phone rang. It was my husband calling to say he was coming to pick me up.

As I waited for my husband, this Scripture came to mind "For your Father knows what you need before you ask Him" (Matthew 6:8). God meets our needs before we are aware of them. As human beings we need to be forgiven for our sin. We don't recognize that easily. So God responded first by sending His Son. In Jesus' work on the cross we see the nature of loving God and our own human need for salvation.

If God knows what we need, why do we pray? Because when we pray, God reveals His nature to us as He meets our need. When we need forgiveness, God shows us He forgives us through Jesus Christ. When we need love, God points to His

Son on the cross. When we need hope, God shows us the empty tomb and the risen Lord.

Our greatest need is God. And God came to us in Christ to satisfy our greatest need.

JUNE 8

My summer is usually filled with outdoor activities. The pool in our neighborhood opens; the mornings are warm enough and light enough to go bike riding; and the evenings cool down so I can walk. I enjoy all the extra physical activity. Usually I put a physical challenge in place for myself. I've used summer to train for a marathon and a half marathon. One summer I trained for a century, which is a hundred-mile bike ride. Giving myself a goal keeps me motivated during my workouts.

I apply this same thinking to my life of faith. I set some specific goals for myself that will push me to spend more time with God. In the past I have memorized Scripture, chosen a specific topic for study or read the works of a church father such as Augustine. Setting a goal helps me to draw closer to God in Christ.

For some people goals include the foreign mission field or work in local missions, while others volunteer for camps and vacation Bible school.

Perhaps God is challenging you to do something different with Him this summer. He is always directing His people to join His ministry through the Spirit. Paul said to the church in Colossae, "See to it that you complete the work you have received in the Lord" (Colossians 4:17). God has something for all believers to do this summer that will grow us deeper in faith and further His kingdom. What's God calling you to do?

JUNE 9

Summer is finally here. A hot sun has the temperature close to 90 degrees today. I spent time after work sitting at the pool enjoying the heat and talking with neighbors. However, after about an hour of the sun shining on my face, I began to sweat. Since it was getting into late afternoon, I decided to walk home.

There was little shade on my walk home, and the intense sunshine beat down on my shoulders. Without shade there was no escape from the sun's heat. Then quite unexpectedly a soft breeze blew across my face, cooling me down. That refreshing wind was a welcome companion as it whisked away the sun's heat as I walked.

Life can get intense. Things like grief, bitterness or anger can sometimes beat us down. Our days become routine and stale because we have only enough energy to combat these stresses. At the end of the day we collapse into bed, dreading the morning. This is not life, but survival.

It's when we are in these ruts that we should ask God to send us the soft breeze of the Holy Spirit. When we pray to God, He will send His refreshment to us through the Spirit, who enters our stagnant days with the promise of eternal life and resurrection hope. Through the Spirit, God in Christ renews our hearts, transforms our minds and replenishes our souls with His life.

"The Spirit gives life" (John 6:63).

JUNE 10

When I first started working as a gymnastic coach, I knew nothing about the sport. I had not been a gymnast. I had never executed a flip. I had no experience or understanding of the sport. It would have been very easy in those early days to give up, quit and find another job. Instead, I chose to work at understanding gymnastics.

Had I given up, I would have missed out on many valuable friendships and memories.

When I first started reading the Bible, I didn't know anything about Scripture. So I read the Gospels, because they contained the stories of Jesus. At first I didn't understand what I had read. But, as I continued reading, I could picture the surprised looks on the faces of the Pharisees when Jesus performed a miracle. I could imagine His walking along the beach and sleeping in the boat while a storm raged. I got to know Him through the stories. As I read, the Spirit taught me more about Christ, His life, death and resurrection.

If I had given up, I would have missed out on a valuable friendship with Jesus Christ, and I would not have grown deeper in faith and knowledge of God.

Yes, the Bible is hard to understand. But the Spirit is in the world to open our eyes to the truth in Scripture. Jesus said, "But when He, the Spirit of truth, comes, He will guide you into all truth" (John 16:13).

JUNE 11

Today at work a coworker asked me to address a specific situation with an athlete. She then told me what to say and what the consequences should be. Even when I worked things out exactly as she wanted, she still went back and addressed the situation.

This is a perfect example of how we sometimes behave with God. We want Him to handle the circumstances of our lives, yet we tell Him exactly how to handle the situation. Even after He responds, we still go back and address the situation ourselves.

We think we know better than God does about what should be done and how it should get done. Quite simply we lack trust in God. To learn to trust God, listen to the words He spoke to Job, "Who is this that darkens my counsel with words without knowledge? Brace yourself like a man; I will question you, and you shall answer me. Where were you when I laid the earth's foundation? Tell me, if you understand" (Job 38:2-4).

We do not and cannot understand the world or our circumstances as God understands them. He sees everything from start to finish. He possesses infinite wisdom but we are finite thinkers. Yet, we are convinced we know best.

Come to trust God as Job did so you can say to Him, "I know that you can do all things; no plan of yours can be thwarted" (Job 42:2).

JUNE 12

My attitude today was abhorrent. I thought about things that were not honoring to God. There were times my words were sharp. I was short-tempered when patience was needed, abrupt when the situation called for kindness and disagreeable when I should have been pleasant. Today my transgressions were crystal clear to me.

I would be totally discouraged and disgusted with myself were it not for the words of King David, who said, "For I know my transgressions, and my sin is always before me" (Psalm 51:3). David, it seems, had a day very similar to mine.

David also knew the cure for this type of day: God. He wasted no time getting before God and confessing His sin. He didn't try to convince God that his sin was no big deal. He didn't list the reasons for his sins or justify his behavior. He simply confessed, "Against You, you only, have I sinned and done what is evil in your sight" (Psalm 51:4).

His confession cleared a path for him to see the nature of God. As David admitted his sin God responded with His mercy, His unfailing love and His compassion. Through confession, David met His Savior and Redeemer by the power of the Holy Spirit.

God responds to me just as He responded to David. As I admit my sin, God shows me my Savior, Jesus Christ, who died on the cross to forgive me for this day of transgressions.

JUNE 13

My husband does the gardening. He has already planted tomatoes and peppers in our vegetable garden and has just finished planting zinnias, pansies, and day lilies in the flower garden.

Each garden is unique and has a specific purpose in the yard. Flowers add cheer and bright colors to the yard. Fresh picked vegetables bring robust flavor to summer meals.

The Bible also tells us about two very important gardens: The Garden of Eden and the Garden of Gethsemane.

God created the Garden of Eden to supply all of Adam's needs. The garden was full of the presence of God, and He shared what He had created with man. However, Adam became dissatisfied with God's provisions and care, and he rebelled against His Creator. God banished Adam from the Garden for his lawlessness.

Because of Adam's sin, God brought His Son Jesus Christ to earth. He had come into the world to obey the will of God and to complete the plan of salvation. His journey to the cross took Him through the Garden of Gethsemane, where He prayed for the strength He needed to carry out God's divine plan.

In the Garden of Eden Adam succumbed to disobedience and sin and became estranged from God. In the Garden of Gethsemane Jesus Christ remained obedient to God and carried the sin of mankind to the cross and reconciled the world to God.

"My beloved has gone down to His garden" (Song of Solomon 6:2 NASB).

JUNE 14

At the gym we tell our athletes that they must be comfortable being uncomfortable. In other words, we ask them to get out of their comfort zone. This phrase is cliché, but, simply put, if a gymnast is not willing to push herself beyond what she feels safe doing she will not be able to progress in this sport. I am not suggesting that a gymnast take undo risks to succeed. But what I have noticed is that a comfort zone is a zone of complacency. Gymnasts who are content with their gymnastics will not achieve new skills.

Complacency is a condition we often allow to creep into our faith. We snuggle into our understanding of God and decide that the knowledge we have of God will make us a good person and get us to heaven. However, this thinking does not address our real problem of sin. Any talk of sin or being a sinner makes us uncomfortable, but until we allow the Holy Spirit to address the sin in our lives we cannot move into a deeper understanding of God in Christ.

When God starts moving, our lives become uncomfortable. He convicts the sinful nature within us and makes us confront our sin. We do not want to confront our sin. We want to deny our sin. Denial does not remove our sin. Denial is how we stay comfortable with our sin. God will not allow us to remain in our sin; instead He exposes our sin and insists that we surrender it to Jesus Christ. Then through faith and by the power of the Holy Spirit, God moves us to the cross. There we see what Jesus Christ has done so that we are saved from sin and death.

It is a very uncomfortable feeling to know that Jesus Christ died for our sin. We want anything but that to be true. And this truth agitates our sinful nature, which battles against Christ. A sinner at the cross is uncomfortable until the grace of Christ brings comfort.

"For it is by grace you have been saved, through faith" (Ephesians 2:8).

JUNE 15

This morning one of my young athletes had a difficult time connecting her bar routine. Her teammates had finished their work, and they were moving to the next event. She had wanted to go with them, but she hurried her routine and fell. She did this two more times. Finally, I explained to her that she had kept falling because she wasn't focused on her routine, but on what the others were doing. When she focused, she finished her routine.

We have similar struggles in our Christian faith. We don't focus on Christ, but, instead, we concern ourselves with what He may call us to do. We hesitate to follow Him because, quite frankly, we are afraid of what He will ask of us. We worry about the work God will call us to do instead of keeping our eyes locked on Jesus.

Our focus needs to be getting to know God in Christ. If we are preoccupied with thoughts about what God might make us do, we will never learn who Jesus is. The goal and focus of the Christian life is Christ. We should not worry about what He will ask of us. We are simply to know Him. When we know Christ, we know God. Stay focused on knowing God in Christ.

"Now this is eternal life: that they may know you, the only true God, and Jesus Christ, whom you have sent" (John 17:3).

JUNE 16

The other day I had to wash my hands numerous times to get Crazy Glue off my fingers. As I held my hands under the running water I remembered the Roman governor Pontius Pilate.

Pilate tried to wash Jesus Christ's innocent blood off his hands. He knew if he released Jesus and didn't carry out the wishes of the angry mob his political career would be over. So he washed his hands of the situation and surrendered Jesus to His enemies saying, "I am innocent of this man's blood. It is your responsibility!" (Matthew 27:24)

The crowd was eager to crucify Christ and they shouted, "Let His blood be on us and on our children" (Matthew 27:25).

Everyone was guilty of spilling Jesus' blood. Only Christ's hands were clean. And the irony is that the only way the hands of Pilate and the mob could be cleansed was if they held the pierced, bleeding hands of Jesus. Christ's blood was shed for the mob that called for His crucifixion. It was shed for Pilate and for the soldiers who nailed His hands to the cross. The blood that spilled from His hands was shed for all the sinners of the world, including you and me.

God let Christ's innocent hands be pierced by the dirty hands of sinful man so that by faith the hands of sinful man could be washed clean by His blood.

JUNE 17

Financial planners say one of the keys to saving money is to pay yourself first. The advice from planners is that people should take a few dollars from their paychecks and put them into investments or savings accounts. The same system works for time. If you need time for yourself, you have to plan it into your day and guard those hours from intrusions and distractions. Equally important is carving out time for your spiritual life. Time alone with God is imperative to living a life of faith.

When you make your spiritual life a priority, you are making God a priority in your life. This is what Jesus meant when He told His disciples, "Give to Caesar what is Caesar's and to God what is God's" (Mark 12:17). God deserves to be a priority in our lives; after all, He made us a priority when He sent His Son, Jesus Christ, into the world. In sending His Son, Jesus Christ, God expressed His greatest desire: to save the world from sin and death.

Since God made us a priority it is only fitting that we give God special attention. It is easy to rush through the day without giving Him a thought. So, meet with Him first, before the craziness of the day begins. Ask the Spirit to guard these hours from distractions and intrusions. First thing in the morning, bring to God praise and thanksgiving for all He has given us in Christ.

JUNE 18

My house was very noisy this morning. My husband and daughters were hurrying to get ready for work. Music played in one room, and the television was on in another. A hairdryer whirred in one bedroom, while in the kitchen a blender whipped a smoothie. One daughter left only to return a few minutes later to print a shipping label she needed before heading out the door again. The house was at noise capacity when the phone started to ring. This was 'way too much activity so early in the day.

Finally, my daughter and husband left for work, and all phone calls stopped. I inhaled and started to write and study Scripture. As I focused on Jesus Christ in the Scriptures the stress of the morning was washed away by His words, "Take my yoke upon you and learn from me, for I am gentle and humble in heart, and you will find rest for your souls" (Matthew 11:29).

My soul did rest. It settled into the Word the way tired feet snuggle into comfy slippers. The angst and weariness in my soul was washed away by Christ's encouraging words.

So many times during the day our souls are overwhelmed by the noise, stress and demands of our day. We will go to the snack machine, Starbucks or even the gym to alleviate the tension. Yet, only the Scripture will sooth the weary soul. Jesus invites His followers to step out of the world and go to the Scriptures, where He is waiting to bathe our souls in His rest.

JUNE 19

When the shooting in the Charleston, South Carolina, church was first reported, Americans expressed outrage and remorse for such a senseless act. Today reporters gave us glimpses into the lives of those mothers, fathers, daughters, sons, sisters and brothers who were killed. And a drape of sorrow covers the land.

However, grieving family members have risen above Dylann Roof's hatred by offering him forgiveness. The love of Christ that had drawn the victims to church has now been manifested in the world through their families. Their words are those of the Savior who said, "Father forgive them" (Luke 23:34), as He hung on a cross dying for all sinners.

By living out their faith in God and by extending the forgiveness of Christ to Roof these families have overcome hate. They are people of great sorrow, pain, and anguish through which the light of God's love now shines in the world. They have shown the depth of their commitment to the Lord by living according to His Word. Their message is full of the power of the Holy Spirit, "But I tell you: Love your enemies" (Matthew 5:44).

Have you been wondering where God is during this time? He is abiding with the grief-stricken families and revealing Christ's loving presence to the world through them. Through their suffering, Christ is made visible in the lives of these families who have chosen to "do good to those who hate you" (Luke 6:27).

"Love never fails" (1 Corinthians 13:8).

JUNE 20

Because of recent heavy rains the neighborhood swimming pool has risen even with the concrete pool deck. It looks like an infinity pool. It is difficult to know where the deck stops and the water begins.

Fullness gives us a different outlook. When a meal fills us up, we appreciate the way food satisfies our hunger. When our homes are full of family and friends, we are content. Meaningful work fills our days with productivity.

When we think of ways to fill our lives, we should also be thinking about filling our lives with God. Paul prayed for the Ephesian church that the members would know the depth of Christ's love, and he said, "to know this love that surpasses knowledge—that you may be filled to the measure of all the fullness of God" (Ephesians 3:19).

Our frame of mind and our vision of life are transformed when God in Christ fills our hearts. When God fills us He gives us His Spirit "without limit" (John 3:34). As God saturates our hearts with His Holy Spirit, we have immeasurable love for God and one another. We have an ample supply of Christ's peace, His peace, "which transcends all understanding" (Philippians 4:7). When the fullness of Christ dwells within us, we are forgiving, gracious, and truthful. Our minds think of ways to praise Him, worship Him and enjoy Him.

Being full of God is being full of Christ and His love.

JUNE 21

This morning's Scripture reading at church was the story of young David slaying Goliath. King Saul had placed his armor on David, but it was so bulky David could not move easily. Instead, David armed himself with the power of God, five stones and a slingshot. David told Goliath, "All those gathered here will know that it is not by sword or spear that the Lord saves; for the battle is the Lord's and He will give all of you into our hands" (1 Samuel 17:47).

David stripped himself of every encumbrance. He moved toward His enemy with confidence in God and the simple weapons God had made available to him.

When problems arise in our lives we go to God, but before the last word of our prayer has been uttered we clamor to the world for solutions. However, the world's solutions are like Saul's armor, burdensome and clumsy. They are no help.

When problems arise in our lives, God offers us Himself through the power of the Holy Spirit. Regardless or our circumstances, God asks us to be like David and strip ourselves of all but faith in Him. In Jesus Christ, God sheds the world from our lives and gives us grace and freedom to move through our problems with Him.

It does not matter what enemy we face; God battles for us. He fills us with the confidence and faith of Jesus Christ, so we can confront our foe with the certainty that victory is ours through the Spirit.

JUNE 22

Tonight the forecast calls for violent thunderstorms. The winds are already increasing. A pink hue from the setting sun is reflecting off the bottom of a cumulus cloud in the west; in the east, the cumulonimbus clouds are gray and heavy. My prediction: If the storm has high winds, intense lightning flashes and loud thunder claps, many people will lose sleep tonight.

The disciples had a harrowing experience in a storm one evening on a lake. Theirs was one of several boats caught in a squall. As waves broke over the side of their boat and the vessel was filling with water, they began to panic. Finally, it occurred to them that they should wake Jesus, who was sleeping in the stern.

As the storm screamed and raged, Jesus responded, "Quiet! Be still!" (Mark 4:39). And the storm obeyed. Not only was the disciples' boat saved and all the disciples safe but all the boats and crews that were on the lake that night were also saved from the storm because of Jesus' words and His divine authority.

When Jesus exercises His authority in one person's life the affect is that many people become witnesses to His divine nature. When God in Christ touches one person's life with His authority, the lives of those around that person are also influenced by the Spirit. Christ does not isolate His authority; He reveals it so that all men can come to salvation.

JUNE 23

A week before I wrote these words, the shooting at Emanuel AME Church in Charleston, South Carolina, prompted Governor Nikki Haley to call for the removal of the Confederate flag from the Capitol grounds. The governor said, "This flag, while an integral part of our past, does not represent the future of our great state."

Although some people consider the flag a symbol of slavery and racism, it certainly wasn't the cause of the shooting, and taking it down will not be the cure. Racism can be conquered only through the power of God in Christ.

If the flag is going to come down, then the churches of South Carolina and all around the United States should raise the cross. Christ's cross of love and grace is the cure for sin, racism, death, and hatred. Christ came into the world, was nailed to the cross and died for our sins. When His dead body was taken down from the cross, sin seemed to win. However, almighty God raised Christ from the dead, and through the glorious resurrection, God's love and grace are alive in the world through the Holy Spirit.

The message of Jesus' cross and the good news of God's love in Christ belongs to the church. Let the church raise Her voice and proclaim the truth of Christ's reconciling work on the cross. "This is how we know what love is: Jesus Christ laid down His life for us" (1 John 3:16).

JUNE 24

Tonight's Bible study centered on this passage, "Blessed are those who are humble, because it is they who will inherit the earth" (Matthew 5:5 ISV).

We often think of a humble person as one who doesn't seek attention. He or she possesses talents and gifts but are modest about them. A humble person does not lack pride; instead, he or she recognizes the greatness in others.

The book of James says, "God opposes the proud but gives grace to the humble" (James 4:6). He opposes the proud because pride acknowledges the self as sovereign. Pride is the belief in one's own worth, merit, and superiority. Pride looks at Christ's cross, sneers at Jesus' sacrifice and resists the work of the Holy Spirit. Pride tells a person that his own worth and dignity make him fit for the kingdom of God. God opposes the proud, because the proud are opposed to everything that is God.

A humble person, however, acknowledges the sovereignty of God. To be humble is to believe in Christ's worth, merit and superiority as God's Son and Savior. People who are humble recognize God's greatness and through the work of the Holy Spirit learn to live under Christ's authority. They live in submission to God and allow the Spirit to work freely in their lives. The humble receive God's grace through Jesus Christ.

Jesus showed us how to live a humble life under God's authority through the Spirit; let the Spirit dwell in you so you can live a humble life before God.

JUNE 25

It's seven o'clock in the evening and the first time today the sun has come out. It has been a day full of rain and clouds, and I have been cooped up inside. Now as the sunlight comes through my window, I think, *What a waste to have sunshine now. It will be dark shortly.* But the sun will come out when the sun will come out. When it shines isn't up to me.

The lateness of the sunshine made me think of the thief on the cross next to Jesus. His punishment indicated he had wasted his life in violence. The man admonished the criminal on the other side of Jesus, "We are punished justly, for we are getting what our deeds deserve" (Luke 23:41). He then acknowledged Jesus' innocence and said to Him, "Jesus, remember me when you come into your kingdom" (Luke 23:42).

As Christ hung on the cross, He shone the truth of His saving grace into the man's heart. His death saves all people who believe in His atoning work. The forgiveness, salvation and reconciliation Christ offers the thief He extends to all through the Holy Spirit.

From an earthly perspective, it looks as though the Son arrived late in the man's life. However, through His death, Jesus secured the man's eternal life. The time of transforming a life belongs to the Son, and it is never too late for the Son to shine.

JUNE 26

Rain. Rain. Rain. Rain. There has been nothing but rain at home for the last two days and much of June. This morning, my husband, Chris, and I headed for a long weekend away from home. And, guess what? Rain. Rain. Rain. Rain. We drove in rain all day. I can't seem to drive far enough to avoid this wet intruder that continues to disrupt my plans.

Sin. Sin. Sin. Sin. Like the rain, it just keeps coming into my life. It is an intruder that disrupts my days and keeps me awake at night. It causes me to do things that I don't want to do, and it prevents me from doing the things I want to do. When I sin, I am ignoring Christ's work of salvation. In other words, I am not letting Christ be my Savior.

Cross. Cross. Cross. Cross. I must take my sins to the cross daily. I need to meet my Lord in prayer and allow Him to cleanse me of my sin through the work of the Holy Spirit. I must allow Christ's work on the cross to thwart my sinful nature. I need to meet Jesus in His Word so He can teach me about His sacrifice for my sin. I must ask Christ to empower me with His Spirit so I can live a godly life and leave my life of sin behind.

Saved. Saved. Saved. Saved. "But when the kindness and love of God our Savior appeared, He saved us, not because of righteous things we had done, but because of His mercy" (Titus 3:4-5).

JUNE 27

Chris and I were invited to attend a surprise fiftieth wedding anniversary party for our friends who live in eastern Kentucky. We live in northern Illinois, and the last time we were together was more than 20 years ago, so our presence at their party was unexpected. It was great fun to celebrate this occasion and reconnect with them. As with all good friendships, we felt the time evaporate, and we talked as though we had seen each other only the day before.

One day, Christ is going to return. Matthew 24:50 says, "The master will return unannounced and unexpected" (NLT). That day will be a glorious celebration for all believers. We will be united to God in Christ through the Holy Spirit. We will enjoy the fullness of God's presence, and that which we lost in the garden because of our sin will be restored to us.

When Christ comes and takes us with Him into the fullness of the kingdom it will be as though we had never left the Garden. Everything will be as it was before our rebellion. Jesus showed us how completely He will reconcile us to God in the miracle of the withered hand (Matthew 12:13), and when He restored another man's sight. (Mark 8:25). Jesus showed His power to restore completely when He was on earth and when He returns the next time He will restore the world to its original, perfect condition.

JUNE 28

It has been a wonderful weekend of catching up with friends. We have sat together at tables and talked about memories from the past, learned about what is happening in our lives currently and even spoken about current plans.

When we come together with Christ at the communion table, we share a similar experience with God. At the table, Christ shows us the sin in our life. He reminds us that He died on the cross to forgive all our sin, and then He opens our eyes to what life should continue to be through the Holy Spirit's guiding and directing our steps.

The communion table is the sacred place where God and man come together in Christ. At the table, Christ calls us to remember His sacrifice for our sin. He invites us to break bread with Him so we can remember that He broke the chains of our sin and has set us free from death. When we come to the table, we honor Jesus because we keep His request to "Do this in remembrance of me" (Luke 22:19).

At the communion table, we quiet our hearts before the Father, humble ourselves before Christ and receive the friendship of God through the Holy Spirit.

Come to the table.

JUNE 29

Today, I messed up when it came to relationships with my family. I said one thing wrong and just kept going. By the time an hour had passed, I had messed up so many times I didn't even know how to ask God to help me.

To regroup, I stepped back, went to my office and started reading Scripture, beginning in 2 Peter. As soon as I reached 1:5-7 the Spirit was already at work giving me a list of behaviors I needed to work on. These were the behaviors I had conveniently ignored earlier. Sometimes the Spirit pours salt in a wound to get my attention.

Let me paraphrase the verses. Through the power of the Holy Spirit, I am supposed to bear this fruit: goodness, knowledge, self-control, perseverance, godliness, kindness and love (2 Peter 1:5-7). However, today my test paper came back with a zero at the top of the page.

Had I not gone to Scripture, I would have more than likely started tomorrow where I left off today: failing to remember to cultivate the fruit that honors Jesus Christ in my thoughts, words and deeds. On days like today, when I fail, He lifts me up with His word through the power of the Holy Spirit, and He teaches me what to practice.

Peter wrote, "I will always remind you of these things, even though you know them" (2 Peter 1:12).

JUNE 30

Recently the Oklahoma Supreme court ruled 7-2 that a 6-foot granite monument of the Ten Commandments must be removed from that state's Capitol grounds.

Of course, many people, including Oklahoma Attorney General Scott Pruitt, are upset about the ruling. I, however, agree with the court's decision.

The Oklahoma Capitol building does not need a monument to the Ten Commandments. The responsibility to teach the Ten Commandments belongs to the Christian church, pastors and parents. Christians are angered when a state building takes down a religious symbol. However, when was the last time a Christian was angered that The Ten Commandments were not displayed on church grounds, in Sunday school classrooms or even on church signs?

The moral decay of our nation is not the result of taking down granite monuments. It is the result of many churches' failure to teach Scripture to the people. The task of teaching Scripture belongs to the church. Besides championing the Ten Commandments, the church must proclaim Christ's cross and the teaching of His suffering, death and resurrection in worship through the power of the Holy Spirit. The Holy Spirit makes the Ten Commandments relevant to our lives and fills us with the grace of Jesus Christ, so we may live according to the moral conduct of God's holy kingdom.

Now let the church in Oklahoma and in every state teach the Commandments and the Gospel to the people. "So then, the law is holy, and the commandment is holy, righteous and good" (Romans 7:12).

July

JULY 1

My daughter wears many different fragrances, but her favorite is Adam Levine for Women Eau De Parfum. When she sprays it on, a sweet, light scent fills her room and wafts gently down the upstairs hallway in the house. When I smell that clean, delicate scent, I know she is going out for a special occasion.

In John 12:3, Mary washes Jesus' feet with a very expensive perfume. As she pours the fragrance on her Lord, the aroma fills the house. I would imagine it was an intoxicating and wonderful smell to those in the house. This perfume was also used to mark a very special and somber occasion. According to Jesus, "It was intended that she should save this perfume for the day of my burial" (John 12:7).

Spices and perfumes were used to cover up the odor of decay in dead bodies, but in the case of Jesus Christ His body would never "see decay" (Psalm 16:10). So the perfume Mary poured on Jesus was symbolic of the "pleasing aroma" (Leviticus 3:16) His sacrifice for our sin was before God; and it was the fragrance of the resurrection life, which the Holy Spirit would bring into the world after God raised Jesus to life.

When by faith we accept Christ's sacrifice on the cross for our sin and receive eternal life through the Spirit, our life becomes a pleasing aroma to God. When we follow Christ, we receive His fragrance of life through the Spirit.

JULY 2

The news never stops was part of an advertisement for a local talk-radio station I heard this afternoon. This station was assuring its listeners that even when they are asleep the reporters are awake covering everything that has happened during the night. Personally, I liked the old days when radio and television stations signed off the air from midnight to six the next morning. Those silent six hours gave us a break from the world. I am speculating, but I think we slept better.

Around-the-clock-news coverage oppresses our psyches. The spirit of the world uses the news media to burden our lives with fear, conflict, struggle and turmoil. We are weighed down by the ongoing stories of violence, greed, and disorder. As we listen to the media drone on about the world's problems, we become acutely aware of our weakness and inability to provide solutions for the issues.

However, God has equipped Christians to deal with the world: He has placed the life of His conquering Son into our lives through the power of the Holy Spirit. Jesus overcame the world in the resurrection. His triumph over the grave proves His power to save the world. When Christ lives within us He silences the world and teaches us to live above its fear and despair. Then He ministers to the world through us.

1 John 4:4 encourages us: "The One Who is in you is greater than the one who is in the world."

JULY 3

Last weekend I had a delightful conversation with a high-school graduate. With great energy and enthusiasm she described her dreams of going to college and becoming a teacher. Young people, between the ages of 18 and 25 who are making plans for their futures fascinate me. Their visions and dreams are pure and untainted by the realities of life. Their words are seasoned with passion and intensity.

As we grow older, we tend to let our dreams fade. Realities have made us tired, and we think that dreaming requires too much work or effort. Yet life is empty without dreams.

Through the power of the Holy Spirit, God fuels us with dreams and visions. We live in the day of the Risen Lord, and because He is alive among us, His Spirit remains in the world, filling believers with the vision and dreams of God. In Joel 2:28 God says, "I will pour out my Spirit on all people. Your sons and daughters will prophesy, your old men will dream dreams, your young men will see visions."

All who believe in Jesus' resurrection and the Spirit are filled with the eternal life of God. When God fills us with His dreams and visions they are not just for this world but for the world to come. Our dreams will not fade because our bodies grow weak or tired. In God we will always be dreamers, and He will make those dreams real through the Spirit.

JULY 4

As we celebrate America's freedom, most of us have traditions that more than likely include family, friends and fireworks. Picnics and parades are organized. People gather together in public areas eagerly waiting for the sun to set and the night sky to fill with dazzling firework displays. We don't mind that each July Fourth is similar to that of the preceding year, because we think it is important to celebrate freedom.

Each week on Sunday we have an opportunity to celebrate one of those freedoms. We are free to worship without fear of persecution. Soldiers have died to secure that right for us. Mothers have buried their sons and daughters who sacrificed their lives on the battlefield so we could attend worship. Fathers have carried home the folded flag that draped across the coffin of their fallen children. We say we remember those who have shed blood for our freedom to worship, but we don't really remember unless we are living with the empty rooms.

How many Christians will honor the dead by exercising their right to worship this coming weekend? Who will attend church and honor the fallen Son of God who died to set us free from sin and death? Jesus died to save us, and others died to give us the right to worship Him freely.

Exercise your freedom to worship. Go to church. Thank God for His Son, and pray for those families who have lost their loved ones so we could gather to worship.

"If the Son sets you free, you shall be free indeed" (John 8:36).

JULY 5

The world tries to convince us we are not sinners. Many people today are believing this lie. Scripture, however, is very clear, "all have sinned and fall short of the glory of God" (Romans 3:23). Unless we recognize our sin we will not recognize our Savior, Jesus Christ.

The Holy Spirit dwells in the world to expose our sin, which is not the terrible thing we think it is. God exposes our sin so He can reveal our Savior. Each time God shows us our sin, He presents His Savior. There is no time lapse or lag between the time the Spirit exposes our sin and the time the Spirit reveals our Savior. Sin exposed; Savior revealed. Sin exposed; salvation offered through Christ. Sin exposed; Christ carries sin to the cross. Sin exposed; sinner set free from sin and death through the sacrifice and blood of Jesus Christ.

God does not expose our sin and leave us dangling in guilt and remorse. He immediately responds with the grace and mercy of Jesus Christ. He shows us our sin so He can show us Christ's dying on the cross to set us free from our sin. He shows us Christ so we can be saved.

All sinners "are justified freely by [God's] grace through the redemption that came by Christ Jesus" (Romans 3:24).

JULY 6

Several of my friends are experiencing grief. During this time, they manage to breathe because it is involuntary. They move through the ordinary routines of the day, showering, dressing, cooking and talking thanks to muscle memory, because their minds are filled with thoughts and memories of the absent loved ones.

We cannot escape grief. The passing of a loved one will affect all of us sometime. And each of us will have to cope and find comfort and strength to deal will our losses.

For those of us who have found faith and truth in Jesus Christ, we can move beyond coping with death to hoping in eternal life. Jesus experienced separation from His Father through death, and then He knew the unspeakable joy of being reunited with the Father in the resurrection. Since He has known both the anguish of death and the joy of the resurrection, He is our strength and comfort in grief.

Jesus Christ died on a cross so He could conquer death through the power of the Holy Spirit who brought Him back from the dead. Death for Christ was not permanent but temporary. He said to His disciples, "The Son of Man is going to be betrayed into the hands of men. They will kill him, and after three days He will rise" (Mark 9:31). In Christ, all who believe will be raised to life. Death is only temporary; life in Christ is everlasting.

"Death has been swallowed up in victory" (1 Corinthians 15:54).

JULY 7

I listened to a podcast last night that said small churches were making a comeback because people want to worship where someone knows their names and where they know the names of others. Megachurches offer anonymity not intimacy.

Meanwhile, in the past two days in two different conversations, my daughters have expressed their distaste for matchmaking websites. They want to meet people the old fashioned way, in person while sharing an activity. The Internet offers cyber interaction but not social interaction. Maybe technology has finally driven us to the point of wanting to be together, in community with one another, in face-to-face conversation, instead of downloading a Face Time app.

I look at these two situations and see similarities: small churches' wanting to attract people and people wanting a place to have personal interaction. I see possibility for the church not only to meet the needs of those tired of isolation because of technology but also to offer community and relationship. I don't know what this type of outreach will look like, but I know that through prayer and study of Scripture, the Spirit will open the eyes of the church members He has called to this ministry.

The church is built on its relationship with Jesus Christ, so it can offer relationship to others through the Spirit. Let the church "proclaim to you what we have seen and heard, so that you also may have fellowship with us" (1 John 1:3).

JULY 8

At this time, the shooting of Kate Steinle, allegedly by illegal immigrant Jose Ines Garcia Zarate in San Francisco, California, has put the city's sanctuary policy under attack. We can argue over this policy; we can debate illegal immigration and we can accuse politicians, including the president, for doing nothing to secure our borders, but none of this rancor will ease the pain of the Steinle family.

Policy will not change the reality of Kate's death for her friends and family. They are suffering. In fact, the world is suffering. We need only to look at the news in the past few weeks to see how deeply we are suffering as a nation. But our politicians can do nothing to ease our suffering and pain.

However, someone has the power and has done something about our pain. God sent His Son into the world so He could come together with us in our suffering. Jesus Christ came to suffer with us and then to suffer for us on the cross. In Jesus Christ, God came to earth to join us in our suffering and to overcome our suffering at the cross. By faith we triumph with Christ over suffering. Just as the Holy Spirit lifted Jesus' burden of suffering by raising Him to life, so the Spirit will also lift our burden of suffering and raise us to life in Christ.

If we have received comfort from our suffering through Christ, let us comfort others through the power of the Holy Spirit. Paul reminds us that God "comforts us in all our troubles, so that we can comfort" (2 Corinthians 1:4) others.

JULY 9

The smoke detector for the upstairs hallway of my house is sitting on my printer. I need to replace the battery. So, currently, it cannot detect smoke. If a fire breaks out in my house, the detector would not give its shrill cry and alert my family to potential danger.

I am reminded that God has given us a sin detector in the Person of the Holy Spirit. Unfortunately, there are days when I disengage from the Spirit, behaving in ways unacceptable to God and rush into potentially dangerous spiritual situations.

However, the Spirit convicts me of my sin and then brings me to Christ in whom my "transgressions are forgiven" (Psalm 32:1). He fills me with remorse for my sin against God and then brings me to Christ, who "create[s] in me a pure heart" (Psalm 51:10). He shows me how sin separates me from God and then opens my eyes to God's reconciling work in Christ.

I am powerless to detect sin in my life unless I stay connected to the power of the Holy Spirit. The Spirit leads me to the Scriptures and shows me in the word my areas of weakness. He calls me to pray and sit with Him so He can warn me about places in my life where I am vulnerable to sin. He fills my heart with gratitude for Christ's saving work on the cross and leads me to repent before God.

Listen for the Spirit's warnings.

JULY 10

A few months ago my husband bought new tires for our car. Things were good until recently when the car started to shake and shimmy on the highway. So he returned to the garage where he had purchased the tires. The mechanic did several hundred dollars' worth of work to the car. It did not fix the problem. My husband has been back three times trying to get the job done right. Instead of fixing the problem, the mechanic has now made the fault ours. Now it seems to me the garage is trying to take advantage of us. I am done with this garage.

I get tired of jobs not getting done right the first time.

I find solace in knowing God did the job of dealing with my sin right the first time. He does not have to go back to redesign His plan for salvation. The work is finished and completed in Jesus' death on the cross. When Christ died for our sin, He died for the sin of the entire world: all the generations of history have been saved through Jesus.

Paul wrote, "For we know that since Christ was raised from the dead, He cannot die again; death no longer has mastery over him. The death He died, He died to sin once for all; but the life He lives He lives to God" (Romans 6:9-10).

God's work of salvation, redemption and reconciliation was done right the first time in Jesus Christ.

JULY 11

I have had such fun today. Before the rains arrived, I walked for two hours, biked for an hour with my sister and then sneaked in another walk with my neighbor. I talked to some friends who were having a garage sale and spoke with a neighbor I hadn't talked with for several months. I am going to the Starlight Theater with my family to watch my niece in a performance of *Mary Poppins*. Everything today revolved around relationships, and it was fun.

I thought about the joy and celebration that awaits us in heaven. There will be no hindrances to relationships. We will be free to see Christ in all His glory and the Father in all His fullness. Paul says, "When Christ, who is your life, appears, then you also will appear with Him in glory" (Colossians 3:4). The Spirit will wrap us in the eternal essence of love. That calls for dancing and singing and rejoicing.

When we are reunited with God in His eternal kingdom, we will know this unbridled joy. I am looking forward to that glorious day.

"They will enter Zion with singing; everlasting joy will crown their heads. Gladness and joy will overtake them, and sorrow and sighing will flee away" (Isaiah 35:10). What a glorious day awaits us!

JULY 12

I had planned to memorize Scripture on my walk this morning. However, I talked with two friends instead. After church I had planned to write, but had a nice visit with my niece and mom. After that visit, my mom and I ran errands and took an unexpected trip to Bed, Bath and Beyond to pick up a clock radio for my aunt. When we finished the errands, I had some time for lunch and then went to feed my sister's dogs because she is out of town. After keeping the dogs company, I had two nice phone conversations with friends.

Jesus Christ put people first during His ministry on earth. "A large crowd came to [Jesus], and He began to teach them" (Mark 2:13, see also 1:45, 10:1). As His follower, I am called to put people first in my life.

Everyone I spent time with today taught me something. I was blessed to see the world through the eyes of my 10-year-old niece. My aunt showed me how to struggle with physical afflictions with grace and dignity and humor. And my friends open my eyes to new ideas. And all of them showed me how God was supporting and sustaining them in their day.

We learn about God when we share our days with people, and we learn about people when we share our days with God.

JULY 13

Each day before work, I make a goal to exercise patience with the gymnasts. Only a few minutes into the workout, and my goal is a casualty. Then my feelings chide me for failing.

Feelings and faith are not the same thing. Feelings are based on perception, and to base knowing God by our feelings becomes problematic to a true understanding of God. If we feel happy, then we may determine that God is near to us. However, if we are feeling sad or lonely we may decide God is not around. Too often we root God in our feelings. God is a Person not a feeling.

Since God is invisible, building an awareness of Him through our senses is extremely difficult. On the other hand, faith is based on the reality of God in Christ and His work in the world. By faith we are shown God through Christ. Jesus was very specific, "When a man believes in me, he does not believe in me only, but in the One who sent me. When he looks at me, he sees the One who sent me" (John 12:44-45).

On days when my feelings try to best my faith, the Holy Spirit shows me the cross of Christ. Jesus did not go to the cross because He felt like it. His feelings would have steered Him into hiding. Instead He said, "Now my heart is troubled, and what shall I say? 'Father, save me from this hour?' No, it was for this very reason I came to this hour. Father, glorify your name" (John 12:27-28). Jesus had faith that His Father would bring Him through the hour of His crucifixion to the day of His resurrection.

Our faith has as its bedrock Christ's confidence in God.

JULY 14

My sister has two dogs, which we occasionally watch. When my sister is gone, one of the dogs, Bandit, leaves waste deposits in her house, which I have to clean up.

Today, he was groomed, and he looked very different. I thought he behaved differently, too. I was hopeful that the haircut had changed him. However, walking downstairs I discovered that Bandit had made deposits all over the basement floor. Changing the look of the dog did nothing to change his character.

Jesus rebuked the Pharisees for keeping up appearances but doing nothing to transform their character. He called them "whitewashed tombs." He said they strived to "look beautiful on the outside but on the inside are full of dead men's bones and everything unclean" (Matthew 23:27).

Sadly, most of us are Pharisees. We spend an enormous amount of time making our bodies look good by working out, eating right, using cosmetics and even choosing certain types of clothes. At the same time, we invest very little time in improving our character. We can be all dressed up and still grouse about our spouse or complain about a friend or even be angry at God.

Transformation of character starts by giving the Holy Spirit access to our hearts and allowing Jesus to open our minds to God. We can dress in fine clothes, which will wear out, or we can be clothed in the righteousness of Christ, which leads to eternal life.

JULY 15

There are many times I say things I wish I hadn't. But words trip off my tongue and out of my mouth before I have a chance to stop them. Lately, I have tried to be deliberate about my word choices, speak carefully and think first. I have had minimal success.

Today I came across this verse in John 12:49: Jesus said, "For I did not speak of my own accord, but the Father who sent me commanded me what to say and how to say it." Jesus wasn't just talking about speaking the words the Spirit had given Him; He was talking about the attitude with which He was to deliver His words. Jesus relied on the Spirit for the content of His words and the attitude of delivery.

There were times in His ministry that He delivered His message in a "loud voice" (John 7:37). I would guess that on the day He cleared the temple, His words were shouted over the noise of the chaos. When He spoke with the disciples at the Last Supper, His words were filled with sadness. On the cross, though at times barely audible as He gasped for air, His words were delivered with mercy. And when He was raised to life and stood before the disciples in His risen glory, His voice was full of joy.

As disciples of Christ what we say and how we say it must be given to us through the Spirit.

July 16

Folding bath towels is one of my least favorite household chores. But today the monotony of the task was interrupted by thoughts of Christ's wrapping a towel around His waist and washing the feet of His disciples. What struck me about this scene from John chapter 13 was that the author had just commented, "Jesus knew that the Father had put all things under His power" (3). Jesus knew He had power, and He exercised that power by washing the disciples' feet and drying them with a towel.

Let's look for a minute at what He didn't do with His power. He didn't strike down Judas Iscariot, who was about to betray Him. He didn't exercise His power to reroute His course to the cross. He didn't use His power to wipe out the Roman soldiers who would arrest Him. He didn't throw lightning bolts or whip up a huge storm to send Jerusalem into chaos.

He used His power in the most dramatic and compelling way; He used it to show His disciples the "full extent of his love" (John 13:1).

On the cross, Christ used His power from God to love His disciples. He used His power of love to destroy sin and death. He used His love to bring His disciples forgiveness and unite them to God. He used His power to open the eternal kingdom of God to all who believe in His name.

Christ's disciples in every age are shown the power of His love.

JULY 17

Facebook had a story about the rescue of a trapped golden retriever. The scared animal fought being rescued. At one point the rescuer said to the dog, "I'll come to you." He came close, scratched her nose and then could free her.

Like the golden retriever, we get scared, especially with all the violence we have heard about lately. This world has us running and hiding. We want a safe place, but we fight being rescued too.

God has come to us in the person of Jesus Christ to deliver us from the fears of this world. Jesus said, "For I have come down from heaven not to do my will but to do the will of Him who sent me" (John 6:38). Jesus is familiar with the violence of this world. His own disciple, Judas Iscariot, betrayed Him to the Pharisees, who used false testimony to accuse Him of rebellion against Rome and blasphemy against God. They took Him to Governor Pontius Pilate who turned Him over to be crucified on a cross. The violence of this world tried to stop Him from rescuing us, but God conquered sin and death by raising Christ to life.

Still we fight God and want to reject Christ's cross. But for those who believe, Jesus is our Deliverer and our shelter from this world.

Christ empowers all believers with the Holy Spirit, so they can live in the world without fearing it.

JULY 18

Tonight is a night for quiet. Politicians have been speaking incessantly since the Orlando tragedy. Reporters have editorialized every aspect of the investigation. Talk show hosts and radio hosts have asked experts an untold number of questions. Neighbors asked neighbors about the shooter's motives. Questions are flying everywhere. We talk and talk and talk, trying to find answers, but the answers won't come to us through human agencies.

So tonight I urge you to sit in quiet and listen to what really matters. Hear the cries of those mourning. Tune your hearts to the sounds of those weeping for their loved ones. Be attentive to the sounds of suffering around you. Listen to the world groan.

And, then, hear God say, "Be still and know that I am God" (Psalm 46:10). Know that God's Son, Jesus Christ, was One who suffered. Know that the Only Begotten of God agonized on the cross to take away our sin. Know that His mother, Mary, stayed at the foot of that gruesome cross weeping for her son. Listen to God groan for the world.

The Orlando tragedy, like all tragedy, will leave us with more questions than answers. Why does man do what man does? Why did this man do what he did?

And then ask God to answer this question for you: Why did One Man, Jesus Christ, die on a cross? God desires to answer this question for you through the Scriptures and by the power of the Holy Spirit. Listen to God through His word, and you will find the answers to all your questions.

JULY 19

Obedience to God is difficult for me. I know what it means to be obedient. It means following the will of God in Christ in my actions, words and motives. However, many times, I only try to obey God so He will give me what I want. I have outcomes in mind that I think He will honor if I obey Him. I negotiate obedience with God. I have in mind an if-then scenario. If I obey God, then He will give me my desired outcome. Placing conditions on obedience is not obedience to God.

True obedience is not about my outcomes, it is about how God in Christ works in me to fulfill His plans. I cannot be obedient to God unless the Spirit empowers me. When I want my own outcomes for obedience I am rejecting the work of the Spirit in my life.

Only Christ has lived in full, active obedience to God. While on earth He was pure in motive, action and word. When the hour of Jesus' ultimate test of obedience had come, He said, "Now my heart is troubled, and what shall I say? 'Father, save me from this hour'? No, it was for this very reason I came to this hour" (John 12:27). His motive and the Father's motive were one. He did not concern Himself with the outcome but only in remaining "obedient to death—even death on a cross" (Philippians 2:8). Jesus was obedient; God determined the outcome: salvation for all who believe.

In this world I may not know the outcome of my obedience. That doesn't matter. What matters is remaining obedient to God in Christ through the Spirit.

JULY 20

When we express time in our finite experience, we use words such as *sooner, later, yesterday, tomorrow, today, earlier,* or *after.* However, the Scriptures refer to infinite or immeasurable time. Time came to my attention while I was reading a verse in John. Jesus is washing His disciples' feet but Peter objects to His servitude. Jesus replied, "You do not realize now what I am doing, but later you will understand" (John 13:7).

Our faith lies between what we "do not realize now" and "but later you will understand." When something happens in our lives we want to see what God is doing now. We don't want to have to wait until later to understand. For us, later is like tomorrow; it never comes. So we grow discouraged in our faith. We pray and wait, and still we hear, "You do not realize now what I am doing." Jesus wants us to be focused on who He is, not what He is doing and when He is going to do it.

Jesus came into measurable time so He could reveal to us immeasurable God. On the night He washed the disciples' feet, He knew His earthly time was almost over, but His immeasurable life in the eternal kingdom was about to be revealed through the resurrection. His time on earth would end in death on the cross. His life in eternity would continue through the resurrection. Jesus, the Incarnate God, tasted death; Jesus the divine Son of God never dies. Because He lives, Jesus is the object of our faith now and the hope of what we do not yet realize.

JULY 21

Today the sky was full of sunshine, not even a cloud passed overhead and dulled the brightness of the sun. The treetops shimmered with light, and my sunglasses couldn't completely shade my eyes from this dazzling day.

When I stand with Christ in the "unapproachable light" (1 Timothy 6:16) of His glorious kingdom, I will dwell in the radiance of God's glory. I will never again fear the darkness, because it will be gone, swallowed by Christ's victory over death.

In the meantime, as I wait for the marvelous day of sharing the eternal kingdom with Christ in all His fullness, I can walk in the light through the Holy Spirit. Jesus said, "I have come into the world as a light, so that no one who believes in me should stay in darkness" (John 12:46).

Christians sometimes forget that the darkness of death and sin, which at one time overcame us and blinded us to the reality of God, has been vanquished by Jesus' death on the cross. When the darkness of ignorance was so deep and blinded us from knowing God, Christ died and shattered the darkness. The Light of God shone in the darkness, making it possible for all who believe in Him to "walk in the light of the Lord" (Isaiah

2:5). Faith in Christ floods our hearts with His light and opens our minds to the living God among us.

"Let there be light" (Genesis 1:3).

JULY 22

Right now my faith seems a bit thin. What I mean is distractions rule my prayer time; Scripture study yields few insights into God; and my ears seem deaf to the Spirit's voice. I consider my faith life bland.

Not long ago, the opposite was true. Scripture study was productive; my prayer time was alive; and I could readily tune my ears to God's voice.

I have experienced living in plenty with the Spirit. However, staying encouraged when faith appears to fall on lean times with the Spirit is difficult.

As I wrestled with this issue of want of Spirit, Paul's verse in Philippians 4:12 came to mind, "I know what it is to be in need, and I know what it is to have plenty. I have learned the secret of being content in any and every situation, whether well fed or hungry, whether living in plenty or in want."

Usually this verse is viewed according to physical needs; but it applies to spiritual needs as well. Right now I am living in want of the Holy Spirit. God put this want in my life so I will hunger for Him and desire the abundance of Christ.

Still, I fight God when my faith seems to lack the bounty of the Spirit. Instead I must learn to be content, accepting all things as a gift from God. The Spirit's work in my life is up to

God. Faith means willingly accepting whatever comes to me from the hand of God.

JULY 23

The context of John chapter 13 is the Last Supper, when Jesus and His disciples gather for their last meal. As it was being served, Jesus leaves the table, removes His outer garment, wraps a towel around His waist and washes the disciples' feet. After this John writes, "When He had finished washing their feet, He put on His clothes and returned to His place" (John 13:12).

This particular sentence in John seems to foreshadow coming events in Christ's life. The final days of His earthly life are coming to an end. The Son of God came to earth wearing the clothing of man, His outer garment of flesh wrapped around His divine nature. Very soon, however, He will be clothed in sin and death on the cross, where God's Servant will complete God's work of salvation.

Once His reconciling work was completed, God removed His shroud of death, and by the power of the Holy Spirit raised Him to life.

The shroud of death removed, Christ put on His glorious raiment of the resurrection. "The body that is sown is perishable, it is raised imperishable; it is sown in dishonor, it is raised in glory; it is sown in weakness, it is raised in power" (1 Corinthians 15:42-43).

After He had risen, He returned to the heavenly kingdom to take His place beside God. "After the Lord Jesus had spoken to [the disciples], He was taken up into heaven and He sat at the right hand of God" (Mark 16:19).

JULY 24

For the first time in its thirty-eight-year history our gymnastic club had an athlete compete in an elite-level championship meet. This milestone was accomplished through years of dedication not only by this gymnast and coaching staff but also by other coaches and athletes who shared their knowledge and experience with us over the years. In other words, we didn't do this alone.

As Christians, we are also surrounded by other believers who help us on the journey of faith. Some of our fellow believers are still in our lives; others have gone on to the kingdom, but their work and writings still influence us. Hebrews 12:1 refers to those who have inspired us by their faith as "a great cloud of witnesses."

The Christian faith is difficult to live in the world. We cannot do it alone. The Father, Son and Spirit are always working in our lives, and God uses believers from the past and the present to enlighten us as we travel on this journey. The Bible is full of people like us, who struggled to live a life of faith in this fallen world. Through Scripture, the Spirit uses their experiences to teach us the deeper things of God. Martyrs, pastors and theologians have also shared their wisdom of and insight into

God. Through their stories, we are encouraged and strengthened to "press on toward the goal to win the prize for which God has called me heavenward in Christ Jesus" (Philippians 3:14).

JULY 25

According to someone (the ambiguous *they* in our country's leadership), each of us must use words that are politically correct when speaking to others. The same thinking has been adopted by the church, but the church calls it *inclusive language*.

So, in keeping with the prevailing attitude of our time, I would like to share with you the most inclusive word in the English language and all languages: *sinner*, which applies to every one of us. Paul wrote in Romans 3:23, "For all have sinned and fall short of the glory of God." And again in Romans 5:12, "Therefore, just as sin entered the world through One man, and death through sin, and in this way death came to all men, because all sinned."

I find it interesting that in our quest for inclusive language the word *sinner* is disappearing from our churches.

When the church draws attention to our sinful human condition it proclaims the message of equality and salvation for all. Sinners are all equal in God's sight, and they are gathered together by the Holy Spirit on the ground of redemption at Jesus's cross to receive Christ's grace and salvation.

The church must preach the doctrine of sin and the doctrine of redemption through Jesus Christ so all people can be healed of sin and reconciled to God.

God has given His church the message of equality and inclusion: "Christ was sacrificed once to take away the sins of many people" (Hebrews 9:28).

JULY 26

I met two cyclists riding in the park this morning who invited me to join them on their ride. They were going to take two laps around the park road before heading back to the bike trail and home. I have biked on the park road for years, but these two fellows took me down a path I had never noticed before. It was a beautiful stretch of trail through the heart of the park. After ten years of riding in the park, I thought I knew every trail. Obviously, I was wrong.

Sometimes I read Scripture without really paying attention to the text. That is true especially when I read familiar passages. I glide over them thinking God has already taught me what I need to know from those passages. I rush over the words, not even pausing, because I am certain I know the lesson God will teach me. However, I have come to realize that even in the familiar texts the Spirit will show me a new path to a deeper understanding of God.

Scripture says, "For the word of God is living and active" (Hebrews 4:12). The risen Christ remains the teacher of His Word, and the Holy Spirit applies His teaching to my heart and mind. Together the Son and Spirit expose my sin, give me new insights into the cross and draw me more deeply into the knowledge and presence of God. These Divine Persons show me God's beautiful heart and everything He has done for me and the world through Christ.

JULY 27

I was restless trying to figure out what to write for tonight. Some days my thoughts just don't seem to come together. But then a friend sent a message encouraging me to look at the sunset. So without delay, I hopped on my bike and rode to the two highest points in the neighborhood, just in time to snap a picture of God's handiwork.

I love the sky. It is vast, mysterious and full of beauty. Sunrises and sunsets, in all their magnificence, still give us only the tiniest glimpse of the marvelous glory contained in the heavens. Stars, planets and moons reveal the splendor of space, and the sun stretches its radiant beams from horizon to horizon, filling us with awe.

Jesus Christ came to earth to give us a glimpse of God's majesty and glory. His miraculous signs were just a peek at the power and strength of the living Lord. His touch healed the sick and raised the dead. His words were the words of eternal life. And when His arms were stretched across the beams of the Roman cross, God's love poured into the world carrying forgiveness and salvation to all who believe.

One day the Son of Man will be seen "coming with the clouds of heaven" (Daniel 7:13). Jesus will come again to earth, and the sky will be full of His glory. So, I am going to watch the heavens; because when He comes, I want to behold His entrance.

JULY 28

In an unusual moment at the end of practice today, my coworker and I exchanged some harsh words. He was frustrated by a situation and spoke without thinking. I could feel anger building inside of me, so I left the workout.

Still seething when I got home, I quickly changed clothes and went for a swim. Physical activity helped me burn off steam and put the circumstances in perspective. I knew we had to work this out before tomorrow.

Blessedly, my co-worker, who is a man of integrity, apologized for his words, which gave me the opportunity to forgive him. Of course, I am going to forgive my co-worker. There have been untold times in my life when I have had to ask a friend to forgive me.

It's not usually big things that ruin relationships. It's the festering little things, like misspoken words or misguided actions that we ignore, that eat away at relationships. Yes, my coworker and I could have denied any wrongdoing, but there would have been no avenue for repairing the relationship, which, at that moment, suffered some damage. His apology allowed me to extend forgiveness so our relationship could be reconciled.

Forgiveness is not something that comes easily to us. Our human nature would rather hold grudges. Still, as believers, we are expected to extend forgiveness to others because God in Christ has forgiven us.

"Bear with each other and forgive whatever grievances you may have against one another. Forgive as the Lord forgave you" (Colossians 3:13).

JULY 29

My good friend became engaged today. Her happiness is evident in the words she writes and the pictures she posts on Facebook. My heart, and the hearts of all her friends and family, are overflowing with joy for her and her fiancé. We all want to dance, sing and celebrate the love these two have for each other.

When we find love in the world, we have found God in the world. Where love is, God is. Love is from God, and love is the nature of God. Scripture says, "God is love. Whoever lives in love lives in God, and God in him" (1 John 4:16). If we know love, then we know God. Love is God, and He cannot be separated from it.

When we choose to love one another, we are testifying to God's love in the world. We can love one another only because God's love comes to us through Jesus Christ and the power of the Holy Spirit. And it is through Christ's strength of love within us that we can love one another. Scripture also says, "This is love: not that we loved God, but that He loved us and sent His Son as an atoning sacrifice for our sins" (1 John 4:10).

God loved us through His Son Jesus Christ, and when we love one another we are revealing Christ's love for us. "No one has ever seen God; but if we love one another, God lives in us and His love is made complete in us" (1 John 4:12).

JULY 30

Lately, I have been butting heads with some of my gymnasts. They have stubbornly refused to conform to my expectations for the team. They ignore my warnings to work out safely, and, instead, practice unsafe gymnastics. Their resistance to complying with my instructions makes me grouchy. Every day when these athletes arrive at my event, I know I am going to be beating my head against the proverbial wall trying to get them to listen.

This morning I decided to stop trying to change them and let God change me instead.

As Christians, we sometimes butt heads with others because we want them to conform to our expectations. And if a person doesn't see things our way, well, frankly, we get a little cranky. We tend to insist that people bend to our way of thinking. Not surprisingly, this usually creates walls and resistance from others.

We need to be in the world as Christ was in the world. He said, "I have set an example that you should do as I have done for you" (John 13:15). We shouldn't want people to think like us; we should pray people will be open to God in Christ.

We can't change anyone; the process of transforming a life belongs to the Holy Spirit. However, we can let God in Christ transform our own hearts and minds. When we open our lives to the transforming work of the Holy Spirit, then our lives testify to the transforming power of the Spirit.

JULY 31

Tonight, we will experience a rare cosmic event: a blue moon. With the weather cooperating in northern Illinois, we will be able to see with little difficulty this second full moon of the month of July. Two full moons in one month will not happen again for three years.

Of course, a blue moon isn't really blue: The lunar orb will maintain its usual characteristics. It will shine in the reflected light of the sun, still be its normal yellow and white and will trace a path from horizon to horizon across the night sky.

Christians should be like a full moon shining in the world through the reflected light of the Son. We should be filled with the Holy Spirit so that our actions and words reflect the integrity and characteristics of Christ.

Jesus said, "Let your light shine before men, that they may see your good deeds" (Matthew 5:16). When the Holy Spirit reflects Christ's light through our lives, then we become His luminaries in this dark world. By the power of the Spirit, our light illuminates the darkness and shines on the cross so others will come to know the salvation of God.

When the light of the Lord is reflected in our lives, then the world will see the accomplishments of God in Christ bringing redemption and reconciliation to all mankind. Believers filled with the Holy Spirit light paths in this world so that others can see Christ and know the saving grace of God.

August

AUGUST 1

Today I am heading to a baseball game. I grew up playing baseball with my dad, who taught me everything I needed to know about the game. Eventually, I became a pretty good player.

When I became a Christian, God used a baseball analogy to give me my first understanding of the Trinity. I compared the Three Persons working together for the salvation of the world to a baseball organization. At that time, God the Father is the General Manager of the team and responsible for all aspects of the organization. Next, Jesus Christ, God in the flesh, who lived among us, is the manager and involved in the daily decisions of the game and the welfare of the players. Finally, the Holy Spirit, who still resides in the world today, is the third-base coach. He receives directions from the manager and flashes them to the batters, so they know what to do. All three, the GM, the manager and the coach worked together to achieve team victories.

Sure, the analogy is simplistic and might not stand up to theological scrutiny. However, baseball was what God used to get me thinking about the mystery and work of God in Three

Persons. All Three Persons worked together at the cross, brought Christ's victory over sin and death, raised Jesus to life and secured salvation for mankind.

God uses the simple things in our lives to teach us His profound mysteries. Jesus said, "I have spoken to you of earthly things" (John 3:12).

AUGUST 2

I am frustrated. I am frustrated at God. I have been banging on my computer keyboard for well over an hour, but I have no reflection to show for it. My day was fine until this point. I started with church, had a nice visit with my sister at my neighborhood pool, went for ice cream with my daughter and even talked with my mom. So I was certain in all this ease that the reflection would be easy to write.

I don't know why I think God owes me a reflection. He owes me nothing. I owe Him. I owe Him more respect than throwing a hissy fit because the reflection isn't finished when I want it to be. I owe Him my admiration for putting up with me when I am in this foul mood. I owe Him my gratitude for sending His Son, Jesus Christ, into the world. I owe Him my thanks for letting Christ bear on the cross my burden of sin and death. I owe Him my life, because His Son secured my salvation and redemption with His blood. I owe Him all that, but I can't pay Him. Instead, He sent Jesus to pay my debt, so I could be reconciled to God through Christ.

Tonight, while I was being a jerk about this reflection, He was loving me, forgiving me and administering His grace to me through the power of the Holy Spirit.

"While we were still sinners, Christ died for us" (Romans 5:8).

AUGUST 3

If I had to count the words I spoke each day, I, no doubt, would use fewer words. So much of what I say could be left unsaid. My words simply pour from my mouth each time it opens.

I need to put more thought into what I say and how I say it. Jesus said, "So, whatever I say is just what the Father has told me to say" (John 12:50). Each word Jesus spoke was in accordance with the purpose and will of His Father. He wasted no words. When He spoke, the words of life reached the ears of His listeners.

As a Christian, my words need to be filled with the Holy Spirit so they carry Christ's message of eternal life into the world. My words need to testify to Christ's life, death and resurrection. I need to speak not on my own but according to what God in Christ has taught me through Scripture about His love, forgiveness and mercy.

One way for me to speak according to God's will is to pray without ceasing that the Holy Spirit will hold back my words until I have listened closely to Christ. My words need to be seasoned with praise and thanksgiving for God through the Holy

Spirit. I need to follow the advice of the apostle James, who wrote, "Be quick to listen and slow to speak" (James 1:19).

Before I speak, I need to be quick to listen to God and slow to speak to others.

AUGUST 4

I didn't have to work today, so Sally and I went to Chicago, met a good friend and spent the day meandering down the lake front, taking pictures in Millennium Park and strolling in and out of designer stores on Michigan Avenue. We talked, we walked, we shopped, we ate and we enjoyed being together. Spending time together deepened our relationships with one another.

God calls us to spend time with Him. Unfortunately, we rarely give God a thought before quickly scarfing down a Pop-Tart and rushing out the door to begin our day.

Even if we do get some quiet time with God, it is rarely without interruption; we often spend the minutes making mental lists and thinking about all we have to do. Basically God is absent from our noisy days and quiet moments.

We need to find ways in our day to meander through the Gospels with our Lord and listen to Him teach us through the Spirit. We need to stroll through the Psalms with Christ, so He can teach us to pray. We need to read with Christ God's promises in the Old Testament, so the Spirit can show us how Jesus has fulfilled them through His work on the cross. We need time free of interruptions to strengthen our faith and deepen our relationship with God in Christ.

"Yet the news about Him spread all the more, so that crowds of people came to hear Him" (Luke 5:15).

Be among those who hear Him.

AUGUST 5

Yesterday my friend who is responsible for the online portion of the ministry started a marketing campaign for the Godnesia Facebook page. He suggested I repost an old blog that he felt would resonate with readers. I have gone back and forth several times in my mind trying to decide if this is something that I should do.

The problem is I have never done a repost, because reflections are my time to sit "at the Lord's feet listening" (Luke 10:39) to what He has been teaching me through the day. Writing has become my window into seeing the faithfulness of God each day. In my mind, reposting means I am relying on myself instead of depending on God just to get more likes for my page. Like equals praise.

Many of us teeter between wanting praise from men and wanting praise from God. Praise from men is tangible and praise from God more difficult to discern. Praise from men means we depend upon men. Praise from God means we depend upon God.

We tend to make decisions based on what we can see. But faith is being certain of what is unseen. The oscillating will stop when we surrender to the Holy Spirit and let Him make us dependent upon God.

AUGUST 6

Tonight I enjoyed myself at a party. What I enjoy most about a party is the stories people share. One friend told of the humorous pranks he played on co-workers. Another friend told of her frustration with technology and retail stores. There were stories about vacations, siblings and children. Each story gave me a deeper understanding and appreciation for my friends.

Stories remind me of how fortunate we are to have the Bible. The men and women of the Scriptures are our ancestors in the faith. In the pages of Scripture, we can read not only about the victories of King David on the battlefield but also about his infidelity with another man's wife. We hear the story of Lot's escape from Sodom and Gomorrah just before the cities were destroyed by God's wrath. We meet Hosea, who was sure to have heard whispering behind his back, since he married a prostitute. There are the adventures of Paul and, of course, the accounts of our Lord and Savior, Jesus Christ.

When we gather for church on Sunday, we come to hear God teach us through the stories of our progenitors. Through the people of the Bible, God reveals Himself and His love for us in Jesus Christ. The Holy Spirit uses the stories in the Scripture to give us a deeper understanding and appreciation for God in Christ.

Get to know the relatives; through them, we learn about God, His work in Jesus Christ and His ongoing work in the world through the Holy Spirit.

AUGUST 7

Since getting off work this afternoon, I have been sitting mindlessly in front of the television. I have watched three episodes of *N.C.I.S* and an episode of *Parks and Recreation*. I did manage to get my haircut and go to the grocery store. The work week has made my mind tired.

I loathe a weary mind because it diminishes my ability to focus. In spite of my inability to discipline my thoughts, God will bring discipline to my mind. Scripture says, "So letting your sinful nature control your mind leads to death. But letting the Spirit control your mind leads to life and peace" (Romans 8:6 NLT). On nights like this, when I struggle to form a coherent sentence, the Spirit of God will still keep my mind and thoughts attuned to Christ.

When I can't trust my thoughts because my mind is weary, I will trust the Spirit to guide my thoughts. When my mind is fatigued it does not have the mental energy to fight off sinful thoughts. However, because I have faith in Jesus Christ, He sends His Spirit to guard my mind and thoughts against the guile of the sinful nature. When my sinful nature wants to fill my mind with hostile thoughts towards God, Christ sends His Spirit to subdue those thoughts and keep my mind centered on God.

"Love the Lord your God with all your heart and with all your soul and with all your strength and with all your mind" (Luke 10:27).

AUGUST 8

This morning as I tied my shoes and prepared to walk, I let a bright, clear sky convince me to add two miles to my usual route.

Walking each day keeps my heart strong, builds my stamina and gives me endurance for my daily routine. Walking also gives me some time alone or allows me an opportunity to contact friends. Walking meets my needs physically as well as emotionally and even spiritually.

Scripture lays out the ways that we are supposed to walk with God. In 2 John 1:6, John encourages us to "walk in obedience to His [Christ's] commands" and that we should "walk in love."

Jesus told His listeners to "walk in the light" (John 12:35 NLT) of God's revelation so they would not be overcome by the darkness of ignorance. God told the prophet Micah that the people of Israel must "walk in the name of the LORD our God for ever and ever" (Micah 4:5). And God reminded Solomon, "If you walk in my ways and obey my statutes and commands as David your father did, I will give you a long life" (1 Kings 3:14).

It is the Holy Spirit who teaches us to walk in love and obedience to God. Through His power our souls are filled with the good things of God, and we are energized to do the work of the kingdom God has called us to do in Christ.

Take a walk with the Spirit, and keep your heart strong for God in Christ.

AUGUST 9

In 1 Kings 19:1-9, the great prophet Elijah flees for his life from Queen Jezebel. He is tired, overwhelmed and afraid. He finally sits down under a broom tree and prays, "I have had enough, Lord. Take my life." Then he falls asleep. An angel comes to him, not once, but twice, with bread and water. At the second visit, the angel says, "Get up and eat, for the journey is too much for you." Strengthened by the food he could travel for many days to safety.

Most of us have days when we have "had enough," and we can't seem to find the strength we need to overcome the fatigue of daily life. We might try remedies such as vacations, the snooze button, comfort foods and so on to no avail. Instead we must find our strength as Elijah did in bread and water.

Jesus declared, "I am the bread of life. He who comes to me will never go hungry, and he who believes in me will never be thirsty" (John 6:35). Jesus Christ is the sustenance God provides for us each day so we can be strengthened to continue this journey of life. When we pray and praise Him He comes to us with the food of His Word and the water of life, His Holy Spirit. When we feed on His Word and drink from the well of the

Spirit of life, we are empowered and strengthened by God in Christ to continue on our journey.

AUGUST 10

Recently, a major big-box retailer decided to use gender-neutral marketing in the toy department. Girls' and boys' toys will no longer be separated and housed in different aisles. Toys will now all be lumped together under the category Kids. (Is this going to be a problem for adults who still like to play with toys? Sorry, I digress.) Children know what they like to play with, and I would venture to say that they don't care what aisle they have to walk down to get the toy.

I grew up in the '60s. I was a tomboy. When all the girls were jumping rope and playing jacks on the playground, I was playing baseball with the boys. When little girls were wearing dresses, this little girl was wearing pants. When all my friends were putting ribbons in their hair, I was getting mine cut as short as possible because I hated ribbons. All I'm saying is affirmation for my choices didn't come from retail stores; they came from my accepting and loving family. All those hours I spent playing with the boys, guess what? I still knew I was a girl.

We can make aisles of toys gender neutral, but the truth is gender isn't neutral. Genesis 1:27 says, "So God created man in His own image, in the image of God He created him; male and female He created them."

Affirmation comes to us from God, in whose glorious image we have all been created.

AUGUST 11

This morning one of my gymnasts was lacking confidence on a particular beam skill. I could tell by her body language that she was doubting her ability to execute the skill. She kept wiping her hands on her legs, positioning and repositioning her feet and brushing her hair away from her colorless face.

My job became to talk her through the fear. I insisted she stop the fidgeting and then begin reciting her cue words for the skill. Once she focused on the words, she could perform the skill.

Her lack of confidence reminded me about the number of times I lack confidence in Almighty Christ. My doubts surface unexpectedly, but when they arise my behavior usually reflects the uncertainties I am feeling toward Christ. I am easily agitated and somewhat restless. Questions about God ransack my thoughts. I wonder about His presence in the world and in my life. I struggle to give Him the praise or thanksgiving He deserves. And I am disgusted with myself for the fear that doubt creates in me. Unfortunately, my disgust doesn't dissipate my doubts.

To alleviate doubt I must retreat to the Word and let the Spirit focus me on the Scriptures and the marvelous stories of God's work in Christ. In the Word, I hear Jesus tell Thomas,

"Stop doubting and believe" (John 20:27), while the Spirit carries the truth of these words to me.

When I focus on the Word, the Holy Spirit restores my confidence in Almighty Christ.

AUGUST 12

There are days I get Chronic Ego Flare-up (CEF), a condition in which my ego starts screaming for attention. My whacked-out ego seizes my thoughts and badgers my mind with rantings, grumblings and complaining. Suddenly, I am debating myself about my pay scale at work and whether I am being paid what I am worth. Or I am eager for credit for my smallest accomplishment. During this time I even wonder if I was put on earth to do much greater things than coach. The issues that come to my mind are not usually things I think about except when I am having a CEF attack.

My inflated ego means I have decided to govern my own thoughts, words and deeds and to ignore the claim Christ has on my life. In other words, when my ego goes postal I am staging a coup against God for control of my life. I have yet to discover what triggers these flare-ups; I do know the remedy is Christ's cross.

As my sinfulness escalates, God in Christ shows me His cross. Through the work of the Holy Spirit, I am made aware of Christ's sacrifice on my behalf. The Spirit awakens me to Jesus' absolute submission to God and the glory the Son brought to the Father through His death on the cross. After

Judas left the Passover meal to betray Jesus, Jesus said to the disciples, "Now is the Son of Man glorified and God is glorified in him" (John 13:31).

When the Spirit leads me to Christ's cross, my ego is abased; then I submit to God's authority over my life.

AUGUST 13

As a child I dealt with unpleasant happenings in my schedule, whether it was a big test at school or a dentist appointment, by looking forward to something enjoyable. I thought this was my own coping technique.

Then I read through the last conversation Jesus had with His disciples just a few hours before His arrest and crucifixion. His words were not only about His coming suffering and death but also about the resurrection life. Jesus is teaching His disciples about the eternal life that awaits Him after the unpleasantness of death has passed. He looks forward to His glorious resurrection.

We all cope with death. Whether we are facing our own mortality or the loss of loved ones, death is agonizing.

But Christ helps us cope with death by offering us the same hope He offered His disciples when He said, "Because I live, you also will live" (John 14:19). When we focus on Christ's risen life and His eternal life in the kingdom of God, we no longer need to dread the unpleasantness of death; instead, we can focus on the wondrous, glorious eternal kingdom of God offered to us through faith in Jesus Christ.

Christ came into the world so He could die on the cross to save us from sin and death. Then through the power of the Holy Spirit He was raised to life, so that in Him we might also have life. Death has been overcome by life. Now that is worth thinking about.

.

AUGUST 14

Completing tonight's reflection presents a challenge for me. I am without Internet access and must write and post from my phone. I can only imagine the number of mistakes I will make without my Word program helping me with spell check and grammar.

This challenge reminds me of how difficult it is to lead the Christian life without consulting God in Christ through the power of the Holy Spirit in His Word.

God has given us His Word in the Person of His Son and the Holy Scriptures. John 1:1 says, "In the beginning was the Word and the Word was with God and the Word was God."

When I try to lead the Christian life without reading Scripture and being taught by the Holy Spirit, I cannot tell if I am walking in the light of God's truth. However, when I consult the Scriptures and call on the Spirit, then God leads me into all truth.

Use God's Word program, and let the Spirit illuminate your hearts and minds with the truth of Christ's life, death and resurrection.

AUGUST 15

A friend made a slight alteration to a typical chocolate-chip cookie recipe. She substituted coconut oil for ordinary butter. The oil infused the dough with a light flavor of coconut, which made the cookie special. The swap between butter and coconut oil did not change the appearance of the cookie; anyone looking at the cookie would think it was chocolate chip. Only a sampling of the cookie revealed the change in flavor.

When I became a Christian the Holy Spirit infused my sinful nature with the Holy nature of Christ. I was still a sinner, but I was a sinner saved by grace. My outward appearance did not change; friends were still able to recognize me. However, inwardly, my heart was changing. At first, I found it difficult to detect the changes the Holy Spirit was making to my life. Then, slowly, I began to realize my old behaviors were not acceptable to God. When I became angry, the Spirit awakened a remorse in me over my anger. I was still impatient with others, but the Spirit made me aware of the damaging affects impatience had on my relationships with people and God. And the Spirit was teaching me to use my tongue to encourage others and honor God.

I have a long way to go, but the Spirit will continue to change my heart, and one day I will "become mature, attaining to the whole measure of the fullness of Christ" (Ephesians 4:13).

AUGUST 16

We are creatures of routine. Most of us have a morning ritual that helps us get ready for our day. During the holidays we look forward to celebrating family traditions. We will frequent the same restaurants, watch reruns of our favorite television shows or see movies we enjoy more than once.

Traditions and routine give us a sense of comfort and security.

We applaud routine and traditions in our daily lives; however, when the church offers us tradition and routine in worship we call it boring.

Each Sunday the order of worship is a ritual that helps us make our ascent into the presence of God. The liturgy chosen for the week is a part of the greater church calendar, which helps us to understand the special seasons of the church. The sacraments are the means of grace that draw us ever closer to God in Christ through the Spirit. These traditions and rituals of the church increase our awareness of God, let us see our own sinfulness and receive the comfort and assurance of the forgiveness Christ offers each of us through His work on the cross and the eternal life won for us in His resurrection. And it is the Holy Spirit who uses the Scripture readings, the traditions and the rituals of the church in worship to grow us deeper in faith in God in Christ.

Paul said, "So then, brothers, stand firm and hold to the traditions we passed on to you, whether by word of mouth or by letter" (2 Thessalonians 2:15 ESV).

AUGUST 17

The clouds tonight were ominous and filled with rain. These steely gray clouds stretched across the sky, creating a ceiling over several miles of the city. I enjoyed watching them move slowly across the heavens, as though they were scouting the perfect place to drop rain. I sat at the stoplight near my neighborhood hoping I would make it into the house before the clouds decided to burst.

As I sat at the light, I compared the size of these storm clouds to my own size. No contest: They were large and vast; I was tiny and fragile. I often wonder how we humans can think we are so big and strong when we can't even stop a cloud from moving across the sky, stop the rain, catch lightning or control thunder booms. And yet, our fallen, sinful egos insist that we are greater than God.

Still God knows we are frail beings. The Psalmist wrote, "For He knows how we are formed, He remembers that we are dust" (Psalm 103:14). And when our egos unashamedly treat Sovereign God with contempt, He responds not with contempt for us, which would be deserved for our disrespect, but with compassion through Christ and the Holy Spirit. Again, the Psalmist writes, "As a father has compassion on His children, so the Lord has compassion on those who fear him" (Psalm 103:13).

As with all of nature, clouds display God's might while revealing man's weakness.

AUGUST 18

Some of the gymnasts on the team have a difficult time accepting change. They resist making schedule changes, advancing to a more difficult level of competition or altering bad technique that would allow them to achieve a new skill or strengthen current skills.

Most of us fear change, and this fear often prevents us from pursuing the truth about God. Many of us learned about God as children or pieced together our understanding of God from statements made by other people. Once those thoughts become ingrained in our thinking, we fail to revisit them to see whether they are actually true. Our understanding has come from a hodgepodge of philosophies, ideas and notions, but not usually from Scripture. Only by reading Scripture with the Spirit can we know whether our thoughts about God in Christ are true. The Spirit discerns for us through Scripture the truth we possess about God.

The Spirit is in the world to guide us into what is true according to the reality of God the Father. The Spirit of truth works through the Scriptures to align our thoughts and hearts with what is true about His existence. Through the Spirit of truth, we learn the facts of Christ's life among us, His death to save us and His resurrection to bring us life.

Jesus said, "But when he, the Spirit of truth, comes, He will guide you into all truth" (John 16:13).

AUGUST 19

The great resource of the Christian life is prayer. However, for many, prayer is a frustrating exercise. And many think it yields no results. Perhaps a different perspective of prayer would be helpful. Prayer is not about what we can get for God. Prayer is a ministry God calls the Christian to.

Prayer is the act of entering the throne room of God so Christ can imbue us with His Spirit, so we can intercede on behalf of others, whom the LORD has impressed upon our hearts. All around us are people who have no strength to make it to God on their own. They are people of despair, not prayer, and they need an intercessor to stand in their place before Christ when circumstances do not let them stand before Christ themselves.

What circumstances or conditions could cause a person to be in such despair that he or she cannot come to Christ? A few examples might be:

- Unbelief. If a person is convinced of his or her own sin but does not know the truth of God's redeeming work in Christ, fear will hinder them from going to the Savior.
- Grief. This is sorrow so great that a person is broken and suffocating in sadness. Such a person is so weak and blind they have neither the energy nor sight to find their way to Christ.

- Evil. This is when Satan grips a soul so tightly that the person is being strangled by wickedness and he or she knows only that Christ is an enemy.

God equips mature believers with the Spirit so they can be effective ministers of intercessory prayer. In this way those called to this ministry will bring those in need of reconciliation to Christ. And Christ will hear and answer.

Paul wrote, "All this is from God, who reconciled us to Himself through Christ, and gave us the ministry of reconciliation" (2 Corinthians 5:18).

AUGUST 20

Today, I lost my cool, opened my mouth, said the wrong things and now I feel like a schmuck. Why don't I just shut up when I get angry? My behavior today was another shining example of why I will never be a good Christian.

There is no such thing as a good Christian. Paul said, "I know that nothing good lives in me, that is, in my sinful nature. For I have the desire to do what is good, but I cannot carry it out" (Romans 7:18). God's work of salvation, redemption and reconciliation has been completed through the death and resurrection of Jesus Christ. Because of my faith in Jesus Christ and His atoning death on the cross, I am not a good Christian, but a saved sinner.

Still I fight against the Spirit's insistence that I obey the living God. Each time the Spirit opposes my sinful nature, my sinful nature opposes the Spirit. Paul said in Galatians, "For the sinful nature desires what is contrary to the Spirit, and the Spirit what is contrary to the sinful nature. They are in conflict with each other, so that you do not do what you want" (5:17).

Like Paul, I want to be obedient to God in Christ through the Spirit. I want to be less angry, and I want to shut up when I am mad. This transformation will happen only when I learn to surrender to the Holy Spirit before my sinful nature deceives me into disobedience to God.

AUGUST 21

The crickets are in full voice tonight. The sky is clear and bright, and a slight breeze is stirring the air. The cooler temperatures carry with them a reminder that summer is passing and fall is coming. Seasons come and go, but each season brings a unique kind of hope. In summer we look forward to long, lazy sunlit days filled with friends and family. The vivid, vibrant colors of fall give us a hope that there is always beauty in the world. Winter may be harsh, but it's pure-white snow, which cause disruptions, reminds us that some of our most amazing moments in life come from an interruption to our schedule or plans. And spring gives us the hope of new birth.

Our lives also have seasons. Solomon wrote, "There is a time for everything, and a season for every activity under heaven" (Ecclesiastes 3:1). The seasons of our lives remind us of God's presence in our days. Our life from birth to death is filled with seasons. But these seasons carry hope from God. When we enter a season of mourning, Jesus said, "Blessed are those who mourn, for they will be comforted" (Matthew 5:4). When we weep, Jesus meets us in our sorrow. In a season of silence, God can be heard. During the season of love we learn, "God is love" (1 John 4:16). When the time is right for searching, God can be found.

God in Christ is in all the seasons of our lives.

AUGUST 22

This morning at 5:30 as I started my bike ride the heat and humidity were already making their presence known. The steamy, thick air stuck to my clothing and skin. And the heaviness of the air made breathing a bit difficult as I pedaled along my route. This drippy weather causes my body to move more slowly and unresponsively as it pushes through the wet air.

As I rode along I realized how much sin is like hot, humid air. Sin clings to the soul and makes the heart heavy. There are days when my sin weighs down my soul. On these days, my soul is unresponsive to Christ's call on my life. I push through the day slowly, my soul bogged down by the reality of my transgressions.

But then the sweet refreshing wind of the Holy Spirit blows into my soul, and revealing my Savior. Suddenly, through the power of the Spirit, I am able by faith to take to the cross of Christ the sin that clings to my soul. At the cross, I repent of my iniquities, and Christ takes my sin to Himself and offers me redemption, forgiveness and new life. As I receive Christ's gifts of salvation the burdens of my soul are lifted, and my heart rejoices in God my Savior.

Let the Spirit freshen your soul with the saving grace of Jesus Christ. "He saved us through the washing of rebirth and renewal by the Holy Spirit" (Titus 3:5).

AUGUST 23

This weekend, a friend and I walked along the Sinnissippi Gardens path and through Anderson Japanese Gardens. Even though I was familiar with these gardens, they looked different from my last visit. Both gardens were full of mature plants and flowers covered with blooms and color. Each time I visit the gardens, I notice something I haven't seen before.

These walks reminded me that Scripture is like these gardens. No matter how familiar we may think we are with a verse or passage, the Spirit can always show us something new. The Spirit will prod us to explore a word differently, point us to another definition or show us a new layer of meaning within the verse. Scripture is never static. When the Spirit teaches us through the Scriptures, He will give us a new understanding and fuller knowledge of God in Christ.

The teachings of the Holy Spirit keep God's word alive and fresh and new in our lives. He illuminates our hearts and minds with His divine perspective on Scripture. He makes certain we see in God's Word all that is necessary to grow us deeper and stronger in faith in Christ.

The Spirit is in the world to teach us the truths of Scripture: "But the Counselor, the Holy Spirit, whom the Father will send in my name, will teach you all things and will remind you of everything I have said to you" (John 14:26).

AUGUST 24

While watching a gymnastic competition recently, I noticed athletes who half-heartedly executed their routines. Forlorn looks covered their faces, their movements were limp and life-less and, instead of fighting to keep their skills on the beam, they gave up and fell off. Their actions demonstrated a lack of commitment to their goals, and, as a result, they won no prizes.

Sometimes we behave in such a way toward Christ. We declare ourselves to be Christians, but we give only a half-hearted effort to following Jesus. We wear long faces, as though we have never heard the Good News that Christ redeemed us through His blood shed on the cross. We move around in the world hopeless and thankless, instead of celebrating the gift of eternal life Christ gives us through His resurrection. And, when our days become troubled we become frightened and want to abandon our Lord.

Nonetheless, God knows our weaknesses and the struggles we have with wholehearted devotion to Him. He knows how quickly our hearts can turn from Him, so He pours His Holy Spirit into us so we can be His steadfast disciples. Through God's Spirit we receive power and might to accomplish the work God has called us to do. With the Holy Spirit abiding in us, we can "press on toward the goal to win the prize for which God has called me heavenward in Christ Jesus" (Philippians 3:14).

AUGUST 25

Yesterday one of my young gymnasts was afraid to try her new dismount on low beam. Her fears convinced her that she could not safely execute the skill. She began to cry as irrational thoughts twisted the truth she was incapable of performing the skill. So I pointed out that using her technique-cue words and looking down the beam would stop her from being afraid. Once she applied her words, success came quickly.

Every now and then we must be reminded that fear is an emotion that turns the mind from the truth of God in Christ. And fear preys on our vulnerabilities—those times in our lives when jobs are lost, illness invades, relationships splinter or death approaches—to fill our minds with falsehoods about God like He is not loving or forgiving. If we listen to the lies produced by our fears, fault lines develop in our faith, which threaten to crumble our confidence in Christ.

The Psalmist wrote, "In God, whose word I praise, in God I trust; I will not be afraid. What can mortal man do to me?" (Psalm 56:4) Fear wants us to listen to its illogical arguments. Fear tells us that God did not save us through the death of His Son. Fear tells us that our sin is too great to be forgiven. Fear tells us that Jesus was just a man and not God. It wants us to turn from God. But God sent His Word, Jesus Christ, into the world to speak words of truth to us through the power of the Holy Spirit. Through the Spirit we can hear Christ say, "Do not let your hearts be troubled and do not be afraid" (John 14:27). When we listen to our fears we cannot hear Christ; when we listen to Christ our fears are silenced.

AUGUST 26

Buying groceries is challenging. Some days I seem to buy too many groceries, and other days I buy too few. I can't predict with much accuracy my family's rate of food consumption.

I can't get groceries right, but God can. After rescuing the Israelites from slavery in Egypt, He provided manna, a type of bread, for more than a million people every day for forty years. God told the Israelites to gather as much bread as each family needed. Scripture says, "The Israelites did as they were told; some gathered much, some little. And when they measured it by the omer, he who gathered much did not have too much, and he who gathered little did not have too little. Each one gathered as much as he needed" (Exodus 16:17-18).

Jesus also managed to feed five thousand people bread and fish so that each person "had enough to eat" (John 6:12).

As I looked at these two crowd stories, I thought about how unique each person would be. There would be large and small appetites. Rich people who could afford bread and poor people who could not afford bread. Regardless of each person's circumstance, God in Christ provided enough bread for all.

We sometimes think God cannot provide us with enough of His grace, love and peace to handle our lives. Yet in these two stories, we see God providing exactly what each person needs. These stories show us that we can depend on God in Christ to provide exactly what each of us needs to grow stronger in faith.

AUGUST 27

The phrase *nothing lasts forever* is one I remember hearing as a child when one of my toys broke. Sometimes it has been used in reference to a break up in a relationship. It might be spoken when a business closes. Or we may casually toss it around in conversation if the context is right. Growing up, I thought this phrase was true for everything. Here's what I discovered this morning while reading in the Gospel of John: This phrase is not true about my relationship with the Holy Spirit.

In John, Jesus says, "If you love me, you will obey what I command. And I will ask the Father, and He will give you another Counselor to be with you forever—the Spirit of truth" (John 14:15-17). When we believe in Jesus Christ and His work on the cross for our salvation, then the Spirit enters into a relationship with us. And our relationship with the Person of the Holy Spirit spans the years of our earthly life and our life in the eternal presence of God. The Spirit is with us now and with us when we enter the kingdom of God.

However, everything the Holy Spirit teaches us about God in Christ through the Scriptures does last forever. He gives us the truth about God and Jesus Christ while we are living in the world, and through Him we will keep all the truth He has taught us about Jesus when we join Christ in the everlasting realm of God.

Something does last forever: The believer's relationship with God in Christ through the Spirit.

AUGUST 28

Two young cyclists bolted across a dark street in front of my car tonight. They blended into the darkness because their bikes had no lights, and they wore no reflective clothing. Fortunately, they were not hurt. However, I made sure they knew they were not visible to drivers and told them to get home. When children put themselves in harm's way, I speak up.

Many people are spiritually in harm's way because of sin, so I have to speak up and tell them that sin and death have been conquered by Christ's blood shed on the cross. I have to speak up so people will know that through Christ God has saved the world and brought forgiveness and redeeming love to all who believe in Him. Too many people wander in the darkness of this world without the light of Christ in their lives, and I have to speak up so people know the cross of Christ is the saving power of God.

People lost in darkness need to get home to the everlasting kingdom of God. I have to speak up and point them to Scripture so they can hear that Jesus said, "I am the way, and the truth and the life. No one comes to the Father except through me" (John 14:6). They do not know that Jesus died so they could have eternal life, so I have to speak up and show them in Scripture where Jesus said, "I have come that they may have life, and have it to the full" (John 10:10).

So I am speaking up.

AUGUST 29

Tonight my husband and I attended a concert in which the band imitated the group the Eagles. The band sounded very close to the actual Eagles. These musicians played many of the Eagles' greatest hits, and it was easy to hear that they had spent many hours perfecting their ability to play the Eagles' music.

While watching and listening to these musicians imitate the Eagles, I thought hat as a follower of Jesus I should be imitating Him in my daily life. I need to study Scripture for many hours with the Holy Spirit to be able faithfully to emulate my Lord in my thoughts, words and actions.

Paul wrote to the church at Ephesus, "Be imitators of God, therefore, as dearly loved children and live a life of love, just as Christ loved us and gave Himself up for us as a fragrant offering and sacrifice to God" (Ephesians 5:1).

To imitate Christ means to live a life of sacrifice to God through the Holy Spirit. We must surrender our personal convictions, desires and values to let the Spirit establish Christ's love, forgiveness and redemption in our hearts. To live sacrificially is to obey the Spirit so that through His help our lives will bring glory to God the Father through God the Son.

When we imitate Jesus through the power of the Holy Spirit our life belongs to God in Christ. "I have been crucified with Christ and I no longer live, but Christ lives in me" (Galatians 2:20).

AUGUST 30

These days the world is a mean and scary place. The media bombards us with images of violence, poverty, hatred and humanity's viciousness, which only fuels our fears. As we watch the news we wonder if there is a way out of this mess.

Every generation has wondered about the mess the world is in. Contemplating the conflicts played out by the generations before ours does not make us sleep better at night, but it should teach us a lesson. Scripture tells us that the nature of the world is evil and corrupt, and it has been since the fall of Adam. In fact, at one point, during the time of Noah, the world was so overcome with sin, corruption and depravity that "the LORD was grieved that He had made man on the earth, and His heart was filled with pain" (Genesis 6:6).

Because of the world's sinfulness, God sent His Son to earth so the world would be saved through Him. Jesus felt the full weight of the world's corruption, depravity and sin as He died on the cross. He endured sin and death for us on the cross, and then by the power of the Holy Spirit He conquered the world when He was raised to life. Through faith in Christ, we also overcome the world through the power of the Spirit, and we are assured by Jesus' word, "Do not let your hearts be troubled and do not be afraid" (John 14:27).

Get some new facts about God to mull over from Scripture. you can start with "Do you not know? Have you not heard? The LORD is the everlasting God, the Creator of the ends of the earth" (Isaiah 40:28).

AUGUST 31

Several days a week, the gymnasts break up into smaller teams to compete in running relays during the practice. The girls always want to pick a team name and ask me to give them a category to choose from. On one of these days I picked baseball team names. One girl, whose parents are diehard Chicago Cub fans, chose the team name Cardinals. I jokingly reprimanded her choice. She countered with "the Cubs are bad."

Her statement would have been true in the past; however, it was not true during the time of my writing these words. This season the Cubs are young, energetic, talented and exciting. The team is 19 games over .500, and it is currently tied with the Pittsburgh Pirates for the top spot in the National League Wild-Card race. This team has been playing some of the best baseball Chicago Cub fans have seen in years.

We all tend to cling to old opinions, particularly negative ones, about teams, stores, foods, restaurants, and even people.

And at one time or another most of us have heard something about God. For many people the first thing they hear about God from another person is negative. Unfortunately, they will stay with this old opinion for years. They will quote it and build a faith upon it, without questioning the validity of that opinion. For instance some people may hear from others that God does not answer prayer, or that He is angry and judgmental. Some might even hear that God is just a myth or that God is an idea created by men of little intelligence.

Knowledge of God should not come through other people's perspectives but through the reading of Scripture and the teaching of the Holy Spirit. Sadly, many people would rather stay in the rut of old thinking than know the truth about God in Christ. If all we have are old negative opinions about God and we allow ourselves to be stuck in those, we miss what God is teaching us about Himself, Christ and the Holy Spirit in Scripture.

September

SEPTEMBER 1

During practice I started making up songs for the younger gymnasts to sing while we were working on bars. The lyrics were ridiculous, and we all laughed our way through the bar workout. Singing silly, zany songs together made the gymnasts happy. Singing turned an ordinary bar workout into something outrageous and special.

Singing songs is an important aspect of our life with God. The Scriptures are full of many instances in which God tells His people to sing or the people raise songs of praise to God. For example, God told King Jehoshaphat to put together a choir to lead his army into battle against three enemy armies. The choir's singing confused the enemies, and they destroyed one other. Jehoshaphat and his army never even threw a spear (2 Chronicles 20). King David encouraged the people to "sing to the Lord a new song" and "make music to the Lord with the harp, with the harp and the sound of singing" (Psalm 98:1, 5). King Hezekiah instructed the people to sing during worship (2 Chronicles 29:25-28). And at the last day, when God calls His people home, we will all be singing: "The ransomed of the Lord will return. They will enter Zion with singing; everlasting joy will crown their heads. Gladness and joy will overtake them, and sorrow and sighing will flee away" (Isaiah 51:11).

Singing is the hallmark of God's people. "I will sing of your love and justice; to you, O Lord, I will sing praise" (Psalm 101:1).

SEPTEMBER 2

Among the disciples chosen by Jesus was Judas Iscariot, son of Simon, who would betray Him. Judas had spent three years with Jesus, seen Christ perform miracles, heard Jesus teach and even let the Savior wash his feet. In spite of witnessing all this, Judas did not recognize that Jesus was "the Holy One of God" (John 6:69).

Over the years I've wondered how it was possible Judas did not understand Jesus was God's Messiah. Or maybe Judas did know Jesus was the Savior and rejected Him.

When I think about Judas, I also find myself thinking of my own life. Yes, I believe Jesus is "the Christ, the Son of the living God" (Matthew 16:16), but sometimes I betray my Lord when I choose to sin instead of resist sin through the power of the Holy Spirit.

Each time I sin against God in Christ the darkness of ignorance fills my mind, and I fail to hear Christ declare, "I am the light of the world" (John 9:5). When I sin, I am rejecting Christ and his work of salvation in my life.

Fortunately, because I believe, Christ will not allow me to live in the darkness of my sin. Instead He sends His Holy Spirit into my life "that the God of our Lord Jesus Christ, the glorious Father, may give you the Spirit of wisdom and revelation, so that you may know Him better" (Ephesians 1:17). It is the work of the Holy Spirit in my life that makes me different from Judas.

SEPTEMBER 3

I have a wall hanging in my office that says FAITH. I had fixed it to a wall with an adhesive. But tonight when I came up to my office, I noticed the two strips of adhesive were still on the wall, but FAITH had fallen off the wall and lay behind my desk. In other words, my FAITH had fallen. I chuckled before it occurred to me that for many people their faith may fall.

Many things in this world can cause our faith to waver: personal tragedy, unsettling news reports or, maybe, a prayer that we think has gone unanswered. Whatever dislodges faith from our hearts must be rooted out by God in Christ through the power of the Holy Spirit.

Faith means we have confidence in Jesus Christ's saving work on the cross and His ongoing work in the world through the Holy Spirit. When our faith fails, we have lost confidence in Christ. Getting faith back requires time in Scripture and a study of the cross, so we can remember the almighty power of God, who raised Jesus from death to everlasting life.

Our faith can rest assured in Christ's victory over sin and death and in the knowledge that Jesus prays for our faith to remain strong. In Luke 22:32 Jesus said to Simon Peter, "But I have prayed for you, Simon, that your faith may not fail." Christ is praying that we will not lose confidence in Him.

SEPTEMBER 4

Peter wrote, "For this very reason, make every effort to add to your faith goodness; and to goodness, knowledge; and to knowledge, self-control; and to self-control, perseverance; and to perseverance, godliness; and to godliness, brotherly kindness; and to brotherly kindness, love. For if you possess these qualities in increasing measure, they will keep you from being ineffective and unproductive in your knowledge of our Lord Jesus Christ" (1 Peter 1:5-8).

According to Peter self-control is an essential part of growing deeper in faith and knowledge in Jesus Christ. Yet, sinful humans do not possess self-control naturally. As sinful creatures we have no desire to exercise self-control or to discipline our thoughts and actions. To us, the idea of control brings to mind of God's Law, which we rebel against because it makes demands that conflict with our self-centered desires. According to the Law, our arrogant thoughts and prideful actions must be destroyed. Self-control means putting to death those sinful desires so our lives honor Christ and serve our neighbors. However, we do not have the power to put the Law's commands into effect.

So how can we possibly exert self-control? Controlling our sinful actions and desires becomes possible only through the power of the Holy Spirit. In fact, self-control is a gift of the

Holy Spirit (Galatians 5:23) given to us so we can know the truth of Scripture: Jesus Christ is the atoning sacrifice for our sin. The Spirit brings us to Christ's cross, and when our sin is exposed the Spirit applies the gift of self-control to our hearts and minds. The Spirit convicts us of our sin, so we can repent of it, mortify it and be sanctified by the truth. Through Christ we are redeemed from sin, reconciled to God and regenerated by the Spirit. In this process, we continue to grow deeper in faith and knowledge of Jesus Christ.

SEPTEMBER 5

When the competitive gymnastic season is over, we design workouts to build our gymnasts' strength. Conditioning increases, and coaches focus on cardio workouts, endurance exercises and strength development, so the gymnasts are fit and strong for the next season. Good coaches spend many hours developing strong athletes. Still the athletes must do the work if they are to improve.

We Christians must also build strength and endurance in our lives of faith. But sin has weakened our resolve to put time and energy into strengthening them. We let distractions trample the time we could set aside for spiritual matters. Some days we pray, some not. Some Sundays are set aside for church, most not. Occasionally we read passages of Scripture, but usually not.

Paul knew the struggles of growing a strong faith. He wrote to the church in Rome, "For I long to see you, in order that I may impart to you some spiritual gift for your strengthening" (Brendan Byrne, *Sacra Pagina*, Romans 1:11).

Paul knew spiritual weakness makes the church vulnerable to heresies and false teachings. Also, preaching the message of the Gospel, which the world so desperately needs to hear, is neglected when the church is not strong.

However, God strengthens His Church, so it can fulfill His purpose and will in the world. The gift that God imparts to His church and disciples is His Spirit. By the Spirit working in the church, disciples grow strong in the knowledge of God in Christ in the Scriptures, and they are brought to repentance, are made righteous by the blood of Christ and are sanctified and are empowered to live lives obedient to God. Strengthened by the Spirit, the church carries the Gospel into all the world, thereby reaping a harvest for Christ.

September 6

I am going to a Chicago Cubs baseball game tonight. Watching baseball live is a very different experience from listening to a game on the radio, viewing it on the MLB app or seeing it on television. At the stadium, I can more readily witness the talent and prowess of the players. A camera lens or announcer's perspective cannot adequately describe the abilities of the players.

The experience of seeing the Cubs live reminds me that a day is coming when I will be in the fullness of the living Christ. Right now, I hear Him speak to me in the Scriptures through the Spirit, who shows me His movements in the church throughout the world. But there are times in this life when difficulties, sin and chaos obstruct my view of His movements among us.

However, on that glorious day when He returns, nothing will impede our view of the risen, almighty Lord. Being in the fullness of Christ will be a totally different experience, one that my imagination cannot even adequately describe. As Paul said, "Now we see but a poor reflection as in a mirror; then we shall see face to face. Now I know in part; then I shall know fully, even as I am fully known" (1 Corinthians 13:12).

On the day of Christ's return, we will know Christ as He knows us. We will see Christ in all His glory, and He will share His glory with us. And all Christ's attributes—compassion, mercy, kindness, peace, and love—will fill our being.

September 7

Does anyone still use the expression *When the cat's away the mouse will play*? This weekend when the head coach and several other coaches were away at competitions, the gymnasts who remained at the gym made this phrase their mantra. They behaved very differently because the head coach was not in the gym.

Human beings constantly play the cat's-away game when it comes to God. Many people think God is aloof and disengaged from life on earth. Sinners carry on in the world as though God is not only absent from the world but also not returning any time soon. So the little sinful mice carry on in rebellious and reckless ways, disobeying the laws of God and acting shamefully as though God is blind and unaware of their lawless attitudes and actions. Sinful human nature always behaves as though God's away.

However, Scripture is clear: God came down from heaven in the person of Jesus Christ so He could show us how involved and committed He is to the fallen world. Jesus Christ came into the world as the Revealer of God. He came into the world to testify to the truth that God is present and to demonstrate how to live a holy life before God through the power of the Spirit.

God is not aloof and far off in an ivory tower. He remains in the world in the Person of the Holy Spirit. And the Spirit is in the world to pour Christ's grace into the hearts of sinners so they will stop racing down the road of perdition, be redeemed and lead obedient lives to the omnipresent God.

Jesus is the "Son of God, who has come into the world" (John 11:27).

SEPTEMBER 8

Working with young female gymnasts presents many challenges, not the least of which is battling growth spurts. Physical changes affect an athlete's performance. When a gymnast grows she suddenly finds herself struggling to execute her skills. Her body is noticeably weaker, and it takes several weeks for her strength to be sufficient for her new body to perform well. During the growing cycle, a gymnast can become very frustrated. Skills that were so recently easy to execute are now difficult and a struggle. Still, as she pushes through, her new body will grow stronger, and her skills will return. She will find she has even developed some new skills in spite of the difficulties.

The Christian life also has growth spurts. At times our relationship with God seems familiar and, frankly, easy. When we study Scripture, God unlocks mystery after mystery. Our prayer life is rich and full and dynamic. Our faith in Christ is strong, and the Spirit illuminates our thoughts with God's promises and assurance.

And then we wake up one morning, and everything seems to have run dry. God seems distant. Scripture seems confusing, and we struggle to find meaning in the passages that we read. The fruits of the Spirit seem to be rotting on the vine. We are short-tempered, and everywhere we turn, the Spirit points out our sin. Faith has become a struggle, and doubts dominate.

Don't give up in the struggle. These are spiritual growth cycles. God through the power of the Holy Spirit grows our faith stronger in knowledge and understanding of Jesus Christ. When we are weak Christ is strong.

"Likewise, we are weak in him, yet by God's power we will live with Him" (2 Corinthians 13:4).

SEPTEMBER 9

In the past few weeks, my heart has been burdened to pray for others who are going through difficulties in their lives. And today, as another difficult situation was brought to me, I realized that there are not enough hours in my day for prayer.

Paul said we are to "pray continually" (1 Thessalonians 5:17), and while I would like to be in prayer constantly, I simply can't. My human frailty prevents me from praying all day every day. I have to meet my physical needs of rest and nourishment. I have to meet my job responsibilities, and I have family obligations as well. When all those needs are met, I am tired and need sleep.

Fortunately, when I am too weak to continue in prayer, God in Christ continues in prayer on behalf of those I have put before Him. Jesus Christ lives eternally to pray continually for the world and its needs. The Lord never forgets those friends I lift before Him. He prays until the Father answers. And He prays for us all the time, every day both now and in eternity.

"Therefore He is able to save completely those who come to God through him, because He always lives to intercede for them" (Hebrews 7:25). Jesus Christ lives in the eternal kingdom praying before God on our behalf. What we cannot finish in prayer, Christ completes. Therefore, every prayer we utter to Christ, Christ brings before the Father for us.

When we are weak in prayer, Christ remains strong in prayer. When we tire in prayer, Christ remains strong in prayer. When we forget to pray, Christ always remembers to pray. Christ "prays continually" for us before the Father through the Spirit.

SEPTEMBER 10

My heart is heavy tonight because several of my friends are coping with difficulties. Some of them have been diagnosed with cancer; others are staggering under the weight of grief; a few have strained family relationships and some are enduring financial hardships.

We all know the heartache of helping friends cope with difficult situations. We don't like to watch our friends and family go through troubles. We want to fix everything for them. We draw close when they seek comfort from us. We stay away when they need to be alone. When they call us, we respond to their call. When they ask us to pray, we pray. We would never deny a loved one help, but sometimes the burdens weigh on us. Our human strength is not sufficient to carry the load of cares that are sometimes placed on our shoulders. We need the shoulders of Christ to bear the load. Jesus said, "Come to me, all you who are weary and burdened, and I will give you rest" (Matthew 11:28).

When we need to rest from our burdens, we can know that God calls us to place the load on His broad, strong shoulders. God has proven Himself reliable to the task of carrying our burdens, because Christ Jesus already bore the burden of our sin on the cross. He was "crushed for our iniquities" (Isaiah 53:5), and He carried our sorrow. Yet even the weight of our sin could not conquer Him. Through the power of the Holy Spirit, God raised Jesus from death to life. His resurrection life will never grow faint or weaken but will remain strong, almighty and eternal. The risen Lord can carry our burdens, and He invites us to unload them on Him.

"Praise be to the Lord, to God our Savior, who daily bears our burdens" (Psalm 68:19).

SEPTEMBER 11

I keep a digital copy of everything I write on my desktop computer and two separate thumb drives. The thumb drives are home to hundreds of pieces of writing, which represent thousands of hours of work. I do not want to lose them. I also have the work stored on the thumb drives so I can take one of them with me when I travel so I can work on the pieces when I am away from my desk.

These writings are important to me, so I make sure they are safely housed and nearby when I need them.

As important as my own writing is to me, the writings God has inspired through men by the Holy Spirit are even more important to me. So, I make sure that I keep a copy of the Bible in my backpack. I have a version of the Scriptures downloaded on my Kindle and on my phone. In addition, I spend several hours each week memorizing verses so I will always have the Word of God in my mind. When the words of Scripture are committed to memory, the Holy Spirit can always use them to transform my thoughts and apply the truth of the Bible to my heart.

We probably all have books or writings or sayings we cherish and keep with us. Make Scripture one of the books you cherish. Through the Word of God in Christ, we are "transformed by the renewing of your mind" (Romans 12:2) through the power of the Holy Spirit.

SEPTEMBER 12

A few of my gymnasts were floundering in practice. After watching them wander through assignments and fail to complete tasks, I decided they needed more individual attention. So, I sat with each one and wrote out a specific assignment for each event. So far, so good. My gymnasts then began to complete the assignments.

There are many days I flounder in my faith. Don't misunderstand, I am not talking about doubt. I am talking about days when my relationship with God seems to stagnate. My prayer and study time lack focus. Scripture readings barely seem applicable to my situations. I nearly exhaust myself trying to be a "good Christian." The more human effort I apply to the situation, the more my soul grows empty.

I've come to realize that an empty soul is not necessarily a bad thing. An empty soul means the Lord has spent me in His service. Once the service is completed, the Lord calls me in from the world to take refuge in the eternal presence of God. The Lord will hide me with Him to rejuvenate, regenerate and refresh my weary soul. In other words, God gives me some individual attention, allows me to rest from my labors and instructs me through the power of the Holy Spirit. He tucks me away for a while in the shelter of His presence before sending me back into world to proclaim the Good News of Christ. "You are my hiding place; you will protect me from trouble and surround me with songs of deliverance" (Psalm 32:7).

SEPTEMBER 13

I was reading in Exodus the story of God's bringing water forth from the rock for the Israelites. God told Moses to take his staff and go to the rock. Then God said, "I will be standing there before you on the rock" (Exodus 17:6). According to the Jewish Midrash "This implies 'In every place where a man leaves his footprint, there I too will stand'" (*The Torah: A Modern Commentary*, 513).

Wow, everyplace I leave a footprint, God is standing with me. This is closer than "me and my shadow." In other words, His Eternal Presence is inseparable from my life. God closer to me than my own thoughts. When I inhale, the Spirit fills me with His life. David said it this way, "Where can I go from your Spirit? Where can I flee from your presence?" (Psalm 139:7)

In God's desire to be close to us, He sent His Son from heaven to pave a path of redemption in the world. Christ left divine footprints in the dust of the sinful world. He left bloody footsteps in the dirty ground on the road to Calvary. His nail-pierced feet trod over Satan, leaving the footprints of love's victory over death and sin in the darkness of hell. And, finally, His risen body returns to the heavenly realm.

Christ walked among us and died for us so God could be close to us through the Spirit.

SEPTEMBER 14

Jesus said "I am the vine; you are the branches. If a man remains in me and I in him, he will bear much fruit; apart from me you can do nothing" (John 15:5).

Our sinful nature is always trying to pull us away from God in Christ so we can pursue our own agenda. Our corrupt nature has convinced us that God wants what we want. With that motivation, we create ministries, programs and projects without giving God's will and purpose a thought. Our fallen nature has us believing that anything we do with good intentions is what God would have us doing. Just because we think something is a good idea, doesn't mean God thinks it's a good idea.

Remember God's promise to Abraham to make his descendants as numerous as the sands? Remember Abraham's wife, Sarah? She was growing old and was barren. She thought it was a good idea to help God's plan along by allowing Abraham to sleep with her maidservant, Hagar, who then became pregnant. Then when the maidservant gave birth, Sarah resented Hagar and mistreated her. God had promised that Sarah would have a son. But Sarah preempted God's action and took matters into her own hands. We are all like Sarah. We ask God for something and then race ahead to fulfill our request on our own.

In His discourse on the vines, Jesus explains that we need to stay connected to Him through the Holy Spirit so others will come to know God in Christ. "This is to my Father's glory, that you bear much fruit, showing yourselves to be my disciples" (John 15:8).

SEPTEMBER 15

The other day at practice a young gymnast came to me crying. Her words were not something I hear often. She said, "I'm sorry." I was surprised and asked her why she was sorry. She replied, "I haven't listened to you and made the corrections you asked me to make." Then she hugged me, and I hugged her. I explained that my instruction and correction were meant to keep her safe when she is executing skills on the events.

When she walked away from me, all I could think was how much I am like my athlete when it comes to my relationship with God. Over and over He instructs me and corrects me through the Holy Spirit so I can lead an obedient life unto Him, yet I do not accept His teachings. Soon I am overwhelmed with remorse because I have failed to listen to Him.

When I ignore God in Christ, my soul becomes agitated and my thoughts stray from God. I wallow in self-pity and blame the world for my resentful behavior and cranky attitude. The fault lies with me because I fail to yield to the work of the Holy Spirit in my life. But the Spirit will persist until my remorse turns to repentance, and repentance moves me to confession. Confession brings forgiveness from God and sanctification from the Spirit.

"If we confess our sins, He is faithful and just and will forgive us our sins and purify us from all unrighteousness" (1 John 1:9).

SEPTEMBER 16

My gymnasts can give me several reasons each day for why they cannot complete an assignment I have given them. These gymnasts use excuses as a tool to keep from doing things in the workout they do not wish to do.

I give God an earful of excuses to try to justify my sin. My sinful nature does not want to obey the commands of God, so I use excuses to exonerate myself before Him. I use my list of excuses to try to hold God at a distance so I do not have to do what He is asking me to do: repent of my sin, leave it behind and live an obedient life through the Holy Spirit. I have a stockpile of excuses I use to try to explain away my sin to God.

However, Jesus said, "If I had not come and spoken to them, they would not be guilty of sin. Now, however, they have no excuse for their sin" (John 15:22). I have no excuse for my sin. In Jesus Christ I have a solution for my sin problem. Yet, I would rather use an excuse than go to Christ's cross, where I have to see what my sin has really done. I see Christ hanging on a tree being punished for my sin. I realize my excuses will never exonerate me, only the righteous work of Christ and His blood can exonerate me before God.

SEPTEMBER 17

Last week I insisted that one of the gymnasts move a new beam skill from a low beam to a high beam using mats stacked under it for safety. She didn't appreciate my assignment, and a glaring look communicated her annoyance with me at that moment. Today, however, she raced across the gym to tell me she had executed her new skill on the high beam. Her displeasure over the assignment had vanished, because she had gained new understanding and she was proud of her achievement.

God calls me to a life of obedience to Christ through the Holy Spirit. Yet, there are times when His command to obey Him seems particularly difficult, and I resist compliance. Instead, I mutter under my breath at God and tell Him the flaws I see in His request. Then I do many things to avoid Him. These avoidance tactics are my way of expressing my displeasure toward God.

Fortunately, God in Christ does not hold my recalcitrant behavior against me. Through the Spirit He shows me my sin so I can repent, receive forgiveness and gain a greater understanding of Christ's love.

"If you obey my commands, you will remain in my love, just as I have obeyed my Father's commands and remain in His love. I have told you this so that my joy may be in you and that your joy may be complete" (John 15:10-11).

A life of obedience to Christ is a joyful life in God.

SEPTEMBER 18

At the beginning of the Revolutionary War, Thomas Paine wrote this famous line: "These are the times that try men's souls." His words resonate with us today. These days test our souls. And like our forebears, we must choose either to face our current difficulties with courage or shrink away from the challenges that confront us. Our souls will either languish in hopelessness or be strengthened through adversity.

We have come to the point it seems that our leaders have abandoned us for their own selfish gains. We cannot turn to them, for they are at the heart of our struggles. We feel like sheep without a shepherd. Our leaders pose as wolves in sheep's clothing, attacking the flock. Yet, we are not alone, for Jesus Christ has made it clear that He is the Good Shepherd who has lain down His life for the sheep.

Though our leaders have abandon us, God has not abandoned us in these days of testing. God who delivered the Israelites, sent His Son to redeem the world and made visible His strength through Christ's resurrection will empower us with His Spirit to face our difficulties. The words God spoke to Joshua He still speaks to us today: "Be strong and courageous. Do not be terrified; do not be discouraged, for the Lord your God will be with you wherever you go" (Joshua 1:9).

Though the times will try our souls, God in Christ will strengthen our souls through the power of the Holy Spirit. Be strong and courageous and hope in the Lord.

SEPTEMBER 19

My daughter is going to a special event this weekend, so she and I have been out this evening buying a new dress, shoes and accessories for the occasion. While it is not a black-tie event, it is still an occasion that demands fine clothing. Appropriate dress shows respect to the host of the event.

Jesus tells a parable about a man invited to a wedding who came to the ceremony without proper attire. Because his clothing did not honor the celebration or give respect to the host, he was thrown out of the party (Matthew 22).

When we try to come before God without the righteousness of Christ in our lives, we are like this guest who belittled the sanctity of the wedding by wearing inappropriate clothes. To insist that our sinful nature can enter the banquet room of God and participate in the wedding of the Lamb is foolishness and will be met with God's righteous anger. God, the host of the heavenly banquet, has determined the dress code for His guests. Unless the guest is wearing Christ's righteousness, he will be banished from the feast.

When by faith we come to Christ's cross and receive His righteousness, forgiveness and justification, we are properly clothed to enter the kingdom of God and share in the heavenly banquet. When we believe in His name, He imparts His righteousness to us through the Holy Spirit, so we will be appropriately clothed for life in the presence of God.

SEPTEMBER 20

Today a church I am familiar with held a neighborhood outreach event. The congregation bought supplies for the event and advertised it and opened the church doors, hoping to draw in the neighbors. A few neighbors attended. Some church members were slightly discouraged by the lack of participation and wanted to give up sponsoring these events. I can understand the disappointment. However, to this congregation I would say, *Don't give up; prayer up.*

Surround your neighborhood with prayer. Walk down the block praying for the people you have not yet met. Pray the Holy Spirit will draw them, not just to church, but to God in Christ.

The church should proclaim the Gospel to its neighbors, but it must also remember that the Gospel might not be quickly embraced by people still shackled to the world. In fact, the church's proclaiming the truth of Jesus Christ will be despised by the world. Jesus said to His disciples, "If the world hates you, keep in mind it hated me first" (John 15:18).

The Gospel isn't popular in the world; however, the Gospel is necessary in the world, so the world will come to know the saving grace of Jesus Christ through the Holy Spirit. The message of the Gospel exposes the sin of the world and brings salvation to sinners who come to the cross of Christ and believe in His name.

So, to the small church struggling to give the time, energy and resources to reach its neighbors, don't give up. Instead, pray, proclaim and stay in Christ. Through Him and by the power of the Holy Spirit you will bear fruit. "This is to my Father's glory, that you bear much fruit, showing yourselves to be my disciples" (John 15:8).

SEPTEMBER 21

We are going to a family wedding this week. We will see family members whom we have not seen for several months. We are packing appropriate attire for the rehearsal dinner as well as for the wedding ceremony and reception. I will be reading Scripture, and my husband is writing his toast for the couple.

A wedding requires months of preparation and planning. As each month passes there is an increase in excitement and energy as the wedding day draws closer. Finally, the day arrives, and guests happily arrive to witness the exchange of vows between the couple.

The church is also awaiting a day of wedding celebration. On that day, Christ will return to take His bride to be with Him in the glorious kingdom. Revelation 19:7 says, "Let us rejoice and be glad and give Him glory! For the wedding of the Lamb has come, and His bride has made herself ready."

As Christians, we are invited to the coming wedding. We should be expectantly waiting and praying for the return of the Bridegroom. The church should be in a state of excitement and joy as we wait for Christ's arrival. During this period of preparation and planning, the faithful are given the wedding clothes of righteousness from Christ through His meritorious work of salvation on the cross and in His resurrection. And through the Holy Spirit the faithful are empowered in the world to do good deeds, which point to the truth that Christ and His church will be united as on the day of His return.

What a glorious day this will be!

Alleluia!

SEPTEMBER 22

My office windows are open. Outside the shrill sounds and chirping noises of a cricket symphony are playing in the yard. To my ears this insect orchestra is playing hymns of praise to God. They do not weary in their task of making music but instead create endless songs throughout the overnight hours.

On a night like this, I am reminded the earth will persist in praising God. As people retire for the evening, their sounds silenced in sleep, the earth keeps the endless songs of praise to God going throughout the late and early hours. When the sun dips below the horizon the moon rises and stars twinkle in the dark sky celebrating the Light of God, who has come into the world. Creation cannot stop celebrating the Creator.

As I listen to the songs of the evening and see the glories of the night sky, I am ashamed at my inadequacies to praise God. The crickets do not stop singing His praises, but I seldom seem to lift my voice to praise God in Christ. I am encouraged this evening to open my mouth and joyfully praise God, but even if my mouth never uttered a word of praise to God, He would still receive praise from His creation.

"The whole earth is full of [God's] glory" (Isaiah 6:3), and if I neglect to praise the Lord, then "the stones will cry out" (Luke 19:40). Or, I can learn a lesson from creation and let praise for God fill my mouth.

SEPTEMBER 23

The other afternoon my daughter and I were watching *Cher's Living Proof: The Farewell Tour* on TV. I had seen Cher's concert live. As we watched the performance on television I was reminded of the energy and excitement of that July evening in 2003. As show time approached, the emotion in the crowd intensified until at last Cher appeared on stage. Upon seeing her, the crowd erupted with thunderous applause. People shouted, whooped, hollered and even whistled to show Cher how much they appreciated her presence. There was a moment of pure exhilaration just before Cher stepped on stage, and I was overcome with joy as she started to sing.

If Cher could create that much joy for me, I can only imagine what my response will be when the triumphant Lord Jesus Christ makes His next appearance on earth. There are days when I imagine His return and am overcome with joy at the thought of His coming. I am anticipating that moment when He comes to earth riding on the clouds. "Look, He is coming with the clouds, and every eye will see him, even those who pierced Him" (Revelation 1:7).

Some days my heart swells with gladness and thanksgiving as I think about His returning to gather His people and ushering them into the glorious kingdom of God.

Each Sunday, when I attend worship, I remember Christ's death on the cross for me, and I anticipate the marvelous day when He will return.

SEPTEMBER 24

The daylight hours are getting shorter. When I start walking in the morning it is dark because the sun is still nestled under the horizon. I have to use a flashlight to illuminate my path, so I don't trip and stumble over uneven sidewalks. Likewise, as I am returning home after work, the sun is already hanging close to the horizon, and not long after I pull the car into the garage the darkness settles on the city, making it seem much later in the evening than it actually is.

This time of year when the darkness gradually chews away at the daylight hours, I am reminded of how easily the darkness of sin can creep into my heart. I get used to the darkness. I get used to my sin. Finally, God allows me to stumble over my sin and remember that I don't have to live in the dark, because "God is light; in Him there is no darkness at all" (1 John 1:5).

Living in the darkness of my sin is ridiculous when God has offered me His light in Jesus Christ. Christ died on the cross for my sin. Through His death, the light of God's love and life shines in the world. Those who "put [their] trust in the light" (John 12:36) will come out of the darkness caused by sin and walk in the light of Christ's righteousness through the power of the Holy Spirit.

The darkness of sin has been overcome by the Light of the world. "Walk while you have the light" (John 12:35).

SEPTEMBER 25

The world has convinced us that creating division is better than striving for reconciliation. From politicians to children angry talk and destructive words are filling the news media, social media, school hallways and family homes. Divisions abound and are weakening our democracy, churches and families. Jesus said in Luke 11:17, "Any kingdom divided against itself will be ruined, and a house divided against itself will fall." Jesus makes it clear: Division destroys.

Christians have been given the ministry of reconciliation through the power of the Holy Spirit. Our life in the world must honor our Lord and Savior, who died on the cross, made atonement for our sins by shedding His blood on the cross and then reconciled sinners to God. Almighty Christ is at work in the world through the power of the Holy Spirit reconciling men to God. As followers of Jesus Christ, we must turn our thoughts and actions away from division. We can no longer participate in the madness of division but must do the work of reuniting man with God through the proclamation of the Gospel and the power of the Spirit.

Disciples are in the world as ambassadors of reconciliation and are called by Christ to live lives of unity, harmony, peace and integrity, so the world will know God "reconciled us to Himself through Christ and gave us the ministry of reconciliation: that God was reconciling the world to Himself in Christ, not counting men's sins against them. And He has committed to us the message of reconciliation" (2 Corinthians 5:18-19).

Divisions end in the reconciling work of Jesus Christ.

SEPTEMBER 26

At the gym today on beam, some gymnasts were caught cheating on their assignments. One didn't do the right number of assigned routines. Another left out a tumbling element and another fell but counted the routine anyway. What puzzles me is how these girls think they can get away with the dishonesty when the beam practice is recorded on TIVO. All the coach has to do is rewind the feed and watch the large-screen TV to see if the athlete has spoken the truth.

The situation reminds me that so often I treat God the same way. Too often I behave as though God isn't present. My carnal nature ignores the truth of God taught in the Scriptures, and, instead. I romp through the fields of temptations picking bouquets of carnal desire and worldly lust. When I think God isn't looking I let my heart chase ungodly ambitions, allow pride to blossom and greed to grow in the soil of my corruption. I listen when people tell me to follow my heart, and I don't hear the words God spoke to Jeremiah, "The heart is deceitful above all things and beyond cure. who understands it?" (Jeremiah 17:9)

But One Person understands our hearts—the Holy Spirit. The Holy Spirit searches our hearts and roots out sin and corruption by applying the Word of God. The Spirit dwells in my heart exposing sin, cleansing me from unrighteousness and sanctifying me through the truth that Christ has died for my sins.

God is always present and abiding on earth in the Person of the Holy Spirit. Live accordingly.

SEPTEMBER 27

This morning I was awake earlier than usual. So I did some thinking. And what I thought was this: Worry is putting our thoughts on the things of this world; prayer is putting our thoughts on the Person of Jesus Christ.

Then I thought about churches. And one conclusion I arrived at is this: Churches worry. Many churches today are worrying about finances, bills, attendance and the future. And, sadly, this anxiety is reflected in worship services. Instead of sermons proclaiming the greatness of God in Christ, the church receives weekly a message about giving and serving. These are not bad messages, but they cannot be the only message. Eventually, these messages tire out the congregation, because parishioners enter the sanctuary looking for solace from their personal worries and the hope of the Gospel; instead, pastors thrust the worries of the church and the cares of the world upon them.

The worry of the church belongs to Almighty Christ, but He is not worried. Christ is the faithful Bridegroom of the Church. He died for Her. He prays for Her. He is her head. He is Her faithful partner in this world and the world to come. Consider Ephesians 5:23, "Christ is the head of the church, His body, of which He is the Savior."

But here's the problem: the church is worrying about worldly things instead of submitting to Her Savior in prayer, worship, the sacraments and Scripture reading and study. When the church kneels in prayer before Her Lord, she rises above Her worries through the power of the Holy Spirit.

The church can worry and be powerless or pray and be empowered by God in Christ through the Holy Spirit.

SEPTEMBER 28

As the sun lowered onto the horizon tonight it splashed radiant gold, red, and orange rays across a blue cloudless sky. The beams also passed through several tree branches, making them appear on fire. The sun is always a majestic celestial ball, but its beauty tonight shone from heaven to earth, revealing the splendor of the Creator.

Shortly after the sun went down, a full moon rose in the east, carrying the reflected colors of that dazzling sun into the evening sky. Like the sun, the resplendent moon illuminated the darkness, pointing to the wonder and awe of the Creator. Nature selflessly uses its glory to bring glory to the Maker.

On nights like this, the effulgent sun and moon testify to the glory of God. Their brightness reminds me that one day I will live in the Light of God's everlasting kingdom. In the city of God, the time of the sun and moon will cease because eternity will be filled with the Light of God's glory. Our great God and Savior will illuminate the eternal city. Revelation 21:23 says,

"The city does not need the sun or the moon to shine on it, for the glory of God gives it lights, and the Lamb is its lamp."

Oh, what a glorious day awaits us when we walk in the Light of Christ in the unending kingdom of God. The light of the sun will burn out, and the moon will darken, but the glory of God will shine forever, and the lamp of the Lamb will never burn out.

SEPTEMBER 29

One of my gymnasts just learned a new skill on bars, on which she will be competing at a meet this weekend. She worked hard, drilled daily and became confident about her ability to execute the skill well. Unfortunately, today she made a mistake on this skill, which resulted in a fall. Though she did not get hurt, she did suffer a setback in confidence. Her fear became greater than her confidence, so she could not repeat the earlier success with the skill.

She was frustrated because she was no longer able to perform the skill well. She asked me why she couldn't do the skill. I told her it was because she had a picture of the fall in her mind, and the picture was making her afraid to do the skill. I told her that by thinking more about the proper technique of the skill, she could get the picture of her fall to fade.

As we talked, I thought about the number of times I have planted a scary picture of the world in my mind. When I see media images of disasters, wars, shootings and other tragedies I become scared and fearful of this world. But then I remember that, by focusing on almighty God in Christ, those pictures of this world that make me fearful soon fade in the light of His omnipotence and sovereignty.

When the world appears scary, I will turn to the words of the Psalmist, who said, "In God I trust; I will not be afraid. What can man do to me?" (Psalm 56:11)

SEPTEMBER 30

I have been wondering for some time what it means to live under the authority of God in Christ. And I can honestly say, I am not good at allowing Him to have authority over me. Instead, I try to have authority over Him. How do I do that? By telling Christ what to do with my day. You see, I am guilty of wanting my plans to be Christ's plans; I should want Christ's plans to be my plans.

I go through my day without asking Christ how He wants me to spend my hours, which are usually spent doing the things I want to do and then asking God to bless them. I have had this wrong for many years. So now I must give Christ His rightful position of authority over me. This shift will take a different level of prayer and Scripture reading, and I will be able to live under Christ's authority only through the power of the Holy Spirit.

When I am under Christ's authority, I should be seeking His direction, which means that Christ should direct everything— from what I pray for, read in Scripture and do as a result of the reading. Not one detail of my day belongs to me. Every minute of every hour of every day of my life belongs to God in Christ so He can spend it for His purpose of salvation in the world.

The Son of Man was "given authority, glory and sovereign power" (Daniel 7:14).

October

OCTOBER 1

I was reading during my flight to Houston. As the steward made his way down the aisle past my seat he paused, reached above my head and turned the light on over my seat. He mentioned the light would make my reading easier. He was right.

The strange thing to me was that I was unaware of the darkness and the struggle it was causing me. Only after the steward turned on the light did I recognize the darkness.

The simple gesture sent my thoughts spinning as I suddenly realized how accustomed to the darkness of this world I had become. I had heard the news broadcast of the shooting at Umpqua Community College in Oregon, and I paused for a moment thinking of those families hurt by the shooter. But sadly, it is not a story that surprises me. These stories are becoming way too common, and I expect it will not be the last shooting I will hear about. Russia has bombed Syria, and that will not be the last conflict I will hear about. I grow accustomed to hearing of death and war and shootings. I have grown used to the darkness, its destructive ways and the pain it causes.

If I am going to overcome my acceptance of the world's darkness I need to live close to the source of God's eternal

Light, Jesus Christ. The Apostle John writes, "The light shines in the darkness, and the darkness has not overcome it" (John 1:5). Accepting the darkness is unacceptable for a Christian. I have prayer, Christ's work of redemption and the power of the Holy Spirit to shed divine light on this darkness.

I must depend on the Holy Spirit to guide me into the Light of Christ and to share His Light in the world through the proclamation of the Gospel. As Christians we must never accept the darkness in this world, but lift up prayers to Almighty Christ who is the Light from God who has overcome the darkness.

OCTOBER 2

A friend sent me this quote from St. Jerome, who was both a theologian and Bible translator: "Ignorance of Scripture is ignorance of Christ."

Jerome's statement needs to be painted on every church wall in America. For some reason many people sitting in church today are under the impression they can have an intimate relationship with God in Christ apart from the Scriptures. This simply is not true. Through the Scriptures, God in Christ is revealed by the Holy Spirit. In other words, knowledge of Scripture is knowledge of Christ.

We spend many hours frustrated with God and Christ because we try to know Him through a thousand worldly sources but not through the one source given to us by the Holy Spirit, the Scriptures.

If your faith life is frustrating you because you feel that God seems distant and Christ seems to be a stranger, then perhaps you should spend more time in Scripture.

Paul wrote, "Consequently, faith comes from hearing the message, and the message is heard through the word of Christ" (Romans 10:17).

OCTOBER 3

As I flew out of the Houston airport for home today, the sky was blue and clear and full of light. But as I traveled north I noticed a large band of clouds forming under the plane. Above the clouds the sky was still blue and clear, but I realized the clouds were blocking the sunshine from reaching the ground below. I knew I would soon be leaving the light and landing in a gloomy, rainy day.

I thought how much my sin is like those clouds. When I fail to confess my sin, it takes up residence in my heart and blocks the Light of Christ from filling my life. Through the Holy Spirit God reveals His Savior to me and shows me my need for repentance and confession. Once the Holy Spirit has shown me my sin He opens my eyes to the truth of Christ's atoning work on the cross. He lets me see my need for the Savior and fills me with regret and remorse for my sin against God. The Spirit allows my burden of guilt to weigh on my heart until I come to the cross. Once I am at the cross, God reveals His love, forgiveness and mercy in Christ.

The clouds of sin are continually forming in my heart. I am wired to disobey God in Christ. But Scripture says, "If we confess our sins, He is faithful and just and will forgive us our sins and purify us from all unrighteousness" (1 John 1:9).

When the Holy Spirit moves us to repentance and confession, the darkness of sin is destroyed by the Light of Christ.

OCTOBER 4

Psalm 62:11-12 says, "One thing God has spoken, two things have I heard: that you, O God are strong, and that you, O Lord, are loving. Surely you will reward each person according to what he has done."

In these two verses I notice the intimacy David shared with God and the depth to which David was being taught by the Holy Spirit. David and God were so close that through this prayer the Holy Spirit revealed the promise of the Christ's coming, two of the attributes of God Christ would make visible and the meritorious work Christ would accomplish on the cross for our salvation.

Listen closely and hear the Holy Spirit whisper the wonders of Christ to you as He did David. To us, God has spoken is His Word, Jesus Christ. What the Spirit inspired David to pray, God the Spirit brought into view in the world. "The Word became flesh and made His dwelling among us" (John 1:14).

God in Christ is strong. He was strong enough to endure the cross, demonstrate His love for us by dying on that cross for our sins, offer forgiveness to all who believe in Him and then conquer death through the power of the Holy Spirit. All who have faith in Jesus are not judged according to what we deserve because of our sin, but rewarded according to the righteousness of Christ and all He has done for us.

The Holy Spirit will continue to teach us in Scripture the mysteries of God in Christ through the words He spoke to David.

OCTOBER 5

Years ago while coaching softball I instructed a young player about the proper glove placement on the ground for a back-hand catch. She did not appreciate my suggestion and instead informed me of the number of years she had been playing the game. She had two decades less experience than I did in the game. After I pointed out her inexperience compared to mine, she begrudgingly made the change with her glove.

When that story surfaces in my mind I think about Jesus' words: "A student is not above his teacher, nor a servant above his master" (Matthew 10:24). I also think about the number of times throughout the day when I try to put my experience above that of my Savior's. So often I tell Him what is wrong with my day and how He should fix my situation. I turn to Him, not to seek His advice but to give Him mine. I question His directions and assure Him I can find my own way.

Jesus Christ endured the human experience on levels I will never know. He entered into the depths of human depravity and corruption at the cross when our sin was heaped upon Him. He was perfect, sinless, innocent of human guilt because of sin, yet He became guilty, took the punishment intended for our sins and was condemned and judged in our place.

Christ came into the world and not only experienced the atrocities of sin but conquered sin and death so we would never experience what He had endured for our sake.

OCTOBER 6

One of my gymnasts approaches each new situation in the gym with fear and trepidation. If she has to move a skill to the high beam she surrenders to fear and ends up in tears. When I remove padding from the low bar so she can combine skills, she is reduced to fear and then tears. Bar dismounts, even when it's the single-rail bar over the foam pit, fill her with fear and again the tears flow. She is setting a dangerous training precedent for herself by choosing to be afraid instead of choosing to be confident. If she is not careful, eventually, fear will win out, and she will not be able to overcome it.

As I watched her today, I thought of how many Christians who—when faced with difficult life situations—choose to be fearful instead of faithful. Our first reaction to a situation is rarely prayer; it's fear. The immediate response we have to new or unsettled circumstances is to worry. And as we worry, fear grows greater. Soon we can see nothing except the picture fear has created in our minds. Fear blocks all other thoughts and leaves us trembling and beaten.

However, faith steers us to the Word of God in Christ. In the Scriptures we read the stories of the powerful and awesome deeds God has accomplished through the Savior. Our eyes are opened by the Holy Spirit to see the marvelous works of God, and our confidence in Christ grows deeper and stronger. Once we realize the strength of almighty Christ and see His love demonstrated on the cross, our fear is shattered because "there is no fear in love" (1 John 4:18).

OCTOBER 7

In 2015 the Chicago Cubs' 4-0 victory over the Pittsburgh Pirates in the National League Baseball Wild Card playoff game represented a new era for Cub fans. We became hopeful, enthusiastic and excited about the future.

Jake Arrieta's pitching was typical for this outstanding athlete, who finished the regular season with a 22-6 record, a 1.77 earned-run average, four complete games and three shutouts. He is poised and confident on the mound, and his teammates share his confidence; they seem to play a little harder, run a little faster and make spectacular plays to support his pitching efforts.

When Jesus Christ rose from the dead after His crucifixion, He ushered in a new era of hope in the world. Sinners who had thought they would die estranged from God now found the Way to God opened by Christ's blood shed on the cross. His church is called to emulate her Head's life of sacrifice, love and mercy. She behaves a little differently because the Spirit fills her with the knowledge of God in Christ through the Scriptures, worship and the sacraments. She does not speak like the world, but, instead, proclaims the message of Good News: through Christ's reconciliation, redemption and salvation have come to the world.

The church in the world celebrates the joy of the resurrection so all the world will know "God was reconciling the world to Himself in Christ, not counting men's sins against them" (2 Corinthians 5:19).

OCTOBER 8

Recently I read a Bible study on trumpets. In the Old Testament trumpets were used in a variety of ways, including signaling armies to attack or retreat, moving camps and gathering the people for worship, festivals and other celebrations.

A trumpet has a very clear, sharp, distinct sound. When I listen to an orchestra I can identify the trumpets in a musical piece. In church, particularly at Easter, I appreciate a trumpet fanfare. A trumpet has a versatile sound that when played well communicates a range of emotions from joy to sorrow.

During my trumpet study, I also came across this verse: "If a trumpet does not sound a clear call, who will get ready for battle? So it is with you. Unless you speak intelligible words with your tongue, how will anyone know what you are saying" (1 Corinthians 14:8-9).

I thought about how much the voice of the Church is similar to the sound of a trumpet. The Church has a recognizable voice in the world. It has carried the distinct message of the Gospel through the ages. And it must continue to articulate clearly the words of Christ on earth. Her message is unique, clear and true: Jesus Christ is fully God and fully man and He lived among us, died for us and was raised to life so all who believe can receive eternal life.

The message of the Church needs to continue to sound the clear call to repentance, confession and redemption so all the world will know Jesus Christ, God's Savior.

OCTOBER 9

The Facebook newsfeed is rich with sayings, such as this one: "I survived another meeting that should have been an e-mail." Another was, "Healing doesn't mean the damage never existed. It means the damage no longer controls our lives." Still another one read, "No matter how good or bad your life is, wake up each morning and be thankful you still have one." Of course, I could list many more, but here's the point: We like sayings. Some inspire us or make us laugh or even cry.

In 1 Timothy 1:15 Paul wrote, "Here is a trustworthy saying that deserves full acceptance: Christ Jesus came into the world to save sinners." This is a saying among sayings. It delivers in one line the Gospel message and expresses the eternal truth that Jesus came into the world to bring salvation to all people.

We will probably not see this one on the Facebook news-feed, but it should be placed on every church sign, painted on church walls and proclaimed by pastors everywhere until all the world has heard that "God our Savior . . . wants all men to be saved and to come to a knowledge of the truth" (1 Timothy 2:4).

This is no ordinary saying. This saying is Scripture, and as such, it will be applied in the hearts of men by the Holy Spirit, so they will believe and come to accept Jesus Christ as God's Son, Savior and Lord. By the power of the Holy Spirit this Scripture will transform lives and reconcile sinners to God.

This is a saying worth repeating.

OCTOBER 10

I was having a nice day. Then somebody insulted me, and I became irritated. I thought I had dismissed the remark, but I found myself later in the day angry about the comment. I wanted to retaliate. But I thought about Christ instead, and I became aware of how petty and childish my thoughts were.

So what if I was insulted? Christ was insulted, wrongly accused and lied about by the religious leaders during His trial before the Sanhedrin, which would bring Him closer to His crucifixion. When I want to lash out in anger, I remember that Jesus took forty lashes at the hand of a Roman soldier on the way to the cross. When I am ready to act according to my sinful and corrupt nature, the Spirit reminds me that Jesus Christ carried my sin in His body to the cross and then died.

Sure, at the time, the insult seemed big. But the Spirit showed me what a little thing it was. Insults are little things; God is big. See what God in Christ has done. The perfect, innocent Son of God died on a cross for a world of sinners who were insulting Him, screaming at Him, angry with Him and hating Him. He willingly suffered shame and death so all sinners, including me, could be saved. Christ has suffered so I could be saved. What have I to be mad about?

"Who then will condemn us? No one—for Jesus Christ died for us and was raised to life for us, and He is sitting in the place of honor at God's right hand, pleading for us" (Romans 8:34 NLT).

OCTOBER 11

Today was my first introduction to Patti Smith—singer, songwriter and poet—whose career began in 1975 when her album Horses debuted. I would have just skimmed over the article in *Rolling Stone Magazine*, except this lyric from her song Gloria caught my eye. Smith wrote, "Jesus died for somebody's sin, but not mine."

To me this was a sad and desperate line, so I continued reading the lyrics. She wrote, "My sins, my own they belong to me, me." She actually wants to keep her sins. Her thinking is very worldly. The world will tell us we can manage sin. The world will boast of its sinful and hateful ways towards God. The world is proud of sin. The world honors sin because the world is corrupt. So the world will convince us to keep our sin.

Jesus addressed this very thing when He said, "If I had not come and spoken to them [sinners] then they would not be guilty of sin. Now, however, they have no excuse for their sin" (John 15:22). And He said elsewhere, "If I had not done among them what no one else did, they would not be guilty of sin" (John 15:24).

Our sin does not have to belong to us. God sent His Son into the world to make it clear sin has been punished and atoned for in the body of Jesus. And we have been redeemed through the blood of Christ poured out for us on the cross. Bottom line: Sin doesn't belong to us; our sin belongs to Christ our Savior. Through faith in Jesus Christ and His atoning sacrifice on the cross, our sin becomes the property of the Savior, and our sinful nature is justified, redeemed and sanctified through the Holy Spirit.

OCTOBER 12

It's exciting to be a Chicago Cubs fan these days. Tonight's victory over the St. Louis Cardinals puts the team one game away from the National League Championship series. Cub fans are happy, and we are living in the hope that maybe this year the team could go the distance. When the teller at the bank asked me how I was doing, my reply was, "I'm doing great. I'm a Cubs fan."

Then it occurred to me that this is an exciting time to be a Christian. We live every day in the reality of Christ's resurrection and the hope of His second coming. The Holy Spirit is among us. He is teaching us the lesson of Christ through Scripture. He is answering our prayers.

Jesus said, "I tell you the truth, my Father will give you whatever you ask in my name" (John 16:23). Through the

Words of Christ and the revelation of God through the Spirit, we know the Father loves those who love the Son. Jesus has assured us, "The Father Himself loves you because you have loved me and have believed that I came from God" (John 16:27).

Yes, this is a great time to be a Christian. We have been saved by the grace of God in Christ through His blood shed on the cross, loved by the Father and empowered by the Spirit to do great things in the name of God. Jesus said, "I tell you the truth, anyone who has faith in me will do what I have been doing. He will do even greater things than these, because I am going to the Father" (John 14:12).

Yes, this is an exciting time to be a Christian. So, if anyone asks how you're doing, respond: "I'm doing great. I'm a Christian."

OCTOBER 13

A year before the Cubs won the World Series a fan held up a homemade sign declaring: *I ain't afraid of no goat*, alluding to the curse of the Billy Goat, which dates back to October 6, 1945, when tavern owner William "Billy Goat" Sianis bought a ticket for himself and his goat, Murphy, to watch game four of the Chicago Cubs-Detroit Tigers World Series. Sianis brought Murphy to bring the team good luck. However, Cubs' owner P. K. Wrigley would not let the goat into the stadium, because Wrigley said, "The goat stinks."

According to the legend, an angry Sianis replied, "The Cubs ain't gonna win no more. The Cubs will never win a World Series so long as the goat is not allowed in Wrigley Field." And that was the curse. But now the Cubs have won the World Series and that curse is broken.

Another curse in the world has also been broken. Paul writes in Galatians 3:10, "All who rely on observing the law are under a curse, for it is written: 'Cursed is everyone who does not continue to do everything written in the Book of the Law.'" Why is this a curse? Because humanity's sinful, rebellious nature cannot keep the law. We are lawless beings, thriving on disobedience to the law and rebellion against God. Our failure to keep God's law puts us under punishment and condemnation. In other words, we can't live according to the law, so we will die as lawless people estranged from the living God.

To rescue mankind, God sent His law-abiding, perfect, divine Son into the world to break the curse by taking the punishment intended for us. "Christ redeemed us from the curse of the law by becoming the curse of the law for us, for it is written: 'Cursed is everyone who is hung on a tree'" (Galatians 3:13).

Christ died on the cross and broke the curse of the law, and by His grace, we receive forgiveness and are reconciled to God through faith.

OCTOBER 14

My Bible study group is slowly working through Revelation. I have read through this book several times and find the themes to be hopeful and triumphant. But through the ages Revelation has been a difficult and sometimes troubling book for Christians.

Since I was a teenager I have heard people predict the end of the world based on their reading of Revelation. Since the world is still here, we might want to reconsider how we study this particular book. Or, maybe we should consider studying this book the way we study all other Scripture: by asking questions and praying the Spirit will illuminate our hearts and minds to the wonderful truths the book contains, and look at it in the full context of Scripture.

Revelation is Scripture, and like all the books of Scripture its mysteries must be unlocked for us by the Holy Spirit, and like all other books in the Bible it reveals God in Christ.

This book is a challenge because of all the strange creatures, celestial beings and imagery it contains. Still that should not stop us from seeking the truth of God in Christ written in these pages. We might not understand all of the content. But, we don't understand all there is to know about any book of the Bible. We can understand only what the Spirit teaches us.

This is what John the Baptist meant when he said, "A man can receive only what is given Him from heaven" (John 3:27). Anything we know about Scripture comes to us from God through the Holy Spirit.

Venture into all the books of Scripture with the Spirit, and hear what God has to teach you.

OCTOBER 15

Unless you are a Chicago Cubs fan, you don't understand all the excitement, hope and celebration surrounding the team's 2015 National League Division Series win. Cubs fans have lived through decades of losses, seasons of drought when there have been no championship celebrations, and years of humiliation at being eliminated from the post season before the All-Star break. The Cubs fans' mantra for more than 100 years has been *Wait 'til next year*. This season, next year is *now*, and joy is flowing through the hearts of fans.

I was thinking that unless you are a Christian, you just don't understand the hope and joy that comes from knowing Jesus Christ has conquered sin and death and reigns victoriously for all eternity. Only Christians understand Jesus died on a cross so they could be saved from sin and death through His loving sacrifice. Christians know that God can't tolerate sin in His presence. Sinners can dwell with God only when their sin has been covered, so that is why Christ endured God's punishment intended for our sin. His blood covers sin. Through Christ all are reconciled to God, and those who have faith in Christ will share the jubilation and everlasting life that come from knowing Christ is risen by the power of the Holy Spirit.

This matter is too important to wait until next year. So, Christian, pray God's Spirit will teach all people the truth of Christ's life, death and resurrection through the Holy Spirit.

"For the message of the cross is foolishness to those who are perishing, but to us who are being saved it is the power of God" (1 Corinthians 1:18).

OCTOBER 16

Years ago, there was a popular board game called *Trivial Pursuit*. This was a game of questions and answers. The questions were, as the title suggests, trivial. The information given in the questions were of very little value or significance.

Today as I sat reading the paper, I realized most of the articles were stories that would generate little interest in the next few days. What I read today will be of little value to me tomorrow. The content will be forgotten unless it ends up in a future edition of Trivial Pursuit. The value of these stories lay in the moment, and the moment has passed.

I was reminded that while the importance of these stories is fleeting, there are stories in Scripture that will always be relevant. The Word is not dependent on a moment in history. The Psalmist wrote, "Your word, O Lord is eternal; it stands firm in the heavens" (Psalm 119:89). Scripture is rooted in eternal God, and, as such, these sacred pages are always relevant to humanity's condition of sin, need for salvation and desire for forgiveness. The words of Scripture transcend this world, and we will know them and understand them fully in the age to come through the teaching of the Holy Spirit.

In other words, everything written about this world is trivial. Everything about the Scriptures leads to eternal life.

OCTOBER 17

Jesus heals a man born blind (John 9). Living in total darkness this man was unable to perceive even the brightest light shone in his eyes. Fear and hopelessness were probably his traveling companions until Jesus applied a healing mud to his eyes. Through Jesus the work of God was displayed in his life.

Since Adam's revolt, every fallen creature is born blind. All souls have been plunged into the darkness of sin and death, filling each sinner with fear and hopelessness. Unable to perceive God, the spiritually blind grope, stumble and fall in the darkness of the world. Because of spiritual darkness, sinners cannot recognize God in Christ. "He was in the world, and though the world was made through Him, the world did not recognize him. He came to that which was His own, but His own did not receive Him" (John 1:10-11).

The darkness of sin in the soul is so deep that only Jesus, the Light of the world, can dispel this kind of darkness. Just as Jesus applied a healing mud to the blind man's eyes, so He applies the heavenly salve of grace and truth to a sinner's blind eyes. Once the salve is applied, He tells the sinner to go to the cross, to be washed in His blood, to believe in His perfect sacrifice for sin, to be reconciled to God and to be renewed by the Holy Spirit.

Through Jesus' atoning sacrifice on the cross the work of God's redemptive plan is displayed in the world. All those tired of the darkness can come to the cross and have their souls illuminated by the Light of the world.

OCTOBER 18

After days of repeated mistakes, a gymnast finally managed to make a correction that led to significant improvement in a skill. She needed to make the mistakes, because each one made her stronger. Finally, she had the strength to make the change. Then I told her to repeat the skill again, keeping her effort and technique the same. She couldn't, even though she was convinced that her attempts were the same.

For the last few nights, the Holy Spirit and I have been having the same discussion. I am having a hard time hearing Him. I am struggling to distinguish His voice. I keep thinking that everything is the same, but something has changed because I don't hear Him the same way.

I was frustrated until I read this verse. "I have much more to say to you, more than you can now bear" (John 16:12). God is working in me to prepare me for what's next in my life. Right now, things are unclear. I am not hearing clearly because the Spirit must bring me to the new place. He is making me stronger and teaching me to trust Him even when His words are unclear. He is working in me and preparing me for the things

305

He is going to say. He is getting my heart and mind ready for the lessons that are about to come. Until then, I must accept what is unclear, because everything will be made plain in God's timing..

OCTOBER 19

Apparently my excitement and enthusiasm for the Chicago Cubs over the last few weeks has influenced one of my gymnasts into becoming a Cubs fan. All I can say is "Go Team!" I did not ask her to become a Cubs fan, but somehow my words and behavior regarding the Cubs affected her and she decided to become loyal to the Cubs as well.

We are all influenced by the people in our lives. Human influence produces some change, but it is not always lasting. When another more influential person comes along, we will be affected and changed again. However, human influence cannot produce truly transformative change. Only the divine influence of the Holy Spirit will bring about that kind of change in a life.

The Holy Spirit remains in the world to express God's zeal and enthusiasm for His Son. The Spirit acts and behaves according to the ways of God because He is God. His work confronts the sinner with the truth of God in Christ and influences people into leaving their sinful ways and becoming reconciled to God through Christ.

The Holy Spirit is the eager messenger from God who delivers the truth to the world that Jesus Christ died for our sin, brought the peace of God to all people through His blood shed on the cross and reconciled us to God by conquering death and being raised to life. With great enthusiasm He reveals the truth of Christ and applies it in the hearts of believers who "are being transformed into (Christ's) likeness with ever-increasing glory, which comes from the Lord, who is the Spirit" (2 Corinthians 3:18).

OCTOBER 20

One day at the gym the girls and I started talking about the movie *Legally Blonde*. One of the girls remarked that when she was younger and first watched the movie she did not understand all the lines. Now that she was several years older, she could grasp those same lines. She wondered why she understood them now but not then.

Of course, at eight years old, she had not had enough life experience or understanding of the world to be able to comprehend the humor. But now that she is in junior high, her understanding had matured, and she had gained enough life experience to understand the humor.

I find myself in that position with the Scriptures. I read certain verses and lack understanding of their meaning. Some days all I do is wrestle with them. Then sometime later I come across the verses again, and they make sense. I understand the meaning.

The Spirit illuminates our hearts and minds through the Word, but we are not always mature enough in our faith to comprehend the meaning of particular verses. Then one day we find ourselves staring at the verses with which we wrestled, and, suddenly, they make sense to us. As we grow and develop in our faith, the Spirit will enlighten us with new understanding and knowledge of God in Christ.

"When I was a child, I talked like a child, I thought like a child, I reasoned like a child. When I became a man, I put child-ish ways behind me" (1 Corinthians 13:11).

OCTOBER 21

Recently I decided to incorporate more protein into my diet. Changing my diet, even slightly, forces me to rethink snacks and meals. Finding more sources of protein is essential. As a vegetarian, I rely on beans and nuts to fortify my meals. Natural peanut butter is a good protein source, but I have to find crea-tive ways to put it in my day, since I am eating less bread. I am discovering new combinations of food. One small change has opened my thoughts to many food options I had not imagined before.

When I incorporate more Scripture reading into my day and limit those distractions—like television and social media—that draw me away from time in the Word, things happen for me spiritually. The Holy Spirit shows me more meaning in the Scriptures. However, if I am not reading the Word, then the Spirit cannot teach me through the Word.

But when I sit with the Word, the Spirit reveals something new to me about God in Christ. He pulls me away from my usual go-to verses and introduces me to other passages, which help me see Christ's work on the cross in a more meaningful way. The Spirit brings a fresh perspective to mind about Christ's life, death, and resurrection. As the Spirit reveals more truth in Scripture to me, my soul is refreshed and my heart joyful.

"But God has revealed it to us by His Spirit. The Spirit searches all things, even the deep things of God" (1 Corinthians 2:10).

OCTOBER 22

For the last ten days I went without sugar. I drastically reduced my sugar intake but could not eliminate it altogether from my diet because sugar is in practically everything. I was surprised by the types and numbers of food items that contain sugar.

Sugar and sin are similar in this regard; sin is in everything in my life as well. My corrupt nature has been crucified with Christ. Still the residue of sin shows up in my speech, my thoughts and my actions. Sin lurks within me and rears its ugly head at times when I least expect it to surface. I make the mistake of thinking I have sin under control, but then I fail to read the Scriptures faithfully. And then I skip church occasionally. Meanwhile I will go for a period of time without listening to the guidance and direction of the Spirit. And, pretty soon, I am stunned to discover that sin is rampaging through my heart.

How did I think I could manage sin without my Savior? At what point did I slip into arrogance and put on audacity and tell the Lord that His work was no longer needed in my life?

The meritorious work of Jesus Christ on the cross has brought me salvation through faith. But the work of faith must be fleshed out daily through the reading of the Word so that through the power of the Holy Spirit I can live a life pleasing to God.

"And we also thank God continually because, when you received the word of God . . . you accepted it not as the word of men, but as it actually is, the word of God, which is at work in you who believe" (1 Thessalonians 2:13).

OCTOBER 23

Not too long ago I talked to a friend who had hit a couple of rough patches in her life. The difficulties have affected several areas of her life at once. The people she thought she could rely on for support have not been helpful. Her description of what she is going through made me very sad. She simply stated she was empty inside.

My heart ached for my friend as I listened to her express her emptiness. I had few words of comfort to offer her.

Later, sitting at home, I thought about Christ's prayer for His disciples on the night before His crucifixion. He knew they would endure hours of emptiness in the next few days after He died. He knew because of His death His disciples would be faced with uncertainty, grief, loneliness and fear. So He prayed for them saying to His heavenly Father, "I am coming to you now, but I say these things while I am still in the world, so that they may have the full measure of my joy within them" (John 17:13).

Even now as my friend endures emptiness, Christ prays that she will receive the full measure of His joy through the Holy Spirit. Christ will fill empty hearts with the divine joy that comes from His Father. I need to join Christ in His prayers and ask the Father to fill her empty heart with His divine joy through the power of the Holy Spirit.

OCTOBER 24

Somedays I set a deadline for the evening reflection simply because I have responsibilities later in the day. Unfortunately, my preset deadlines don't often work out. The more I try to make the deadline the less likely that comes to pass. Instead, I become frustrated and annoyed that I cannot get the writing finished.

I treat God this way. Sometimes I pray for something specific, and then I give Him a deadline for answering my prayer, and as my deadline draws near, I become more and more irritated with God when it doesn't look as though it will be met. My prayer time with God becomes a shouting match. Of course, I am the only one shouting. My annoyance increases, and my frustration escalates. Soon, I am not thinking about God at all.

For me to give God a deadline is about the most arrogant attitude I can have toward God. who do I think I am that I can give the living God, the Creator of the universe and the Father of my Savior a deadline? This behavior is my ego run amuck. If I insist that God deliver on my timeline, I have elevated myself above God. My sinful corrupt nature insists that I have the right to dictate to God. I have no right to dictate anything to God.

God in Christ is not my servant; I am His, and, as His servant, I am to "humble [myself], therefore, under God's mighty hand, that He may lift [me] up in due time" (1 Peter 5:6).

OCTOBER 25

Music fills my days. All week long in the gym the athletes have their phones plugged into the stereo. From the youngest member of the team to the oldest, the girls all seem to know the hits. On a regular basis I hear Charlie Puth's "Let's Marvin Gaye and Get it On"; One Direction's "Drag Me Down"; Ariana Grande's "One Last Time" and even Macklemore and Ryan Lewis's "Downtown." At home I get a mix of country, oldies and rap. Just about every genre of music passes through my ears at some point during the week. And Sunday is no exception, as each worship service is filled with praise songs, hymns and responses.

For many people music is an outlet and an escape. We all seem to identify with the themes, emotions and rhythms of a song. We have often heard music referred to as the universal language because it can sometimes express for us what we cannot express for ourselves. Songs stay with us.

God appreciates music, holy songs lifted to Him in prayer. He listens as the angels sing to Him, surrounding His throne and singing songs of praise and laud and honor. And as the angels surround God with songs, so God surrounds His people with songs of salvation. The psalmist wrote about these songs, "You are my hiding place; you will protect me from trouble and surround me with songs of deliverance" (Psalm 32:7).

Each day, unplug from the songs of the world, and listen to the voice of God sing His love songs to you through the Psalms.

OCTOBER 26

Salvation is all divine effort, and a sinner comes to salvation through God's grace. Grace is God's doing everything for our salvation through Jesus Christ's atoning sacrifice on the cross to save sinners from sin and death. "Salvation belongs to our God, who sits on the throne, and to the Lamb" (Revelation 7:10).

However, this is a difficult teaching for fallen humanity to accept. We want to know that by human effort we are able to come to God. Sinners want God to deem them worthy of salvation because of their merits. But all the attempts of fallen humanity to secure salvation through works fall short of glorious God. What we can offer to God has all been corrupted by sin and is an unworthy offering to God. Corrupt, sinful, carnal mankind has no acceptable offering to bring before God.

Neither our merits nor our works can save us from the punishment God has determined for sin. Only the meritorious work of
God in Christ on the cross is an acceptable offering to God, and
through faith in His perfect sacrifice we are saved.

By grace God reveals Himself, exposes the human condition
of sinfulness and turns a sinner to the cross of Christ. By the
"Spirit of grace" (Hebrews 10:29) a sinner repents, confesses
and comes to a complete moral renewal. Christ's "greatest joy
is to give you character, to beautify your example, to exalt your
principles and make each the depository of His own almighty
grace" (Horace Bushnell, "Unconscious Influence," in *The
Treasury of the World's Greatest Sermons*, Wiersbe, 100).

By the Spirit of grace a sinner is saved, regenerated and reconciled to God through Christ Jesus.

OCTOBER 27

As my family has grown older, I have changed the food
items I put in my grocery cart. When my children were young,
the cart was full of formula, baby food and juices. As my children grew, the cart had frozen pizzas, Hot Pockets and other
meals of convenience. Today these foods have been replaced
by gluten-free items, paleo-diet foods and vegetarian foods. At
this point I doubt my food choices will return to those I made
thirty years ago.

My grocery cart made me think about how my heart has
changed since the presence of God in Christ became a reality
in my life. Before God's presence was real in my life, my heart

was hard, dark and disobedient. I lived according to my will and did the things that pleased me. However, after the Spirit opened my eyes to the truth of Jesus' atoning death on the cross, my heart was softened by redemption, saddened by sin and renewed. Through the power of the Spirit, I live in obedience to God's will, and I am determined to please Him.

Since Christ has saved me by His grace, I can no longer live as I did before the transforming work of the Holy Spirit consumed me. My heart belongs to Christ through the Spirit, and I cannot go back to my sinful ways, but must rely on the power of the Holy Spirit to bring me to repentance so He can rid my heart of all unrighteousness, godlessness and licentiousness. Scripture says, "No one who lives in Him keeps on sinning. No one who continues to sin has either seen Him or known Him" (1 John 3:6).

OCTOBER 28

Since this is Halloween week, the gymnasts picked a theme for each day and have dressed according to the theme. Today was imposter day. Several of the girls decided to impersonate me. They know me well: One wore a Chicago Cubs T-shirt, one had one of my TOPs (Top Opportunity Program—run by the United States of America Gymnastics' national coaching staff) T-shirts and all of them wore shorts and tennis shoes. They brought my favorite toys: a yo-yo, several swim noodles and Nerf dart guns. Then they attacked me with the noodles and dart guns. It was fun. I am complimented by their actions, since as the saying goes, *Imitation is the sincerest form of flattery.*

The Bible has much to say about imitation. Consider Ephesians 5:1: "Be imitators of God, therefore, as dearly loved children and live a life of love, just as Christ loved us and gave Himself up for us as a fragrant offering and sacrifice to God." When we live a life of sacrificial love by the power of the Holy Spirit we honor God in Christ. Choosing to love means we choose to reflect Christ and His sacrifice on the cross for our sin.

Look also at Hebrews 13:7: "Remember your leaders, who spoke the word of God to you. Consider the outcome of their way of life and imitate their faith." God has put people of faith in our lives. Look at their lives in Christ, and remember the wisdom of the Word they shared with you and their counsel on spiritual matters. Imitate the people of faith in your life, even as you are a person of faith another can imitate.

The highest praise we can give to God is to imitate His Son through our words and actions by the power of the Holy Spirit.

OCTOBER 29

During the week preceding Halloween, the preschool students wear costumes and parade through the gym. We have seen a variety of costumes, including a school bus, golf caddy, Captain America, Spiderman, Superman and Supergirl. Children young and old seem to appreciate superheroes with their strengths, powers and invincibility.

Society loves its superheroes, because we consider these fictional heroes perfect, since they cannot be defeated or destroyed. And each of us wants to feel invincible and able to conquer the ultimate enemy, death.

But we are not invincible, we are mortal. When God created Adam He made him perfect. complete. God gave Adam all he needed to dwell in His presence, grow in knowledge and love of Him, grasp the truth of God and live forever in the eternal kingdom.

But Adam rebelled against God and died because of his sin. "The wages of sin are death" (Romans 6:23). Adam was no longer able to reside with living God, because death had swept into his soul. By Adam's fall, his whole race tasted death. So, Jesus Christ came into the world to rescue Adam's race from sin and death. By dying on the cross and being raised from the dead by the power of the Holy Spirit, Jesus showed He was invincible God, unconquerable and unable to be defeated by death. If you need a superhero to help you feel safe and secure, look to Christ Jesus who saves us from death and restores us to life with God through faith.

OCTOBER 30

Today I reached into my refrigerator to grab some ingredients for a smoothie, including a bottle of orange juice called Simply Orange. Anyone familiar with this brand knows the company uses nothing but oranges in its juice, no artificial preservatives or added sugar.

The church should adopt this company's strategy and go Simply Gospel, no false doctrines or destructive heresies. Business plans, fundraising campaigns and clever advertising strategies can be surrendered to the Good News that Christ has died, Christ has risen, Christ will come again.

The message of the Gospel, the good news that Christ has suffered and died to set us free from sin and death, should not be an afterthought of pastors and leaders. The cross is the essential doctrine of the Church and must be taught to the faithful so they can grow stronger in Word and deed.

When the Gospel is preached, sinners are transformed through the power of the Holy Spirit. Paul said it this way, "My message and my preaching were not with wise and persuasive words, but with a demonstration of the Spirit's power, so that your faith might not rest on men's wisdom, but on God's power" (1 Corinthians 2:4-5).

We cannot design a business plan or marketing strategy that will persuade a person to believe in Christ. The Spirit, however, will bring sinners to Christ through the Gospel.

"Is it not in your power to preach, not a superficial but a simple gospel, a gospel which makes a man strong to think, strong to do, and strong to bear" (Thomas Kelly Cheyne, "Faith and Progress," *Treasury of the World's Greatest Sermons*, Warren Wiersbe 128).

OCTOBER 31

Any child wanting to be an athlete must go through a learning process in the sport. For instance, girls come into the Gymnastic Academy to learn how to become gymnasts. The process for being a good gymnast takes many years. Gymnasts must learn everything from how to execute skills to how to wear their hair for competition. Girls become gymnasts by participating in gymnastics.

When the disciples said "Lord, teach us to pray" (Luke 11:1), they expected to participate in the learning process of prayer. They knew they would have to learn to pray just as they had learned to talk, walk or even fish. They would learn to pray by praying.

Christians must learn to pray. Oswald Chambers called prayer "a holy occupation" and said that "the job of every Christian is to pray" (*Prayer: A Holy Occupation*, Chambers, 7). However, prayer does not come easily to believers because we constantly trip over our carnal nature. Our corrupt nature doesn't pray for God's will to be done, but for our will to be done. So, the first lesson the faithful learns is that prayer is the process of seeking God, His will and His purpose of salvation in Christ. The second lesson a Christian learns about prayer is that discerning the will of God is impossible without the assistance of the Holy Spirit teaching through the Word of God. Christians also learn that prayer is allowing the Spirit to rule their hearts so they live obedient lives to God in Christ.

Prayer must be learned, for it is the process through which the Spirit forms Christ's life within the believer.

November

NOVEMBER 1

My computer virus protection system detected and removed three harmful cookies from somewhere in the system. I have no idea what that means, except that my computer is now safe. I wish my waistline had a comparable detection and removal system.

We surround our lives with many types of detection and removal systems. For example, most homes have smoke detectors, which warn us of fire, and security systems that alert us to intruders. These systems can warn us of potential danger, but they can't stop the danger once it occurs. Still we will spend thousands of dollars to be aware of any dangers that may be lurking in our lives.

Sin is a danger. It threatens our spiritual lives. Still our response to the danger caused by sin is to deny its existence. We can ignore sin but that does not remove it from our lives or protect us from its consequences. We will avoid reading the Scriptures because we do not want to hear about sin. We think if we discount sin it will just go away on its own. We don't need to look very far into the world or our own lives to discover the lie in that thinking. Sin does not go away on its own.

Jesus Christ is God's own detection-and-removal method for sin. His becoming a man was for the purpose of destroying sin's grip on the world through His death on the cross. God willingly placed His Son in the cradle, so He could willingly go to the cross and save us from our sin.

If we deny our sin, we are also denying the work of Christ the Savior. Jesus said, "But whoever denies me before men, I will also deny before my Father who is in heaven" (Matthew 10:33 ESV).

NOVEMBER 2

Committing my life to God in Christ is not something I can resolve to do. Human effort cannot hold me to Christ when the road is difficult and lonely. For instance, when the Lord calls me to follow Him into the lonesome, harsh, barren desert of pain, despair, or heartache, I hesitate to answer and, instead, consider the dangers of such a place. My resolve melts, and I abandon the trail.

Turning away forces me to examine the true source of my loyalty. My unwillingness to follow Christ exposes my loyalty to the world and my commitment to my sins and carnality. Thomas Watson wrote, "So dear is sin to a man that he will rather part with a child than with a lust" (*The Doctrine of Repentance*, 16).

But I cling to my desire to abandon the world and follow Christ. So, how is this to be done? God says, "Commit yourself to the Lord, and trust in Him forever, for the Lord is an everlasting rock" (Isaiah 26:4, as cited in *Lift Thine Eyes: Evening Prayers for Every Day of the Year*, Christoph Blumhardt, February 10). Commitment to the Lord is dependence on the Holy Spirit. Only by the Spirit's power can earthly thoughts and ambitions be banished from my mind and heart. He surrenders me to Christ, illuminates my mind with the knowledge of God in Christ found in the Scriptures, purges my heart of ungodly filth, frees my soul to trust the Savior and plants me firmly on the path of righteousness.

Only by the power of the Spirit am I able to commit to the Lord and follow Him into the desert.

NOVEMBER 3

The Psalmist wrote, "Worship the Lord in the beauty of holiness" (Psalm 96:9 KJV). Have you ever imagined the beauty of God's holiness? Have you ever sat with the Spirit and asked Him to reveal to you the absolute purity and glory of our heavenly Father? Imagine seeing the beauty of God's holiness in all its fullness, radiating from the heavenly realm and splashing indescribable light across this dark world.

The beauty of the Lord's holiness should be the focus of our praise. Look at the example of King Jehoshaphat: He was about to be attacked by three enemies. In his defense against the enemies, he appointed men to "sing to the Lord and to praise Him for the beauty of His holiness" (2 Chronicles 20:21). In the face of such praise, the enemies turned on one another and died. King Jehoshaphat didn't even send a man into battle. As the

Israelites worshipped, they saw that the splendor of the Lord shown around the battlefield, blinding the enemy and creating such confusion they could not distinguish allies and enemies.

And consider the night of Christ's birth. The shepherds in the field were surrounded by the glory of the Lord. "An angel of the Lord appeared to them, and the glory of the Lord shone around them, and they were terrified" (Luke 2:9).

Psalm 29:2 also says, "Ascribe to the Lord the glory due His name; worship the Lord in the splendor of His holiness." Oh to be able to worship God in this way: To be able to see His beauty as revealed to us by the Holy Spirit. Oh what it would be like to enter a sanctuary on Sunday morning and be greeted by His purity, His holiness, His beauty. Would we ever leave?

NOVEMBER 4

Tonight at Bible study, we looked at four visions in Scripture, which give us glimpses of worship in the heavenly realm. The group referred to Revelation 4 as the base text to which we then compared the visions in Isaiah 6, Ezekiel 1 and Daniel 7.

Similarities among the visions included creatures that had multiple pairs of wings and some that had eyes all over them, a throne upon which God was seated, smoke and burning coals and voices chanting to God. As strange as each of these scenes may seem, one point is clear: Creatures in these images express their perpetual adoration for God. In their service to God, they proclaim His greatness unceasingly. They lift up the glory and wonder of His nature. Nothing in the heavens distracts these worshippers from praising God Almighty.

Our earthly worship should emulate the worship of God in heaven. Worship is a time when we put aside the distractions of life and focus exclusively on God. We should come to church on Sunday mornings, not with our minds filled with thoughts about what we must do for the week, but filled with the expectation of giving our undivided attention to God, who saved us through the blood of His perfect Son and sanctifies us through the work of the Holy Spirit. Our minds and hearts should be filled with adoration for God through the Holy Spirit, and we should pray that we can give God the glory and honor due Him.

These Scriptures are a gift from God so we can learn how to worship Him in Spirit and in truth. What a glorious service that will be.

NOVEMBER 5

Tonight I sat for a few minutes randomly pounding on the computer keyboard. Suddenly a calculator popped up on my monitor screen. I had no idea which button I had pressed to activate the calculator. I looked more closely at the keyboard until I found the calculator button. I laughed at my unfamiliarity with a keyboard I have been using for several years. I can only guess how many other useful functions remain hidden from my sight.

According to Scripture God also keeps things hidden. He doesn't tell us everything. However, He has revealed to us what we need to know for salvation, redemption and sanctification. Moses told the Israelites: "The secret things belong to the Lord our God, but the things revealed belong to us and to our children forever, that we may follow all the words of this law" (Deuteronomy 29:29).

God keeps some things to Himself. But what He does reveal to us belongs to us through the power of the Holy Spirit. Through the Spirit, Jesus Christ, God incarnate, was born into the world. The Son of God no longer remained a secret in the Godhead but was revealed so humanity would know "the only true God and Jesus Christ who He has sent" (John 17:3) and "we could be saved by grace through faith" (Ephesians 2:8).

What matters aren't the secrets God keeps but what He has revealed to us in Jesus Christ.

NOVEMBER 6

Great love stories span the ages: Cleopatra and Mark Antony, Lancelot and Guinevere, and Romeo and Juliet come to mind. These love stories are not only rich with passion but also steeped in tragedy. Cleopatra and Mark Antony bring down a royal house, the love of Lancelot and Guinevere destroys a king and his kingdom and *Romeo and Juliet* ends in the deaths of the two young lovers.

However, the greatest love story of all—one that began before the world was created—is often overlooked: the love affair between Christ and His bride, the church. Christ deeply loves His church. Even though she sometimes proves to be an unfaithful lover by engaging in adultery with manmade idols, Christ forgives her and remains steadfast in His devotion to her. He sacrificed His life on the cross for her, that she might live a faithful life to Him in the world through the power of His Holy Spirit. According to Ephesians, "Christ loved the church and gave Himself up for her to make her holy, cleansing her by the washing with water through the word, and to present her to Himself as a radiant church, without stain or wrinkle or any other blemish, but holy and blameless" (5:25-27).

Christ adores His bride, and He has set her apart for His good pleasure. He has clothed her in righteousness, sanctified her through His pure blood and reconciled her to God so she can be with Him forever in the heavenly kingdom.

NOVEMBER 7

As children, many of us were, at one time or another, afraid of the dark. Our parents would remedy the situation with a night light. Though the wattage of these bulbs was low, it cast enough light into the room to chase away the boogie man.

As adults, we still sometimes find ourselves afraid of the dark in this world. Hostilities among nations, political uncertainty, marital problems and family hardships can all cast shadows across our days. Trouble, anxiety, confusion and skepticism have us wanting to turn on a proverbial night light. We need something to chase away the uneasiness in our hearts.

Psalm 27:1 reminds us, "The Lord is my light and my salvation, whom shall I fear? The Lord is the stronghold of my life, of whom shall I be afraid." The everlasting light of God shines in this world. When we look at God, all the shadows, grays and darkness of this world are dispelled. The inextinguishable Light of God in Christ banishes the darkness of our worries about the day, our angst about life and even our dread of tomorrow.

Christ's light casts away the darkness of this world and opens our eyes to the reality of God's glorious kingdom. Therefore, "walk while you have the light . . . Put your trust in the light while you have it, so that you may become sons of light" (John 12:35, 36).

The Light of Christ shines in this world so we do not have to be afraid of the dark.

NOVEMBER 8

Tonight while I was visiting my mom, she gave me a wonderful gift. She had a collection of 25 pamphlets called Living Selections from Devotional Classics, published by The Upper Room. These little pamphlets present writings from some of the Church's greatest theologians: Augustine, John Wesley, John Calvin, John Knox, Dietrich Bonhoeffer and many more. I am very excited to read these gems.

These men soaked in the Scriptures for hours, listening to the teachings of the Holy Spirit. The Spirit awakened their hearts and minds to God's truth in Christ. Then these men shared their knowledge and wisdom with other believers, so the Spirit could grow the Church stronger. They were instrumental in changing the times in which they lived through their writing and obedience to the Word of Christ in the Spirit. Wesley changed England, Martin Luther started the Reformation, and Dietrich Bonhoeffer inspired war-torn Germany.

Today the Spirit still works in those who study the Scriptures. He illuminates our hearts and minds with the knowledge and love of God in Christ. He brings His transformative work to bear on the world through those faithful to Jesus Christ. He still raises up obedient men and women today who will proclaim the Gospel of our Lord to the world.

When we are diligent in Scripture study, deliberate in prayer and obedient to Christ, we cooperate with God in ministering His saving grace to the world through the Holy Spirit.

NOVEMBER 9

As the weather begins to turn cooler, I look forward to having a fire in my family room fireplace. The dull dark opening in the fireplace soon comes alive as flames dance and twirl, while sparks, like small fireworks, shoot upward from the logs. The crackling sounds of the burning wood soothe me. A fire heats up a room, and its glow sends an invitation to anyone passing by to come and share its warmth and light.

The Holy Spirit is the fire of God in our lives. The fire of the Spirit invites us to gaze into the manger in Bethlehem and see a tiny, infant King. He is the Son of God in the flesh dwelling on earth as the man Jesus Christ. The flames of the Spirit warm our hearts and turn our thoughts to the Savior of God hanging on a tree, dying for our sin. And the red-hot embers of the Spirit burn in our hearts, purifying the sin there and chasing away the darkness.

The fire of God ignites our passions for Jesus Christ, so we can fall on our knees in worship for all He has done for us. The Spirit melts the cold of the world that lingers in our hearts and ignites the love of Christ within us.

Through the fire of the Holy Spirit, we our purified and made righteous through Christ.

According to Hebrews 12:29, "Our God is a consuming fire." Let Him engulf you with the flames of godliness and holiness.

NOVEMBER 10

E News quoted Olympic gold medalist Michael Phelps from a *Sports Illustrated* interview. He said that he was in a "really dark place" after his 2008 and 2014 DUI arrests.

When I heard his quote, my first thought was we are all living in a really dark place. This world is full of the darkness of sin and death. Scripture says, "See, darkness covers the earth and thick darkness is over the peoples" (Isaiah 60:2). Getting out from under this darkness will take much more than worldly methods. Consider Phelps: the glint of his gold medals could not shatter his darkness. Money cannot buy enough light bulbs to permeate the ubiquity of this blackness. There is no power generated on earth that can brighten this darkness.

The only power strong enough to dispel the darkness of sin and death comes from the divine, blood-stained cross of Calvary. Upon the cross, God's beloved Son suffered and died for sinners. The darkness of disobedience and rebellion crept across the sky, hiding the Light of God from view. As Christ hung dying on the cross, the blackness of sin tried to stop the world from seeing His Light shine in the darkness. Matthew wrote, "From the sixth hour until the ninth hour darkness came over all the land" (27:45).

The darkness of this world was banished by the Light of God in Christ's resurrection. We no longer need to dwell in darkness. The light of Christ still shines in the world through the Holy Spirit.

NOVEMBER 11

Many posts on Facebook today expressed appreciation for the servicemen and women who have fought to defend our country and for those who continue to serve. I would like to add my gratitude and prayers for those who put themselves in harm's way, so I have the freedom to write these words tonight.

Most of the pictures and videos showed families being reunited. A few highlighted soldiers who bear the battle scars they received while protecting our land. Both images depict the same thing: sacrifice. These valiant heroes have sacrificed their time, their bodies and even their lives to keep us safe from our enemies.

While we recognize the struggle with our earthly enemies, we should also remember there are spiritual enemies who threaten our world: sin, death and the devil. Sin plunged humanity into death, and death is an enemy we cannot fight alone. So God sent Jesus Christ into the world to show us that the battle against sin and death was won through His sacrifice on the cross. And Christ bears the marks of His battle against sin.

On Christ's hands and feet are the scars left by the nails driven through His flesh. On His back are the marks of the whip the soldiers used to flog Him until He was almost dead. The scar on His side is from the soldier's piercing Him with a spear.

Every time we consider the cross, the Holy Spirit will show us Christ's scars to remind us of the sacrifice He made for our salvation. And, when by faith we join Him in the heavenly kingdom, we will know Him by those scars. And we will join the living creatures of heaven and fall on our knees and worship Him singing: "Worthy is the Lamb, who was slain, to receive power and wealth and wisdom and strength and honor and glory and praise!" (Revelation 5:12)

Tonight as we honor our veterans, let us also honor our Lord, who battled sin to save us.

NOVEMBER 12

I heard a commercial on the radio today for an identity-theft monitoring system, which is supposed to help protect people from identity theft. Within the ad is a disclaimer that says, in essence, no system can keep you totally safe from theft.

However, the radio personality pitching the product went on to say that this service helps you "feel better protected."

According to that last line, a person buying this technology isn't actually better protected; they will just *feel* better protected.

On the night before His crucifixion, Jesus Christ prayed for His disciples, "Holy Father, protect them by the power of your name—the name you gave me—so that they may be one as we are one" (John 17:11). Notice Jesus doesn't pray that the disciples feel protected, but that they would actually be protected. He asks the Father to keep them safe from the guile of the evil one, the rumors about Jesus that would be lies and anything that would take them away from union with God in Christ.

In the book of Acts, God sends His protector, the Holy Spirit, to fill the disciples with the power to preach the Gospel of Jesus Christ to all the world. And Jesus also prayed that God would unite and protect all those "who will believe in me through their message" (John 17:20). In other words, Jesus has prayed for all believers to be filled with the power of the Holy Spirit to spread the Good News of His life, death and resurrection in the world.

God doesn't make us *feel* protected. God protects us by the power of His name through the Holy Spirit.

NOVEMBER 13

Tonight my house is silent, still. The silence is rich and peaceful, and my soul is content to snuggle deeply into its calm.

This tranquility constitutes more than just noiseless air and soundless minutes. A serenity this profound, this easy and this enjoyable comes from the Presence of God.

A silence this pleasant can come only from God through His Spirit. It is a divine quiet that brings rest to my soul and reconciliation to my heart. The weariness in my soul brought on by the commotion of the day melts in the assurance that God is near. So close is God's Spirit to me in this silence that I can hear Him whisper, "I am with you" (Haggai 1:13). And I want to stay wrapped in His presence, like a caterpillar stays wrapped quietly in its chrysalis until the day it becomes a butterfly.

This is the transforming silence of Holy God graciously making His presence known. With the quiet He brings knowledge of Himself through the Spirit found in the Word. In the silence of His presence He affirms, "my Spirit remains among you" (Haggai 2:5). This holy silence filled with the presence of God is an answer to Christ's prayer to His Father on the night before His death. Jesus prayed not just for His disciples but "for those who will believe in me through their message, that all of them may be one, Father, just as you are in me and I am in you. May they also be in us so that the world may believe that you have sent me" (John 17:20-21).

God makes Himself known to us even in silence.

NOVEMBER 14

Today, after the news of a vicious terrorist attack in Paris, we mourn with her citizens. As a country we know the anguish, the shock, the sorrow of a terrorist attack. We remember the uncertainty, the fear, the panic of having the enemy destroy our security and lives. We want those responsible for this despicable horror to perish.

Yet, nothing seems to change. The wicked and evildoers in this world continue to kill and maim and ruin. And like the Psalmist we want to know: "How long will the wicked, O Lord, how long will the wicked be jubilant?" (Psalm 94:3)

Still I cannot lose hope. I must cling to God and not allow these acts of darkness to threaten my faith in Christ. I know the Light of the world cannot be extinguished by evil. And if my faith starts to slip I will remember that the love of God supports me. My Lord and Savior will encourage me through the power of the Holy Spirit to look at the cross of Christ and know with certainty that love conquers all.

I will never understand the ways of evil. And I will always, while I am living on the Earth, wonder why Evil exists. However, I will never allow my why questions to rob me of the truth of God's reality in the world. At the cross, God in Christ condemned the evil one and brought salvation to all who believe.

Yet, tonight as I pray for God's light to shine in the Paris darkness, I also find myself praying the words of the Psalmist: "He will repay them for their sins and destroy them for their wickedness; the Lord our God will destroy them" (Psalm 94:23). I cannot take matters into my own hands, but I can leave these matters in the hands of Almighty God through prayer.

NOVEMBER 15

An editorial in *USA Today* caught my attention yesterday, particularly this quote, "But as 9/11 and the subsequent attacks have shown, even small groups of people can inflict horrific damage and instill even wider fear."

If a small group of terrorists can inflict the world with pain and fear, then a small group of believers praying with the Three Persons of the Trinity can affect the world with healing and hope.

Christ's church started as a small group of twelve disciples, clothed in the power of the Holy Spirit, who took the message of Jesus' death and resurrection into the streets of Jerusalem. Eventually their message changed the world.

Their message was simple, "It is by the name of Jesus Christ of Nazareth, whom you crucified but whom God raised from the dead" (Acts 4:10), that salvation comes. Peter, strong in the Holy Spirit then said, "Salvation is found in no one else for there is no other name under heaven given to men by which we must be saved" (Acts 4:12).

Today, Christ is still alive and among us in the Person of the Holy Spirit. He is almighty Christ dwelling in this fallen world, and His power and strength are greater than evil. Omnipotent God is calling His church to respond to evil with the proclamation of the Gospel and prayer.

Each time the church kneels in prayer, Omnipotent God changes the world. One small group praying with the Three

Persons of the Trinity, God the Father, Son and Spirit, will change the world.

NOVEMBER 16

A few years ago, a young man came to the gym to workout with the tumbling team. He stayed for a couple of months, and, during that time, he occasionally shared his knowledge of the sport with our athletes. The problem was that this young man was struggling through some difficult time, and his anger toward his circumstances spilled over into the way he talked to the gymnasts. His words were often sharp and blunt and rough. He scared many of the younger athletes with his intensity. He rarely smiled, and his countenance was dark.

So today when word spread that he was coming to visit, several athletes who remembered him were apprehensive about his return.

It took only a few minutes to realize this young man had gone through a great transformation. The difference was evident in his smile, the kind words he spoke and the happy expression on his face. This change was so radical it could only be because of God. All of us, athletes and coaching staff, were thrilled with the change. Whatever was in his past had now been dealt with by the Holy Spirit, and he was very enjoyable to be around.

As I contemplated his transformation I came across this verse in Job 9:27, "If I say, 'I will forget my complaint, I will change my expression, and smile.'" The suffering and complaints that this young man had several years ago where now gone, dealt with by Jesus Christ on the cross. And he was freed from whatever oppressed him through the power of the Holy Spirit.

When this young man walked through the door of the gym, I sensed he had become a "new creation"; I knew God had done a miracle in his life. His transformation gave evidence to God's work in the lives of all who believe in Christ through the power of the Holy Spirit.

NOVEMBER 17

I know it is a little early for a Christmas list, but I have mine. I want the world to stop fighting, media to stop talking and politicians to give a damn about the people. I am quite certain that I will not find one of these gifts under the Christmas tree this year.

But I am so exasperated by the fear-mongering media that I told Mark Levin to shut up and then promptly turned off my car radio. When the news is on I turn off television, and I skip news clips on my computer. My ears hurt to the point of wanting to remove them and hide them away in the closet until some good news comes along.

Fortunately, the Good News is here: Jesus Christ arrived in the world two thousand years ago preaching about God's eternal kingdom and offering salvation to all those who believe in His atoning work on the cross. And the Holy Spirit remains in the world to continue to illuminate the hearts and minds of believers to the truth of God's reality.

During these days when the world is so mean and horrible, I take refuge in the truth that God has opened the doors to His eternal kingdom to me through Christ. I do not have to listen to the world yammer on because I can listen to the almighty God speak to me through the Scriptures and tell me about the heavenly kingdom where fighting has ceased, and the only sound is the songs of angels singing praises to God.

Man cannot give me peace or quiet, but Jesus Christ assures me peace is mine through Him. "Peace I leave with you; my peace I give you. I do not give to you as the world gives. Do not let your hearts be troubled and do not be afraid" (John 14:27).

I am looking forward to the day when the world shuts up.

NOVEMBER 18

A snow squall in Chicago created havoc for airport workers, pilots and air traffic controllers this afternoon. High winds and low visibility made takeoffs and landings at O'Hare International Airport dangerous. In the interest of safety, air traffic control diverted our flight to Moline, where we could safely wait for conditions to improve. After almost a two-hour delay, the plane finally touched down on the O'Hare runway; passengers applauded their appreciation to the crew.

As I sat on the tarmac in Moline, I realized that Christ's cross diverted my spiritual destination. Sin put me on the road to destruction and death. Yet, by Christ's sacrifice for me on the cross my eternal destination has been diverted from the road to perdition to paradise. For all who believe that Christ is the Savior and that His shed blood on the cross has brought us redemption from our sin and reconciliation to God, then heaven, not hell, is our final eternal destination.

Paul wrote to the church at Ephesus, "But because of His great love for us, God, who is rich in mercy, made us alive with Christ even when we were dead in transgressions—it is by grace you have been saved" (Ephesians 2:4-5).

Before Adam's heart darkened in disobedience and rebellion toward God, Christ had already rescued us from damnation through His atoning sacrifice on the cross, diverting our course from the road to death to the road to eternal life.

NOVEMBER 19

For the last two weeks, I have been going through the final edits of my next book. My editor and I have combed through the pages several times each. Tonight, I realized the process of editing could go on for weeks. There will always be something to find. So we have decided to make this last round the final edits, and it will go to print within the next few days.

While I was going through this tedious process, I kept thinking that no matter how often I comb through my life and search my heart and mind I will still find sin. There is no way I can remove sin from my life. Just when I think I have one sin under control another one pops up.

This lack of control is the reason I need a Savior. Jesus Christ died on the cross to rid my life of sin. Then because He knew my corrupt nature would keep rebelling against His righteousness, He sent the Holy Spirit into my life to continue the work of sanctification.

There is no way I could make myself holy. However, I can reject sin and be obedient to God in Christ through the power of the Holy Spirit living in me. I must allow Him to do the work of sanctification in my life so I will be fit to dwell in the presence of God.

The work of the Holy Spirit is to make me holy as God is holy (Leviticus 11:45). Let the Spirit get to work in your life.

NOVEMBER 20

The church is dealing with a spiritual immigration issue. All over this country religious leaders are throwing the church doors open to the world. When I speak of the world, I am not talking about a penitent sinner looking for righteousness, reconciliation and renewal from God in Christ through His atoning sacrifice. By the world, I mean the ungodly and wicked who want the message of the cross silenced and fill the church with false teachings, unholy love, destructive heresies, disreputable doctrine, myths and idols. These wolves in sheep's clothing devour the flock, lead them astray and scatter them. They are cunning and crafty and convince the church to embrace lies, false doctrines and ungodly rants, which carry the church away from Christ's cross onto the path of destruction.

The church, therefore, cannot fraternize with the world, but must preach the truth of Christ's cross so the world can be saved.

Almighty Christ has equipped His beloved church with the Holy Spirit of truth, who continues to empower the faithful to "overcome the world" (John 16:33). Christ has entrusted His church with the responsibility of growing believers strong in the faith, so they can share Christ's ministry of incarnation in the world. By the Spirit, the faithful followers of Christ are empowered with the truth of Scripture, strengthened to carry out the will of God in Christ, given boldness to proclaim the Gospel and "brought to complete unity" (John 17:23) through the prayers of Jesus.

The church cannot be deceived by the world but must remain strong in the truth of Christ so the world is saved through Him.

NOVEMBER 21

Some food naturally lends itself to pairing. A few examples of these foods include hot chocolate and marshmallows, hamburgers and French fries, mashed potatoes and gravy, bread and butter and salt and pepper. Have you ever asked someone to pass the salt? I bet you got the shaker of pepper also. And what happens if you politely say, "no thank you" to the offer of gravy on your mashed potatoes? The server will look at you as though you are from a galaxy far, far away. Certain foods were not meant to be separated.

Scripture also talks about a spiritual natural pairing: justification and sanctification. Justification and sanctification are intrinsically linked works of God in the life of a believer. Romans 4:25 says Jesus "was delivered over to death for our sins and was raised to life for our justification." We are guilty of sin before God. But God sent His sinless, innocent Son, Jesus Christ, into the world to die on the cross for all guilty men so they could be made innocent before God through Him.

Once we sinners accept that Christ has made us right with God through His atoning sacrifice on the cross, then Christ sends His Holy Spirit to sanctify us. God works in our lives in the Person of the Holy Spirit to make us obedient followers of Christ. Peter wrote that believers have been "chosen according to the foreknowledge of God the Father, through the sanctifying work of the Spirit for obedience to Jesus Christ" (1 Peter 1:2).

Christ's sacrifice makes us right before God and the Spirit works in our lives to make us obedient followers of Jesus. Justification and sanctification: spiritually, you can't have one without the other.

NOVEMBER 22

In this digital age, keeping our identity safe is an ongoing struggle. My husband and I have each had our identities stolen. Friends of mine have also been victims of identity theft. Even the best safeguards cannot prevent it from happening.

The first identity theft occurred in the Garden of Eden when Satan tricked Adam into disobeying God. Adam had been created in the likeness of God. His character was holy, pure and noble. But Satan stole Adam's identity when he enticed him to sin. The image of God that Adam had borne shattered, broken and ruined by sin. His perfection was destroyed, and the holiness, purity and nobility of man collapsed under the weight of wickedness, rebellion and sin.

Fortunately, God designed a plan to restore human identity. He sent His Son, who "is the radiance of God's glory and the exact representation of His being" (Hebrews 1:3), into the world to bring a new identity to those who believe in His name. Those who believe in Jesus Christ's work of salvation on the cross are given a new identity. When a person receives redemption, righteousness and sanctification from Jesus through the power of the Holy Spirit, our identity becomes one with Christ.

A new identity means our nature is made whole in Christ, and we are fit to dwell in the presence of holy God. Through Christ and by the power of the Holy Spirit, our identity is protected and cannot be stolen. Jesus said, "[N]o one can snatch them out of my Father's hand" (John 10:29).

NOVEMBER 23

There was nothing unusual about my day. In fact, my hours were filled in typical fashion. I ran errands, met a friend for a brief visit, had lunch with my daughter and then promptly went to work. At work, some gymnasts completed their assignments; others didn't. Some athletes were happy; some were not so happy. We laughed, we talked, and we worked. Yep, this was a typical day.

However, when I arrived home some atypical things happened. I received a message from the director of a parachurch organization who wants to meet. After responding to that message, I received another ministry opportunity via a friend. This ministry possibility really excites me because it is edgy and different and a little bit rogue.

Why tell you about the contrast? Because as I was having a typical day the Spirit was working. Any time the Spirit makes Himself known, nothing stays typical. Suddenly, His work changed my typical day into an atypical day filled with ministry possibilities. Of course, ultimately these ministries and my involvement with them depends upon Him. But in the meantime, they are a matter of prayer and a source of encouragement. I think about Jesus when He said, "My Father is always at His work to this very day, and I, too, am working" (John 5:17).

God in Christ is always about ministry through the power of the Holy Spirit. And Christ eagerly shows His followers where they can participate in His ministry through the Spirit. Ministry in the Spirit will always make a day go from typical to atypical.

NOVEMBER 24

The girls at the gym asked which event in Christ's life was most important: His birth or His death. His birth was essential to God's plan of salvation, because God had to become a man if man was going to be saved from sin and death. Jesus was born to suffer and die as a sinner for sinners.

On the cross Christ willingly laid down His life so sinners could be set free from their transgressions. "This is how we know what love is: Jesus Christ laid down His life for us" (1 John 3:16). He endured the punishment that our sins deserved. "He was crushed for our iniquities; the punishment that brought us peace was upon him" (Isaiah 53:5). His blood was spilled so sinners could receive forgiveness from God and be restored to Him through the power of the Holy Spirit. "In fact, the law requires that nearly everything be cleansed with blood, and without the shedding of blood there is no forgiveness" (Hebrews 9:22).

At Christmas we celebrate with the angels that Christ the Savior is born, and on Good Friday we witness God's Savior hanging, bleeding and dying on the cross in our place. Many will not accept the truth of the Lord's sacrifice. Some sinners will look away from Christ's marred and tortured body on the cross and question God's love.

However, those who see the truth of Christ's atoning work on the cross and come to faith in Him will be saved. Christ was born to die on the cross so believers could be made righteous through Him, sanctified through the Holy Spirit and reconciled to God.

NOVEMBER 25

God called Gideon to lead an attack against the Midianites. Before the battle God decreased the size of Gideon's army from 32,000 troops to 300 troops. God said, "You have too many men for me to deliver Midian into their [Israel's] hands. In order that Israel may not boast against me that her own strength has saved her" (Judges 7:2).

There are times when the world seems so big. Unscrupulous, unethical and dishonest men seem to run everything. The wicked flaunt their sexual immorality, lawlessness and shameless deeds. Meanwhile "the fool speaks folly, his mind is busy with evil: He practices ungodliness and spreads error concerning the Lord" (Isaiah 32:6). Against this backdrop the church, with its aging and shrinking membership, seems tiny, and she looks helpless and weak against the wicked.

But God has positioned His church where He wants Her in the world and has made Her exactly what He wants Her to be. Her numbers are small so the world will know Her strength comes from almighty Christ and the power of the Holy Spirit. She is in the world as a witness to the truth that Jesus Christ is the Savior of the world. She lives in the power of the resurrection and proclaims to the world the Good News that Jesus Christ died to save sinners and reconcile them to God. The power of the church lies not in her physical size, but in the strength of Her Redeemer and Head.

NOVEMBER 26

Each day at the gym I watch gymnasts execute skills on the equipment. What surprises me is how many times I must remind the girls to keep their bodies moving. For example, on bars if a gymnast is going to complete a pirouette she must keep her body turning by turning her feet 180 degrees. If she stops moving her feet, the pirouette stops, and she will drop off the bar.

Paul applies a similar theory to spiritual matters. He wrote, "Pray without ceasing" (1 Thessalonians 5:17 ESV). I think Paul means that believers who pray keep their souls continually moving toward God in Christ through the Spirit.

The saved soul desires unity with God. It longs to abide continually in the presence of eternal God, remain in Christ, live in the triumph of His victory over sin and death and stay obedient to the Spirit. Through prayer, the soul delights in redemption, reconciliation and renewal. When a person prays continually, the soul is in motion with God in Christ.

However, the outside forces of the world distract believers from prayer. Sadly when the world rages, believers tend to stop praying and turn to worry or human solutions to their problems. When prayer stops, the soul's pursuit of God stops. Without prayer, a believer begins to doubt, and the soul is flooded with uncertainty, causing great angst.

Prayer keeps a soul moving toward God. Pray without ceasing.

November 27

At the gym today, I watched a young gymnast flawlessly execute a flip flop on a low beam. So, the next step was to move the skill to a high beam with stacked mats underneath. After several tries, she was still unable to land her flip flop successfully on the beam. Overwhelmed by the new environment, she abandoned her technique words and, as a result, could not execute her skill.

I thought about how many times we describe God in terms of His love, compassion and kindness. We contemplate His goodness and give thanks for the salvation He has brought to us in Jesus Christ. Then suddenly our environment changes. We lose our job or have difficulty with a co-worker. An illness invades our body. We have to move. We encounter grief.

Suddenly the words we used to describe God when times were smooth change, and we use words that do not truthfully describe the nature and character of God. We start to question His love, compassion and kindness. Our environment changed, and, as a result, we changed our thinking about God.

God, however, does not change. In truth, God cannot change. "Jesus Christ is the same yesterday and today and forever" (Hebrews 13:8). When our environment changes, we should read the Scriptures and remember that God in Christ does not change. His nature is all loving, all compassionate, all kind and all good. Nothing can change almighty God in Christ. God is always God. Though our circumstances will change,

God will never change. The One who is and was and is to come is always the same, unchangeable God.

NOVEMBER 28

When my family and I were hiking in the mountains this past week, I usually went first. I am a good climber. So, I would lead. I checked the stability of the rocks and made certain there was solid footing so my family could safely follow. As long as they followed in my footsteps, they would avoid stumbles and falls.

God became a man so He could walk among us and guide us along the paths of our lives. He placed His feet on the path of human experience so He could point out the pitfalls of sin and keep us from stumbling and falling into temptation. Every path and temptation known to man has been trod upon by the Son of Man. "For we do not have a high priest who is unable to sympathize with our weaknesses, but we have One who has been tempted in every way, just as we are—yet was without sin" (Hebrews 4:15).

Jesus Christ walked before us so He could show us where to step to be on the solid ground of God. He walked to the cross so we could follow and be forgiven. He walked through Sheol so we would not have to. He stepped into the heavenly realm and left His footprint of grace so we could ascend with Him into God's eternal presence.

Step where the Lord plants His foot, and He will lead you safely home.

NOVEMBER 29

Every coach has an athlete who fights her. By that I mean, at some point athletes will reject a coach's lesson plans, conditioning programs and philosophy. Usually this is a temporary situation that arises when the athlete's stress level increases. During periods of stress, the athlete, at that moment, cannot see that the coach has her best interest at heart; so the athlete takes control of her own workout.

The nature of the coach-athlete relationship reminds me how many times people, including myself, fight with God. Sin deceives the sinner into thinking God does not have the best interest of human beings at heart. Even though Scripture says "Delight yourself in the Lord and He will give you the desires of your heart" (Psalm 37:4), we still let the stress of living in this fallen world darken our understanding of God in Christ. When this happens, we begin fighting with God and insist on controlling our own lives instead of cooperating with the Holy Spirit of God.

God gifts us with His Spirit so we can live above the stress of this world. He fills us with an affection for God in Christ so we will not waste our time dallying with the temporal things of this world. Through the Spirit's power we are able to "live high above a love of things temporal" (*Valley of Vision*, 307), and, instead, "set your heart on things above, where Christ is seated at the right hand of God" (Colossians 3:1).

Earthly things, temporal things are the cause of our stress. God gives us His Spirit so we can live above the nonsense of these days.

"Set your minds on things above, not on earthly things" (Colossians 3:2).

NOVEMBER 30

Flying into Chicago from Phoenix, there was thick cloud cover beneath the plane, yet my view from the plane window revealed a brilliant clear-blue sky with rays of sunlight stretching across the horizon. Approaching the airport, the plane had to descend from the magnificent light into the gray, dark and dreary clouds. On the ground, the plane came to a stop in the dismal gloom of the day.

At the time of this writing, today starts the season of Advent in the Church. This is the time of year when Christians around the world pause to remember "Immanuel . . . God with us" (Matthew 1:23).

Descending from that plane—moving from the light into the darkness—triggered my imagination. I thought of what it was like for the Lord of Light to descend into this world of darkness and death. Then I thought about why He descended: so we could ascend into the land of eternal light and life.

Until His Incarnation, the Son of God had beheld the light and glory of the Father; however, on earth His eyes had to adjust to the shadows and darkness of sin's destructive effects on His creation. His perfect soul knew only eternal life in the everlasting kingdom, but on earth He felt the sting and weight of death.

This was the divine condescension of Jesus Christ, the Son of God. The Infinite Son of the Father became a finite human being to bring salvation, justification and sanctification to the world.

God condescends to man so man can ascend to God.

December

DECEMBER 1

My dad died peacefully in his sleep early this morning. Yet, because of the glorious life of our Lord Jesus Christ, His sacrifice on the cross for sin and the power of God that raised Him from the grave, my dad lives.

Jesus said, "I am the resurrection and the life; he that believes in me, though he were dead, yet shall he live" (John 11:25).

These words from Jesus are the solemn promise of God. Death is no longer a victor. Christ's triumph over the grave brings hope when the clouds of grief gather. His victory over sin and death assures our safe arrival in the Promised Land of the Eternal God.

Today when death snarled and threatened, the Savior stood firm with my dad and gave him safe passage into the heavenly realm. The resurrection is the sure ground upon which we all can stand when we know the truth that Jesus Christ is "the way, the truth and the life" (John 14:6).

DECEMBER 2

When I push through the pain and deep emotion of grief, I see one thing clearly: Jesus Christ is faithful.

Our human nature wants to put the responsibility of getting to heaven on the meritorious acts of our loved ones. Yet, Scripture is plain: "do not put your trust . . . in mortal men who cannot save" (Psalm 146:3).

Passage from this world to God's glorious kingdom is not contingent upon a man's deeds; it rests on the shoulders of one faithful man, Jesus Christ. The Lord conquered death and fulfilled God's promise of eternal life for all who believe in His saving nature. Psalm 33:4 says, "The Lord . . . is faithful in all He does."

When pain threatens to undermine our foundation of hope and pain tries to bully us into denying God's providence, surrender to the Holy Spirit. He will use the truth of Scripture to confirm Christ's great faithfulness to God and man. He will verify the truth of the merciful acts of Jesus and the comforting words of others that God's "love [is] higher than the heavens; [his] faithfulness reaches to the skies" (Psalm 108:4).

When "sorrows like sea billows roll" ("It Is Well With My Soul," Horatio Spafford) into your life, stand on "Christ the solid rock" ("My Hope Is Built on Nothing Less," Edward Mote), and He will bring His enduring faith into your life through the power of the Holy Spirit, and sadness will give way to hope.

DECEMBER 3

My dad's funeral is Friday. Arrangements were made today. We made decisions at the funeral home. The service was planned. Pallbearers were chosen. Readers were decided upon. Flowers picked. Caterers contacted. The obituary was written and submitted. Today was the day of preparation.

In the church calendar, December is the month of preparation, one in which believers prepare for the incarnation of God. The Father took care of every detail before sending His Son into the world. Plans were made, and the details of the plans were spoken by the prophets. "For to us a child is born, to us a son is given" (Isaiah 9:6). John the Baptist came into the world to preach the message of repentance and baptism to prepare the people for the Savior's arrival. A woman was chosen to carry the Son of God. "Mary, you have found favor with God. you will be with child and give birth to a son and you are to give Him the name Jesus" (Luke 1:30-31).

Finally, the preparation was over, and Jesus arrived. The infinite God came into the world through the womb of a young girl. He grew in "wisdom and stature, and in favor with God and man" (Luke 2:52), and when the time was right, He fulfilled all the details of salvation for God the Father: He went to the cross and atoned for our sins.

God prepared for Christ's incarnation. He calls us to prepare our hearts to receive Him.

DECEMBER 4

In the Gospel of Luke Jesus says, "He is not the God of the dead, but of the living, for to Him all are alive" (Luke 20:38).

The human race is afraid of death. We know it to be a natural part of life, but still our hearts tremble when we think about facing life beyond this realm. We know that death is natural, but we view it as unnatural. Our finite minds just have a difficult time grasping the truth that there is life everlasting beyond the temporal borders of this existence.

And within that land of the eternal, God, the Supreme Being of the universe, lives and dwells. He sent His Son into this temporary place so Jesus could teach us about the permanence of the kingdom, but we shunned Him and killed Him. Even after He rose from the grave, skeptics tried to drown out the voice of the Risen Savior, who declared, "I am the light of the world: he that follows me shall not walk in darkness but have the light of life" (John 8:12).

Christ has conquered death through the power of the Almighty God. Death becomes simply the mode of transportation that takes us to the realm of light and life, to live eternally with God the Father, Son and Spirit.

"As the Father has life in himself, He has granted the Son to have life" (John 5:26). And all those who are in the Son walk in life.

DECEMBER 5

Communion was part of my dad's funeral service today. I had the privilege of distributing the wine to the friends and family who had gathered to remember and celebrate my dad's life. What a profound opportunity to offer the blood of Christ to people who have meant so much to me and to my parents.

There is a reason Christ told us to "do this in remembrance of me" (1 Corinthians 11:24). When we come to the communion table, we are reminded of Christ's earthly life and the sacrifice He made for our sin. We are brought to the cross, where we recall that the upright beam represents His condescension to earth and the crossbar represents His divine life in the kingdom.

At communion, we witness His earthly life and divine life become one in His body. The visible church and the church triumphant come together in the holy mystery of God. At the table, the saints in the world and those present in the fullness of God become the "great cloud of witnesses" (Hebrews 12:1) who testify to the truth that Christ has died, Christ has risen, and Christ will come again.

Each time we take communion, the Spirit illuminates our minds with memories of Christ's atoning sacrifice and His glorious triumph over death. We are standing on the sacred ground of Christ's shame and His glory.

Jesus said, "This cup is the new covenant in my blood, which is poured out for you" (Luke 22:20).

DECEMBER 6

Some days it just feels good to be home. The weariness created by the day drains away as I listen to my family tell stories, reminisce and laugh. Comfortable clothes, my favorite chair and a good dinner all help me to relax. Work is far behind me, and the calm of the evening hours quiets my thoughts. The restful hours ahead will prepare me for the coming day.

As a believer, I should have the same fond memories of being in church. The angst created by the world melts away as I listen to the Scriptures read, sermons preached and hymns of praise lifted to God Most High. Like many churchgoers I settle into my favorite pew, exchange pleasantries with those around me and occasionally meet someone new. My soul is nourished as I gather at the communion table with fellow worshippers and hear the sacred words of the Last Supper spoken in the service.

In this holy hour on Sunday morning, my focus is directed on God. I have come to exalt His Name and offer thanks and give honor to the Son of God who came to earth and died for my sins so through faith in Him I can receive eternal life.

Once a week for one hour, it's good to be out of the fray of the world and in the presence of God. It reminds me of all I have to look forward to in the heavenly kingdom.

"I rejoiced with those who said to me, 'Let us go to the house of the Lord'" (Psalm 122:1).

DECEMBER 7

Recently the Rockford Symphony Orchestra and Mendelssohn Chorale put on a Christmas concert. The beautiful music was a wonderful mix of carols and traditional Christmas songs. The profound lyrics filled my heart with the joy of the season. The songs were a reminder of the miracle: God became a man.

This season is about a simple truth: Invisible God made Himself visible to the world in the person of Jesus Christ so all mankind would know the reality of God. At Christmas we remember that God is self-revealing. Immortal God puts on mortality. Infinite God became a finite human being. Imperishable God dwelt in the perishable flesh of man. The Prince of Peace, the eternal King of heaven, humbled Himself before God, put on a suit of skin, and He was placed in a manger.

The omniscient Son of God became a baby boy, who had to grow and learn about His earthly surroundings. The omnipotent Son became dependent on Mary and Joseph for His needs. The baby, who would one day become the man who would feed the masses, cried to be fed. The boy, who probably learned how to hold a hammer from Joseph, grew into the Savior, into whose hands soldiers used a hammer to drive nails through His body to hang Him on the cross.

Jesus Christ willingly descended from heaven to earth to reveal the living God. "That which was from the beginning, which we have heard, which we have seen with our eyes, which we have looked at and our hands have touched—this we proclaim concerning the Word of life. The life appeared; we have seen it and testify to it, and we proclaim to you the eternal life, which was with the Father and has appeared to us" (1 John 1:1-2).

DECEMBER 8

This week God has revealed to me an aspect of my Christian faith to which I had never given much thought: That is hope.

Hope is often used as a synonym for a wishful feeling. We hope for a sunny day or a new car. We use the same word across the gamut, from the simplest desire—wishing for a good grade on a final—to the deeply serious—a successful outcome to a surgery. We use the word hope so ubiquitously that it sometimes comes across as a bland sentence seasoning.

Hope in Scripture has nothing to do with wishful thinking. God has brought hope into the world through His Son, Jesus Christ. Hope means that we place our expectations of salvation, redemption and eternal life in Jesus our Savior. We have hope because we are confident that God has accomplished His will and work through Christ. Hope confirms that Jesus' cradle leads to the cross. Hope assures us that Christ's blood shed on the cross cleanses us from sin. Hope is certain that in His death those who believe receive eternal life. Hope affirms that "God did not appoint us to suffer wrath but to receive salvation through our Lord Jesus Christ" (1 Thessalonians 5:9).

Hope means we are convinced that God's Son lived as a man, died as a man, was raised from the dead as a man and now reigns next to God, from whence He came.

This season, hope in the Christ child. He is the expectation of God come into the world to save the world.

DECEMBER 9

Family stories have always been part of our gatherings. Memories of how our parents met, what our grandparents were like and things family members said or did help us better understand our relatives and ourselves. These stories help each of us get a picture of who we are as individuals and who we are as a family.

Scriptures are stories about God and His remarkable work through His Son. Passing on these stories shapes the community of faith and draws believers into greater knowledge and wisdom of the Redeemer. These stories of God in Christ are the bedrock upon which the Church rests. Each week when we gather as the family of God, we listen to the readings from the Scripture, and these give us a deeper insight into God the Father, Son and Spirit. Through these stories, the Holy Spirit reveals God to the people of God.

These stories belong to all the children of God, and they have been preserved in the world by the Holy Spirit, so each generation can marvel at the miraculous work of God in Christ. The Spirit uses these stories to teach us who we are as children of God and what God requires of His children. "All Scripture is God-breathed and is useful for teaching, rebuking, correcting and training in righteousness, so that the man of God may be thoroughly equipped for every good work" (2 Timothy 3:16).

The Scriptures reveal all that God has done, is doing and will do in the church and through His people.

DECEMBER 10

The other day I was talking with my cousins about the Chicago Cubs. We were discussing the players and the number of them who were on track to win coveted baseball awards this year. We were talking about their statistics, player prospects and game highlights. One of my cousins remarked about how much I sound like my dad when I talk about the game. I was not surprised, because all I know about the Cubs and baseball stems from what he taught me.

As I thought about my cousin's comment I thought how important it is that I sound like my heavenly Father when I am speaking to others. If I am going to carry the words of the Gospel to others, then I have to be a student of the Scriptures. I must let my Father teach me through the Holy Spirit. I must carry those lessons with me and build my faith upon them. My speech and my actions need to communicate love, compassion and kindness. When people ask about God, I need to reply with the truth of Jesus Christ. I need to speak clearly and plainly about Christ's work of salvation on the cross and His forgiveness of sin and His resurrection from the dead.

When I speak, I need to let the Spirit testify to the reality of God in Christ and His saving grace in the world. As a Christian, I need to sound like my Father.

"Speaking the truth in love, we will in all things grow up into Him who is the Head, that is Christ" (Ephesians 4:15)

DECEMBER 11

One of our coaches returned recently from a week at the Karolyi Olympic Training Center in Texas. At this camp, our coach and athletes worked with several of the top gymnastic coaches in the country. After the experience, this coach's enthusiasm and passion for the sport appeared to have grown. With great zeal and intensity, he shared the latest techniques and drills with the girls.

Advent is a time in which we remember God's enthusiasm in sharing His Son with the world. Chapter 9 of the book of Isaiah says, "For to us a child is born, to us a son is given . . . The zeal of the Lord Almighty will accomplish this" (6-7). God's fervor to reveal Himself to a fallen, sinful people was the motivation behind the incarnation of Christ. He was so passionate and enthusiastic about bringing "grace and truth" (John 1:14) into the world that He let His Son become a man, Jesus.

The Son's earthly arrival was announced by an angel and celebrated by "a great company of the heavenly host" who praised God saying, "Glory to God in the highest, and on earth peace to men on whom His favor rests" (Luke 2:14).

God's intense devotion to mankind wrapped His Perfect Son in the flesh, laid Him in a manger, nailed Him to a cross, made Him a sacrifice for sin, raised Him from death and then wrapped Him once again in the glory of heaven.

God's ardor saved the world through His Son.

DECEMBER 12

Since my dad's death, I think about him all the time.

Thoughts of Dad filling my mind are, apparently, very normal. One mother whose son died put it this way, "I used (to think about my son occasionally during the day; now, I can't get him off my mind." These remembrances are healthy and are part of the healing process.

This capacity to remember is a gift from God, and He uses it to build our relationship with Him through Jesus Christ. When Jesus died on the cross, His disciples you can be certain could not get Him off their minds. As they huddled in hiding from the Romans and Jewish leaders there is no doubt they shared memories, discussed His teachings and spoke of His miracles. They dealt with their grief just as we do.

Salvation for us all comes through the cross. Why? Because the cross is where Jesus died. When we see Him hanging on the cross, we cannot get Him off our minds. The cross is where we center our thoughts, and our capacity to remember moves us more deeply into a relationship with God. When Jesus is constantly on our minds we think about what God accomplished through Him for us. We remember His miracles, His teachings, His sacrifice and His glorious resurrection. We remember Him through the image of the cross.

Jesus told His disciples at the Last Supper, "Do this in remembrance of me" (Luke 22:19). In other words, keep Him on your mind; He will bring you spiritual health and healing.

DECEMBER 13

A headline across the CNN network read that most people don't expect to get out of debt. It was sad to think about people carrying that burden without hope of settling the obligation. Debt surrounds us. We think of it primarily in financial terms, but it is a spiritual condition as well.

Spiritually humanity is in debt to God because of sin. We owe God, but, because of our sinful nature, we have nothing within us to settle the debt. So, we are saddled with its burden. The only way out of this debt is through Jesus Christ.

During Advent, we celebrate "Immanuel, God with us" (Matthew 1:23). The sole purpose of Christ's journey into the world was so He could journey to the cross. On the cross, He satisfied the debt we owed to God. Those who believe that Christ paid our obligation have been set free from the slavery of sin and have become slaves to God.

It sounds like we have jumped from the fire into the frying pan. Being a slave to sin leads to death; however, Romans 6:22 states, "But now you have been set free from sin and have become slaves to God, the benefit you reap leads to holiness, and the result is eternal life."

Debt is a fact of our spiritual life. We can carry the burden by living in sin, or we can accept Christ's payment on our behalf and live in God.

DECEMBER 14

Today was a day that never brightened. The fog stayed thick, covering the city in a moist, gray cloud. Car headlights could barely penetrate the gloom. The artificial lighting of store signs, street lamps and Christmas lights could not clear up the dull, drab hours of the afternoon. The only relief from the colorless, dismal, dreary day was the thick darkness of night.

When these bleak days arrive during Advent, I am reminded of how the people of Israel were feeling as they waited for the Messiah. Spiritually their days were gray and gloomy. Sin cloaked the people in despair. Without the Messiah, they had no hope of salvation from their disobedience and rebellion. The longer they waited the more sin swallowed their souls in darkness. They grasped hold of the promise from God that He would send His Savior.

And then, the miracle of the Incarnation occurred. God shattered the gloom and disheartenment of the people by sending a tiny baby, His divine Son. And the Light of the world split the darkness of sin. The Glory of the Lord lay as an infant on a bed of hay, and from the cradle the beams of heavenly light shone like spotlights into the deep dark. "The people walking in darkness have seen a great light " (Isaiah 9:2). The era of gloom and despair and death caused by sin came to an end. Light—divine—inextinguishable Light had come into the world.

DECEMBER 15

My mom and dad had purchased plane tickets on Allegiant airlines for a trip to Las Vegas in December. However, when my dad passed away, Mom contacted the airlines and requested his ticket money be applied to her return flight. The company bureaucracy tied up my mom's request even though we submitted all the necessary paperwork, including a copy of the death certificate, in a timely fashion.

We have received their response. No refunds are issued, even in the case of death. They did, however, manage to blame us for the problem because we didn't purchase Trip Flex, which allows a passenger to change his or her itinerary or postpone a trip without paying a fee, for that flight. That would have cost an additional 75 dollars. We are done with Allegiant.

This world insists we pay for everything. However, in the kingdom of God, He paid for everything. God had every right to charge us for our sins against Him. He could have designed a plan that required us to pay the debt. Instead, He designed a plan of salvation that centered on His own Son. Through His Son's sacrifice, our debt was satisfied. Jesus Christ paid the debt for our sin through His sacrifice on the cross. This is the gift of grace, and it is free to all who believe on the name of the Son of God, Jesus.

Ephesians 2:8 says, "For it is by grace you have been saved, through faith—and this not from yourselves, it is a gift of God." God offers us salvation for free through His Son. It's a good deal; take it.

DECEMBER 16

My mom met with her financial planner to get all her accounts in order. As expected, my dad had arranged things before he died so she would be secure and safe financially. These provisions are concrete, tangible expressions of my father's enduring love for her.

Our heavenly Father gives us tangible, concrete expressions of His everlasting love for us. Jesus Christ revealed God's declaration of His love through the words of the Lord's Prayer (Matthew 6:9-13).

When we see the wonders of an evening sky or the brilliant colors of the dawn we recall that "the highest heavens belong to the Lord" (Psalm 115:16). Each Christmas season we remember the advent of God's kingdom arriving on earth in the tiny, frail body of a baby boy.

When we taste delicious, warm soft loaves of bread, we hear the words of Jesus, "I am the bread of life" (John 6:35). Each Good Friday we remember His love and commemorate the anniversary of Jesus' being nailed to a Roman cross to bring us forgiveness and reconciliation with God. We hear the Lord's words, uttered in agony, "Father forgive them, for they do not know what they are doing" (Luke 23:34). And the reality of His atoning work is present in the Spirit each time we forgive a person, just as Christ has forgiven us.

God provides these enduring expressions of His love so we can know the enduring safety and security of His presence with us.

DECEMBER 17

When my sister moved to town the family dynamic changed. When my dad died it changed again. My sister who lives out of town visits more often now. There is new energy released into the family relationships that wasn't there before. These changes can only make the family stronger.

When John the Baptist started preaching repentance the dynamic in Israel started to change. He made known that God's Savior was in the world. He saw the "Lamb of God" (John 1:29) and confirmed for the people, "I have seen and I testify that this is the Son of God" (John 1:34).

When Jesus began His ministry the dynamic in Israel and all of Judea changed again. His "miraculous signs and wonders" (John 4:48) brought a new energy to the people. His teachings were infused with such authority that the temple guards remarked, "No one ever spoke the way this man does" (John 7:46). Even the Pharisees puzzled over His wisdom "How did this man get such learning without having studied?" (John 7:15)

And when Christ died on the cross, the dynamic changed forever. By faith in the atoning work of Christ on the cross, sinners are brought into peace with God and welcomed into His family. "Yet to all who received him, to those who believed in His name, He gave the right to become children of God" (John 1:12).

Christ chose to die, so the family of God would be made stronger through His sacrifice.

DECEMBER 18

At the bank this morning, the teller and I exchanged a few words about the Christmas season. We acknowledged that it is not only the "most wonderful time of the year" but also the most expensive as well.

Recalling that conversation later, I thought that this was a very expensive season for God as well: He sent His Son into the world knowing the outcome of His arrival would ultimately be HIs death. That was God's extravagant gift to us for our salvation. This is the lavish, reckless love of God. By His ordained will and with unconditional favor toward mankind God placed His Divine Son in a cradle, in enemy territory, fully aware that the cross would be the conclusion. Jesus's glory and holiness in the cradle would, by His life's end, be exchanged for our shame and guilt. As the folk hymn attests, "What wondrous love is this, O my soul, O my soul, what wondrous love is this, O my soul!"

This condescension was the goodwill the angels proclaimed. They rejoiced at His birth knowing that the curse of sin and death would be lifted from the world. God in Christ had made visible His everlasting love toward humanity, and He bore the cost of that love.

As Charles Wesley wrote, "Hark the herald angels sing, 'Glory to the new born king, peace on earth and mercy mild, God and sinner reconciled!'" As you tally your Christmas expenses, ponder also the expense God did not spare this season.

DECEMBER 19

The house is still and quiet as rest comes to all of us. The day is over, and the depths of night's darkness will soon arrive. Tranquility accompanies the silence. Peace is settling into each room, wrapping its strong arms securely around the occupants. Whatever today was is no longer. Whatever tomorrow will be has not yet been determined. What we have is the deep, calm assurance of this silent night.

There was a time when the night hours did not offer such solitude. There was a time when darkness was terrifying, when it was the realm of sin and death. However, God brought peace to the darkness when He sent His Son into the world.

Christ's arrival in the world capsized the realm of darkness, and the terror of sin and death was upended by His light and love. That holy night, when the divine Son entered the human race, "the Lord kept vigil" (Exodus 12:42), protecting, guarding and defending His Son from the enemy, while the baby's mother placed Him safely in the cradle. Once the infant arrived on earth, the darkness was overcome, and the tyranny of sin and death deposed. "The light shines in the darkness and the darkness has not overcome it" (John 1:5).

Even in the darkest hours of the night, Christ's light shines, and we no longer need to be afraid of the dark. Sin and death no longer control the darkness because "Light has come into the world" (John 3:19).

DECEMBER 20

As parents we would like to leave our children an inheritance. It doesn't have to be just financial. I remember many teachings from my dad. For example, he told us we should never burn bridges, and when driving on the highway he always said, "Speed limit take eight." He left us a treasury of one-liners and humorous stories. Above all, he left us words of wisdom to govern our lives. All that he had he gave to his family.

Each of us has something that we would like to leave for others. I write so that I can pass on to my children the lessons God has taught me. Some friends will leave behind music or art work, and others will leave financial stability. The point is we will take what is ours and give it to others.

God has done the same thing for us through Jesus Christ. Jesus said that the Spirit "will bring glory to me by taking from what is mine and making it known to you. All that belongs to the Father is mine" (John 16:14-15).

Imagine that! Jesus through the Holy Spirit is leaving us everything He knows about the Father. The wisdom of God, the grace of God, the hope of God can all be ours through the Spirit when we believe in Jesus Christ. In addition, we are given knowledge of God, teachings from Christ and joy from the Spirit.

As believers, this is our inheritance.

DECEMBER 21

We do not talk of God's supernatural work through the Holy Spirit. Yet, this is the season that He makes that work plain in the tiny body of an infant boy, Jesus.

Jesus Christ's nature—fully God and fully man—defies human logic: He is "Mighty God, Everlasting Father, Prince of Peace" (Isaiah 9:6) who came to earth as a human baby. His arrival arises from God's supernatural power made manifest in the womb of a virgin, Mary, who was told by an angel, "The Holy Spirit will come upon you, and the power of the Most High will overshadow you. So the Holy One to be born will be called the Son of God" (Luke 1:35).

These words, no doubt, overwhelmed Mary. The supernatural work of God exceeds the reason of natural man. He confronts the rules and limits of the temporal world to reveal His infinite world.

If, when you look at the manger you glimpse the "King of Kings and Lord of Lords" (Revelation 19:16), rejoice at His coming and be assured that "this was not revealed to you by man, but by [Christ's] Father in heaven" (Matthew 16:17). Knowledge of the Christ child is yours through the supernatural Spirit of God.

God's Christmas gift is His Son, and the supernatural work of the Spirit empowers us to see and live the truth. Give thanks, all you who see God's infant Son, for "you have been clothed with power from on high" (Luke 24:49b)!

DECEMBER 22

My soul is tired. It is feeling trampled by Christmas preparations. People are crowding into the stores, like me, doing last-minute shopping. Traffic is heavy and moving slowly on rainy roads. About now, I am ready to be a Scrooge and shout "Bah Humbug!" I feel myself slipping into the "weary world" ("O Holy Night," Adolphe Adam).

So, I am hiding in my office listening to Handel's "Messiah." This music reminds me of the wonder and majesty of this season. The lyrics are from the prophecy in the book of Isaiah. My soul is being revived by the beautiful voices and Scripture, "And the glory of the Lord will be revealed, and all mankind together will see it. For the mouth of the Lord has spoken it" (Isaiah 40:5).

The "glory of the Lord" is a tiny baby. Through the miracle of birth God brings the miracle of salvation to the world in Jesus, His divine Son. This infant will draw the attention of all mankind. And mankind will be confronted with the words of God, "This is my beloved Son, whom I love; with Him I am well pleased" (Matthew 17:5).

We will all rush through these next two days. But the gentle nagging of God will insist you peer into the manger and see the

Holy One who is creating all this attention. This baby is the Lord. "Let us rejoice and be glad in His salvation" (Isaiah 25:9).

DECEMBER 23

We're all getting tired. Holiday preparations have taken their toll. But in less than thirty-six hours the stores will close, and for one remarkable day, the city will, basically, stand still. That hush, that indescribable hush that will fall across the city on Christmas Eve is God's gift to the soul.

All year long our souls live in the tension of this physical world. They feel the oppression and burden of being trapped in this temporal realm; meanwhile they long for the invisible world, its resting place. In the world, the soul lives in the tension of looking for solace from the pangs of sin, disobedience and rebellion. It knows the anguish of sin and desires the healing balm of the Lord.

But on Christmas Eve the soul finds its way to the manger of the Christ child, where it finds rest and repose. At the cradle of the Savior, the soul finds its dignity, in the presence of the infant king. And on this glorious night of the Savior's birth the "soul felt its worth," (O Holy Night," Adolphe Adam). The Savior has come into the world, and the shackles of sin will soon be broken, "because He will save His people from their sins" (Matthew 1:21c).

When we feel exhausted physically, we often don't even imagine how depleted our souls are spiritually. Bring your soul to rest and recline in the stable of the Savior. "Be at rest once more, O my soul, for the Lord has been good to you" (Psalm 116:7).

DECEMBER 24

Holiday crowds are thinning. Shop owners are flipping over the closed signs. Cars are leaving the malls, and workers are heading for home. Soon the streets will be empty of traffic. Noise will cease. Silence, like a benevolent relative, will be welcomed into the city on this the holy night of God's arrival.

Our souls will drink in God's peace, and our hearts will be joyful with anticipation as we wait to hear the angels sing, "Glory to God in the highest and on earth peace to men on whom His favor rests" (Luke 2:14).

For one amazing night, the world will take a back seat. It has been stilled by the mighty hand of God, who has moved in history and placed His Son on earth. Tonight, our gaze is upward, our hearts are lifted to the heavenly realms and we listen for the angel to declare the "good news of great joy that will be for all people" (Luke 2:10). As the world stops and the night grows deeper, we see through the eyes of faith "the glory of the Lord" (Luke 2:9) shining in the darkness. And when we look to the east, we believe that the star still shines over the place where Jesus lay.

God has stilled the world so we can slip away to the manger and worship Jesus the Son. "Come on bended knee" ("Thy Kingdom Come! On Bended Knee," Frederick Hosmer) and let the Spirit show you what He showed the Magi: in the cradle lay Christ the King.

DECEMBER 25

"God with us" (Matthew 1:23). Let these words like a spring rain soak deep into the soil of your spirit and bring refreshment to your soul. Then treasure the truth that God the Immortal, Invincible, Invisible God of heaven is NOW keeping company with mankind. Revel in the wonder of Perfect God in the midst of imperfect, sinful man.

"God with us" takes the adage *opposites attract* to an unfathomable level. Holy, infinite, omnipotent God planted His foot on the ground of fallen creation to "draw all people to myself" (John 12:32 ESV). Strangely this mystery, God in the body of a man, calms the heart and soothes the soul while stirring the curiosity of natural man with how and why.

How? God's Spirit came upon a virgin. Why is answered in the words of the prophets, which carried in them God's promise to come to earth. "Shout and be glad . . . For I am coming, and I will live among you, declares the Lord" (Zechariah 2:10).

"God with us." The great "I AM" (Exodus 3:14), Israel's Redeemer and Deliverer is born of a woman, placed in a cradle and given the name Jesus. Fully God, Jesus, the Son, "was the exact representation of his [the Father's] being" (Hebrews 1:3). Everything the Father is, the Son is. Nothing of the Father was withheld from the Son.

God is with us fully and completely through His Son, Jesus, and by the power of His Spirit now and forever more.

DECEMBER 26

Noise doesn't just affect our ears, it disrupts our thoughts, agitates our hearts and disturbs our souls. Because we are in it so often, we accept the uneasiness it produces in our spiritual lives. In fact, we are so conditioned to noise we fail to equate it to spiritual unrest.

After two days of quiet, my ears seem especially sensitive to noise. I can hear the barking dog down the street and the steady flow of traffic on the road behind my house. With Christmas over, stillness and quiet are once again a rare commodity.

Noise is a deterrent to our active progress toward God. Here's a case in point: on Christmas Eve the world lay still, and we could focus on the miraculous birth of Jesus Christ. We paused and listened intently to the heavenly voices proclaiming the Good News of God on earth. Christmas Day, the world continued to slumber, and we could tiptoe past it to the manger. We knelt by the cradle, looked at the face of God and listened to Him breathe. We could hear Him cry. We could hear Him coo. We could her Him fuss. And we could hear the soothing words of Mary comfort and settle her baby.

Jesus Himself rebuked the noise of the world to save a soul (Luke 4:35 and Mark 1:25). Let's reduce the daily noise in our lives, so our soul can hear the pure, clear voice of God in Christ and find rest.

DECEMBER 27

This month—tonight in particular—writing the Evening Reflection has been much more difficult than previously. All day long I note observations, thoughts or interactions that I've had. Then I mull them over with God, and He picks the one we write. However, the writing has been much slower and more arduous than before.

When writer's block hits, I get agitated. I pray and wait. I read Scripture and wait. Then I get a bit mad at God and wait. Then I adjust my attitude and wait. Then I get exasperated and wait. Then I adjust my attitude and wait. Then I surrender and wait. And, finally, I just wait and wait.

The strange thing about this struggle is that the more I wrestle with God, the stronger my faith in Him grows. Our spiritual lives, like our physical lives, need struggle to build strength. To struggle means to strive. And striving means making a strenuous effort toward a goal. In this case, that effort is toward a better understanding of God. My struggle will take me to the point that I finally realize I can't understand God on my own but only through the revelation and testimony of the Holy Spirit. This is how I grow stronger: I become more dependent on the Spirit.

Wrestle, struggle and strive until you know "there is a greater power with us" (2 Chronicles 32:7).

DECEMBER 28

The only thing remaining from Christmas is the extra holiday pounds. Exchanges were finished on Friday. New toys have lost their luster, and stores have lost their appeal. Most people probably stayed at home today to watch their favorite NFL teams fight for a playoff berth. Things appear normal.

But nothing will ever be normal again: God came to earth as a baby boy. The miracle of Jesus' birth is not just the conception but that the Almighty Christ left the glories of the heavenly realm and "made Himself nothing, taking the very nature of a servant" (Philippians 2:7). Jesus came to earth with no ambitions, desires or dreams of His own. He served God's ambitions, desires and dreams of salvation, redemption and forgiveness for mankind. His words and actions were one with the purpose, work and will of the Father. The Son came to earth to serve the Father and through that service "He will save His people from their sins" (Matthew 1:21).

If you have been saved by Jesus Christ, then your gift from God is the Holy Spirit; He will empower you to live as a servant to the Son. Your gift to Christ is surrendering everything to Him through the power of the Spirit, until you have made yourself nothing. As Jesus served God so we should serve Christ. Our wants, aspirations and endeavors should be abandoned to the will of God through the Holy Spirit.

DECEMBER 29

My most productive time with the Lord is early in the morning. I follow a specific order of praise, prayer and worship. Some days when this time ends, I pledge evening hours to a similar pursuit. Unfortunately, by the time the day is over, responsibilities have worn me down and the plans I have dedicated to God crumble.

My effort alone is not enough to accomplish for God the things I said I would. In truth, my efforts are futile and useless. I am so weak, my attempts to accomplish even the simplest spiritual task fails when I use only my human devices. When I am ready to kick myself for failing, Peter comes to mind. He made a grandiose declaration to Christ, "Lord, why can't I follow you now? I will lay down my life for you" (John 13:37). Peter eventually does lay down his life for Christ, but not that night. The night he made this bold announcement he failed miserably. He denied Christ three times. However, once Peter was filled with the Holy Spirit on Pentecost, His words ultimately became truth.

We sometimes make promises to God prematurely and without waiting for the Spirit. Our intentions are good, but they are only intentions unless the power of the Spirit makes them truths. God doesn't need our effort. God needs us to be vessels for the Holy Spirit, so that by the Spirit, God in Christ can accomplish His purpose and will through our lives.

DECEMBER 30

One of the Christmas gifts I bought did not fit the recipient. So, with receipt in hand, I went back to the store and stood in line with many other customers waiting to exchange items. Some people exchanged their purchases for a refund; others took store credit; some traded for the same item and some had simply changed their minds and wanted something else.

There are still busy shopping days after Christmas. Sales abound. Our human nature enjoys exchanging gifts for a better bargain during this period of discounts.

Spiritually we are also susceptible to making exchanges. Look at what the Lord told the prophet Jeremiah, "But my people have exchanged their Glory for worthless idols" (2:11). As strange as this may sound, God knows we exchange our faith in Him for faith in idols.

Most of us will balk at this comment or even deny it. However, we swap God for an idol when we consult the horoscope. We trade the Living God for good luck charms. When we are superstitious we are exchanging God for idols. When we listen to heretical teachings God is exchanged. If we put faith in anything but God in Christ through the Holy Spirit, we are exchanging God's glory for things that "are not gods at all" (Jeremiah 2:11).

Work with the Spirit to identify the idols in your life, and exchange them for the Glory of our Living God.

DECEMBER 31

The final tradition of the holiday season, New Year's resolutions, will arrive shortly after the indulgences of this evening
end. As Christians, we will make a list of spiritual changes we
hope to accomplish. No doubt we will resolve to have a deeper
relationship with God, commit to spending more time in the
Word, attend church more frequently, act more like Christ and
"do to others as you would have them do to you" (Luke 6:31).
Yet, we all know that when life returns to normal, those aims
will drown in the seas of work, family, laundry, fatigue, and so
on.

New Year's resolutions prove the weakness of the human
will. Suffering under the ravages of sin, our will has been left
anemic and fickle. Still we rely on our willpower, only to discover time and again it is unreliable, capricious and
unpredictable. Eventually we recognize that this roller-coaster
ride with the will must be abandoned.

So, let's all save time tonight and surrender our will to the
will of God in Christ. We can conquer our failings by admitting
that the "flesh is weak" (Mark 14:38 ESV) and that it "counts
for nothing" (John 6:63). Once we accept this powerless condition, we can move to prayer and ask God for the gift of the
omnipotent Spirit. In this way this year will be the one in which
we "can do everything through Christ who gives me strength"
(Philippians 4:13).

WORKS REFERENCED IN THIS BOOK

Baumberger, Bernard J. Plaut, Wolf Gunther. *The Torah: A Modern Commentary*. Union of American Hebrew Congregations, 1981.

Blumhardt, Christoph. *Lift Thine Eyes: Evening Prayers for Every Day of the Year*. Plough Publishing House, 1998.

Bushnell, Harold. "Unconscious Influence." *The Treasury of the World's Greatest Sermons*. Edited by Wiersbe, Warren W., et al. Kregel Publications, 1977.

Chambers, Oswald. *Prayer: A Holy Occupation*. Thomas Nelson Publishers, 1993.

Cheney, Thomas Kelly. "Faith and Progress." *The Treasury of the World's Greatest Sermons*. Edited by Wiersbe, Warren W., et al. Kregel Publications, 1977

Stein, K. James. *Living Selections from the Great Devotional Classics*. Upper Room Books, 1950.

Valley of Vision. The Banner of Truth Trust, 2002.

Watson, Thomas. *The Doctrine of Repentance*. Bottom of the Hill Publishing, 2012.

Wright, N. T. *Surprised by Hope: Rethinking Heaven, the Resurrection, and the Mission of the Church*. HarperOne, 2014.

ABOUT THE AUTHOR

Denise Larson Cooper has a passion for Christ and sharing His Word. She is an avid walker and spends many hours in the great outdoors admiring God's creation. She also enjoys photography, leads small group Bible studies and invests the Gospel in all she does. Denise graduated with a Masters of Divinity from Asbury Theological Seminary and worked ten years in an inner-city ministry in Rochester, New York. A wife and mother of two daughters, Denise works as a gymnastics coach in Rockford, Illinois.

Readers can follow her on Facebook at Godnesia.

Her website is located at
https://www.facebook.com/DeniseLarsonCooper